FREEDOM

— AND —

HUMAN ACHIEVEMENT

I0039950

FREEDOM
AND
HUMAN ACHIEVEMENT

JEFF LOVE

DEFIANCE PRESS
& PUBLISHING

FREEDOM AND HUMAN ACHIEVEMENT

Copyright © 2023 Jeff Love

First Edition: 2023

All rights reserved. No part of this publication may be reproduced, distributed, or transmitted in any form or by any means, including photocopying, recording, or other electronic or mechanical methods, without the prior written permission of the publisher, except in the case of brief quotations embodied in critical reviews and certain other noncommercial uses permitted by copyright law.

This book is a work of non-fiction. The author has made every effort to ensure that the accuracy of the information in this book was correct at the time of the publication. Neither the author nor the publisher nor any other person(s) associated with this book may be held liable for any damages that may result from any of the ideas made by the author in this book.

DEFIANCE PRESS
& PUBLISHING

ISBN-13: 978-1-959677-55-0 (Paperback)
ISBN-13: 978-1-959677-56-7 (Hardcover)
ISBN-13: 978-1-959677-54-3 (eBook)

Cover: Lady Liberty, with backdrop of the Constitution, lights the way to Freedom while holding a tablet representing the Declaration of Independence. Individuals are scaling Lady Liberty to lift themselves out of darkness.

Published by Defiance Press & Publishing, LLC

Bulk orders of this book may be obtained by contacting Defiance Press & Publishing, LLC. www.defiancepress.com.

Public Relations Dept. – Defiance Press & Publishing, LLC
281-581-9300
pr@defiancepress.com

Defiance Press & Publishing, LLC
281-581-9300
info@defiancepress.com

*Freedom and Human Achievement is dedicated to
all who have sacrificed to preserve the blessings
of Freedom we still enjoy to this day.*

FOREWORD

I wrote *Freedom and Human Achievement* out of concern that the basic concepts of Freedom and Liberty were under insidious attack through failure to teach their meaning. The flourishing of humanity that they bring were no longer being taught to future generations.

Equally alarming was the cancerous tentacles of Marxism, Socialism and Progressivism that were gaining acceptance on college campuses. Once again fostered by the privileged elite and repackaged as Progressive Democratic Socialism, a supposedly "new and better" way to govern was taught while completely ignoring all of the death, chaos, and destruction these ideas inflicted on humanity in the last century. It is an unambiguous, observable fact that an "elite ruling class" has used manipulation of Government to subjugate the rest of humanity for most of written history.

Freedom and Human Achievement is a comprehensive treatise on Freedom. It shows why humanity flourishes when Free and languishes when oppressed and shows that almost all of the progress of humanity has occurred in the brief moments of history when man has been free from his own Government.

If we fail to pass these ideas on to future generations, humanity could enter a modern-day Dark Age, with today's technology used to subjugate The People.

The manuscript was completed but not published more than ten years ago. It did not conform to the globalism mantra of the day. Freedom and Human Achievement highlights contemporary threats and makes predictions. Instead of updating to current-day conditions and statistics, I am publishing it as originally completed. This gives you the unique perspective to view my predictions with the benefit of contemporary knowledge.

Here are some of the topics:

Tolerance	**Crime**	**Debt**
Cancel Culture	**Militarization of Police**	**Growth of Government**
Divisiveness	**Gun Control**	**Socialism**
Individualism	**Marxism**	**Anti-Capitalism**

TABLE OF CONTENTS

PART I. WHAT IS FREEDOM?

★ ★ ★

CHAPTER 1

THE TENETS OF FREEDOM

THIS IS A BOOK ABOUT FREEDOM, with a capital F. It is based on the premise that Freedom is, as Thomas Jefferson proposed, a natural, self-evident right of all human beings.[1] We will not delve into abstruse or arcane notions of psychological Freedom. I understand the sense in which it may be said that Solzhenitsyn, starving in his Gulag cell, was the freest man in Russia, but when, in the pages that follow, the word Freedom is used, it refers to political, social, and economic Freedom—Freedom from oppressive Government most of all.

It is also my purpose to show that to the extent The People of a given nation are Free, they will achieve great things. They will live happier, more comfortable and more productive lives, and that productivity will have consequences not only for the individual responsible for it, but for others as well, and in the long run, for all humanity. A Free society is dynamic, ever-changing, moving inexorably, although surely not in

---

1. Jefferson used the word *liberty* in the Declaration of Independence. In the historical past, some used *Liberty* and *Freedom* to be synonymous, the former being derived from French and the latter from German. I take Freedom as denoting "rights" which create a condition of opportunity and which cannot be taken away; Liberty denotes the condition or ability to act on those rights. For example, Government may forcibly deny my Liberty to enjoy Freedom, but the fundamental rights embodied in Freedom are inalienable.

a straight line, along a path which can accurately be called progress. By contrast, an oppressive society seeks stasis to define, determine, and lock into place those things which will be allowed and/or allotted. *And it decides which people are promoted as beneficiaries of its munificence or punished through its disapproval,* with the oppressors secure in their privileged positions of power. This is true whether the leaders of such a society are elitists, kings, or commissars.

Thus Freedom, a good thing in and of itself, is also to be sought on utilitarian grounds. Freedom is good because it leads to human achievement.

Historically, Freedom has been a scarce commodity, but we will see that a vastly disproportional share of human achievement is associated with Freedom. We will investigate the long and tumultuous journey of Freedom from its ascendency in ancient Greece to how it is faring in the early twenty-first century. At times the path has been arduous and difficult, even to the point of hopelessness, as in the Dark Ages. At times it has been breathtakingly dynamic, as in the Enlightenment and American Revolution. But at all times it has affected the achievement and well-being of The People depending on its success or oppression.

The American Revolution, and the great documents it produced, initiated an unprecedented level of human achievement that is threatened today as at no other time since its inception. Attack from an aggressor needs no recognition as a threat and will rapidly galvanize almost universal support of The People. However, allowing the philosophical principles that underpin Freedom to gradually be eroded away and discarded is a more insidious threat. Appealing to the greed of those who would live at the expense of their neighbors, assurances that Government will keep us secure and take care of us, distortion of meaning of the words "rights" and "equality," assertion that the Constitution is a "living document" and re-institution of class warfare are some of the tactics being used by political elitists to once again subjugate those who still live with some degree of Liberty. The extent to which the meaning of Freedom can be distorted or blurred makes it more difficult to defend.

In its modern guise, this withering of the Freedom doctrine has taken the form of a collectivism based to some extent on Marxist thinking, but more recently devolving from the economic ideas of John Maynard Keynes, in which individual Freedom is sacrificed in favor of a large, professional bureaucratic state utilizing centralized planning in an attempt to "rationalize" the inevitable rough edges and inconsistencies of Freedom-based societies, and move toward a more bland egalitarianism.

Is it inevitable that decline must follow ascendency once Freedom-driven nations achieve prominence? Many historians certainly believe so because of the classical experience, which they believe to be analogous to the modern American case. In this view, America is seen as being on the brink of repeating the period of decline that has been the fate of every previous country which has risen to the pinnacle of world power.

When observing some of the common threads and societal factors that have preceded the denouement of other great states, a strong case can be made that America has started initiating many of the same policies that have led to the failure of preeminent nations in the past and is sliding downhill toward the precipice of financial ruin at a rapidly accelerating pace. The questions are not whether the threat is real or whether America is foundering; this book will demonstrate the case for both postulates. The crucial questions are *why* we are in decline, whether the outcome is now inevitable, and if not, what can be done to reverse the gathering momentum toward collapse so that America can once again reassert its role of Freedom-based leadership in tolerance, prosperity and achievement for all The People.

America has long been the worldwide leader in innovation and development of (among other things) new technology, supported by an educational system that was once among the best in the world. But in the last quarter of the twentieth century, our public educational system has been in decline. We recently learned that in the 2010 testing against thirty-four OECD countries (Organization for Economic Cooperation and Development) around the world, America's fifteen-year-olds scored fourteenth in reading skills, seventeenth, in science and below-average twenty-fifth in mathematics. If much of our way of life is already teetering on the brink of decline, what does this lack of competitive education portend for our grandchildren's future?

One decade into the twenty-first century, America is suffering arguably the greatest downturn in our economy since the Great Depression, compounded by the fact that America is now the greatest debtor nation in the world. The media reports unemployment at hovering around 9 percent, but the method of Government reporting often distorts the true picture and under reports the problem. Those who have become discouraged and who are no longer looking for work are designated as "marginally attached to the workforce" and are not reported in the unemployment statistics; nor are those with only part-time jobs—many of whom need full time work just to feed their families. The precise number may be unknowable, but at least one recent university study pegs "true" unemployment at more than 30 percent.[2] The most accurate calculation would probably be in between, but the number is not as important as the fact we know unemployment is bad, and we all know families who are affected. In the midst of this crisis, our Federal Government has gone on a binge of spending and debt creation that is unprecedented in the history of our country and perhaps the world. Against the protests of The People, our politicians have created a new health care entitlement program that will most certainly dwarf all

2. http://sfcmac.wordpress.com/2010/09/17/youngstown-state-university-study-americas-true-jobless-rate-at-30-5/

existing entitlement programs, which are currently bankrupting the nation. Only a very limited portion of the new health care program, passed in 2010, has taken effect at the time of this writing, and there are various legislative and judicial attempts to curtail various components of it, or the entire program. It is therefore impossible at this time to say how great a financial burden the program will place on the nation. While many of the upper class and elite are unaffected and oblivious to the problem, Government is intruding into the daily lives of mainstream Americans as never before. Whether because they sincerely support such intrusion into Free decision-making by The People, or simply because they feel they must justify their existence, bureaucrats are engaging in micromanagement of the economy right down to mandating unworkable toilets and even the type of politically correct light bulbs that can be used. The collateral damage to jobs, the economy, and the environment can be seen as clearly as if one had a good light bulb to shine on it, as the last company in America to manufacture light bulbs fires its workers and shuts it doors—out of business as a direct consequence of Government fiat. And the new foreign light bulbs we are forced to purchase are filled with deadly toxic chemicals that are an unintended consequence.

Thousands of new regulations are also being created each year, and they are stifling the growth and profitability of businesses. This has resulted in a mass exodus of jobs to overseas countries with fewer regulations and lower taxes. Those companies which either *must* remain in America or who *choose* to remain are put at a serious competitive disadvantage, which restricts their ability to grow, prosper, and create jobs.

We have not learned from the abject failure of Marxist class warfare that was so destructive in the twentieth century. Some leaders are still working to increase their own power and influence by dividing society into respective interest groups, rather than working toward unity and resolution of our problems. By joining the divisiveness, many seem to be abandoning the heritage of tolerance that is crucial in our multi- cultural society.

We can see that the middle class is shrinking dramatically in size, and the disparity between rich and poor is growing at an alarming rate. If this trend continues, America could end up as just another "banana republic," with elitist landowners, high corporate and Government officials controlling most of the wealth, no more than a nominal middle class, and a vast majority of downtrodden poor living in conditions that resemble the serfdom of Medieval Europe. How can America be losing one of its greatest historical achievements — its middle class?

Many Americans can see this early decline and know that we are on the wrong path but are unable to pinpoint the causes of the breakdown or to articulate those things which need fixing. The problems have grown to such magnitude that they seem insurmountable and beyond our grasp. There is a feeling of impotence to effect meaningful change. We seem to have lost something important that has made us vibrant and that has allowed us to flourish.

This book is going to demonstrate why we are foundering today by presenting a historical perspective of what worked to make America great, but more importantly *why* it worked, and why America is now on the precipice of decline, and what we must do to restore the vitality that led us to greatness. We are abandoning the principles which our forefathers used to reshape the world, and which promote abundance and well-being.

The American experiment in Government, which began just a bit more than 200 years ago, caused an unprecedented flourishing of humanity because Freedom is more than just a word. **Freedom is the driving force of human achievement**.

THE CONCEPT OF FREEDOM

The philosophical case for Freedom derives from the proposition that each individual is endowed with natural and inalienable rights that are universally held and not contingent on laws, customs, or beliefs. Individuals alone hold these rights, which are called "natural" because they derive from the very nature of what it means to be human. They do not adhere to groups of individuals, as groups. Phrases such as "women's rights," or "gay rights," or "minority rights" may be used correctly and usefully when by them is meant that individuals who fall under these classifications enjoy the same rights as all other persons; but they are oxymoronic and inaccurate when they are used to define special "rights" peculiar to the classification.

Rights imply that each individual is sovereign to make the widest possible latitude of choices affecting his well-being so long as he is not thereby *personally* infringing on the rights of others. Incontrovertibly holding natural and inalienable rights insures "Freedom from" one's own Government, or any other entity or authority.

Rights may not be taken away by Government force, coercion or subversion. You may object to this. Government takes away rights all the time, you may say, and you may accuse me of inconsistency, since I complained just a few paragraphs ago that the Government was depriving me of my right to buy the light bulb of my choice. The distinction is this: no matter what the Government does, the *right* remains. That is the difference between rights and Liberty. Government has taken away my Liberty by failing to protect my inalienable right (Freedom). In the Declaration of Independence,

Thomas Jefferson made this point clearly. "To secure these rights," Jefferson wrote immediately after his famous reference to the rights of "life, liberty and the pursuit of happiness, "Governments are instituted..."

Natural and unalienable rights exist. They are not created by the Government.

The Government's job is to make the rights secure by guaranteeing The People the Freedom to exercise them. And if Government fails to do so, Jefferson adds an additional right: In such a case, he says, "it is the Right of the People to alter or to abolish it."

Following on the Declaration by a decade and a half, the Constitution was a brilliant attempt to secure the rights of The People by limiting the power of the Government it created to abridge or contravene those rights. It recognizes and refines Jefferson's short list of natural rights, and in the Bill of Rights—ten Amendments which were part of the Constitution from the beginning, expressly prohibit the Government from interfering with these rights. Since Government has always been the greatest traducer of rights, these prohibitions represent a giant step toward securing them for The People. The Bill of Rights even goes so far as to state that, "The enumeration in the Constitution, of certain rights, shall not be construed to deny or disparage others retained by the people."[3] Some of the rights which are specifically enumerated include the rights of free assembly, association, keeping and bearing arms, the press[4], religion (no matter how strange, so long as it does not infringe on the rights of others, such as perhaps by justifying human sacrifice), free speech, and several important rights involving jurisprudence, including the right of a speedy trial, trial by jury, non-self-incrimination and others.

Among the rights not specifically enumerated, but in the view of

---

3. This is, in its entirety, the Ninth Amendment.

4. This right is often misconstrued to suggest a special class of people, journalists, or "the press." That is not the meaning of the right at all. As with all other rights, "freedom of the press" means simply that all people have the right to state their views on any subject whatsoever on paper and to make and distribute copies of what they write.

The editorial board of the New York Times has no greater "Freedom of the press" than you do. A natural extension of this right is that it applies also to radio, television, the Internet and other modes of dissemination that do not involve an actual printing press.

the author clearly among those retained by The People, and which we will discuss in due course in this book are the rights of personal choice, sovereign death, movement, privacy, property, thought, sovereignty over one's life and body, and the right to be left alone. In addition, there are rights to be free from unrestrained Government and excessive taxation, and another which we will highlight at some extent because of its timeliness and importance: the right to be born free from debt. Some of these rights are relatively noncontroversial. Others are the subject of bitter debate. A few will be challenged by readers who believe themselves to be strong proponents of Freedom. I welcome and encourage a vigorous debate for having a clear understanding of our individual rights is essential if America is to recapture, maintain, and extend its exceptional position as the greatest exponent of Freedom—and therefore of human achievement—in the history of the world.

---------- **CHAPTER 2** ----------

FREEDOM FROM GOVERNMENT

*"The course of history shows that as a
government grows, liberty decreases."*

– Thomas Jefferson

FREEDOM HAS BEEN A RARE AND precious reality enjoyed by only a small segment of mankind. Even today, a majority of the world's population lives under the yoke of oppression. For most, there is no cultural heritage of Freedom. For as far back as they can trace their ancestry, few or none of the generations have known even the most basic of Freedoms. And sadly, there has been little hope for bettering their lives for themselves and their descendants, no matter how industrious or hard working they prove themselves, no matter how bright and intelligent they are, and no matter how hard they apply themselves.

If we examine those few times and places in which the degree of Freedom has risen above the norm, we find that they have produced the greatest leaps forward in almost all fields of human endeavor. The bulk of progress has occurred in those societies which adopted more of the tenets of Freedom, and the well-being and flourishing of humanity have been more or less proportional to the degree of Freedom and Liberty realized by The People. Unfortunately, the reality of most times in most places is that the elite few use the force of Government to confiscate and plunder the wealth created by those who produce.

Since the formation of the State, the greatest oppressor of mankind has always been his own Government. Because Government constitutes the exercise of authoritative power over The People, it has provided a means of dominance by the powerful who manipulate society for personal gain. When one country conquers another, one of its first acts will almost always be to establish a "puppet" Government in the vanquished country, as the primary tool of exerting its dominance and authority over The People living there, and to skim the country's productive capacity on behalf of the conquerors.

The local puppets thus serve the conqueror in order to preserve or establish their own wealth and status. The puppets may be the same elite that was in control before they were conquered. Think of King Herod, for example, or a new favored class, such as the Nazi Party of Czechoslovakia following the Munich capitulation to Hitler. Either way, the local leaders must now kowtow to the new masters.

Similarly, when a coup, revolution or civil war brings new native leadership to power in a given country, the almost universal result is that an old group of oppressors—the Russian czars, say—are replaced by a new one—the Bolshevik commissars. *Only one country* stands apart, in that for the bulk of its existence The People have escaped the shackles, oppression and elitism that have long dominated the rest of the world, and that is the United States of America.

Those who wish to control the lives and thinking of mankind will tell you that Freedom means *Freedom To* … History and reason teach us exactly the opposite.

Real Freedom means *Freedom From* … The Forefathers of the American Revolution recognized that first, foremost, and above all else, Freedom means freedom *from Government.* This is one of the primary cornerstones upon which all other tenets of Freedom must be built.

Unfortunately, most Americans today do not even realize that our

Forefathers viewed Government as a significant threat to Freedom, and that the Constitution's stated purpose of establishing justice, ensuring domestic tranquility, providing for the common defense, promoting the general welfare, and securing the blessings of Liberty, was fulfilled in their plan by *restricting* the activities of the Government, not by *expanding* them. Modern Americans have nonetheless been taught in public schools to view Government as a benevolent benefactor, an iconic Uncle Sam cartoon character whose purpose is to solve all humanity's problems, and who therefore must be given ever more authority to do so. Many Americans thus believe that almost any problem should be referred to the Government for solution. Some believe Government should take care of The People from cradle to grave with no concern about where the resources to do so will originate. And they do not understand that the trade-off for bigger Government is always less Freedom for The People, and less Freedom brings about a decline in the overall standard of living and advancement in all fields of endeavor, with the possible exception of warfare.

The lesson is a hard one to learn, and sadly seems often to be learnable only the hard way. Survivors of the inhumane oppression of many of the now defunct communist regimes have no illusions about the evils of unrestrained Government, and are some of the most committed and passionate believers in Freedom today.

Unfortunately, only a few of the former Soviet republics and satellite countries were able to install Freedom-based governments following the communist overthrow, now more than twenty years ago. From Kazakhstan to Belarus, and in Russia itself, Freedom is still an unfulfilled dream.

Occasionally, a stark moment drives home the point in an unforgettable way. The now iconic images of a single student standing in front of a tank in Tiananmen Square in Beijing in 1989 were a rebuke to the oppressors of the world's most populous nation, and in a way to the rest of the world for not caring as much about Freedom as he did. Oppressed people do indeed yearn to breathe free, but those who enjoy Liberty often fail to understand how precious it is.

The People of Iran, with many murdered in the streets while protesting the rigged presidential election of Mahmoud Ahmadinejad in 2009—which preserved the power of his regime and the radical Muslim elite behind it—have first-hand experience with the oppression of Government. Hundreds of thousands of innocent political prisoners suffer almost unimaginable tortures daily in the concentration camps of Kim il-Jung's North Korean prison-nation, and those privileged to live outside the barbed wire are better off only by comparison, dependent on food aid from abroad, though they live in a fertile land more than capable of feeding all of them and many more.

Nor need we go very far back in history to remember the stacks of morbid skulls from Pol Pot's late 1970s regime in Cambodia, and its contemporary, Idi Amin's murderous tenure in Uganda. These examples, not to mention Hitler's Germany, Stalin's USSR and many others, demonstrate that any country on any continent is vulnerable to a potential reign of terror, now as much as ever. It has been estimated by every observer who, to my knowledge, has attempted the task that more of The People have been killed by their own Governments in peacetime than in all the wars of history, and there can be no more valid adage than the famous statement that "eternal vigilance is the price of liberty.[5] It is somewhat of a paradox that even with the obvious truths from both history and current events confronting them, many who now enjoy some measure of Freedom refuse to accept the premise that their own Government might become their oppressor. It is apparent that human beings want to believe in their own Government, ignoring the State's predilection to usurp Freedom and Liberty from The People.

---

5. This famous maxim apparently originated with John Philpot Curran (1750-1817), an Irish orator and political leader. It was used by President Andrew Jackson in his farewell address.

Since the phenomenal success of using cutting-edge mass communication for Government propaganda by the Nazis in the 1930s and 1940s, The People have been subjected to a barrage of indoctrination promoting the interests of the State by almost every country in the world. The expenditures have been one sided, as no other entity has had the resources or continuity to match the decades-long advertising blitz. This effort has often been fomented by collectivists, determined to promote a move toward worldwide socialism. The breadth of the campaign to sell Statism has been extraordinary, from children's television programming suppressing ideas of individualism adult appeals for more welfare constituents and even entertainment programs venerating not only bureaucrats themselves, but also lawyers, journalists and other favored groups.

FREEDOM TO AND FREEDOM FROM

The struggle for Freedom can be pared back to the differences between the two concepts, *Freedom To* and *Freedom From*. The difference I suggest with these categories is the difference between those who support the primacy of Government and those who believe in the sovereignty of The People. *Freedom To* implies that rights are reposed with the "other" (Government) which then grants privileges to the governed. *Freedom From* is a clear statement of the inherent rights of The People, which are to be protected, or "secured," to use Jefferson's word, against usurpation by the State. The basic conflict is between those who believe all rights arise out of Government and those who believe all rights arise from The People. The struggle is not new, but extends back into antiquity and the well-being of The People has been, and is directly affected by the prevailing side.

FREEDOM TO

Those who believe in Statism believe that all rights arise out of Government, and the State must grant rights and privileges to The People. Government must grant you the *Freedom To* pursue almost any activity, or you face punishment for doing so without permission. The form of Government is relatively unimportant in this regard. Old-style absolute Monarchies were expressly based on the assumption that the King ruled by Divine right, and that he and he alone was the ultimate owner of all the wealth of the realm, from which, according to his concept of his best interest, he doled out in some measure to his subjects, great or small. Ideological Dictatorships in our own times viewed the situation in the same light, except, at least in the case of the Communists, that they denied any of it was in any way Divine. But modern Social Democracies, the prevailing form of Government in Europe and elsewhere (and for that matter the twenty-first century USA too, except that we reject the terminology) also make the assumption that all rights and privileges belong to the Government in the first place, and only through their agency are granted to anyone else, most assuredly to The People. Regardless of its form, those who support the omnipotence of Government believe order is maintained through the use of force, fear, and intimidation. Those who believe in Government control of our lives believe that The People are incapable of governing themselves.

Since the individual has no rights (all rights are reposed in Government), "right" decisions are made by Government and enforced through formalistic laws, and application of force, fear, and intimidation over The People.

It is inherent in the nature of Government to oppress The People. This tendency arises from Government's role as enforcer through the licensed (legalized) exercise of power, because of the collective

24

nature of its function, and most of all because collective power and control are converse to, and therefore antagonistic to, the rights and sovereignty of the individual. Where people's natural rights have been secured by a Government, such as in the early USA, or simply by tradition, it will be the inevitable nature of Government to take them away whenever the opportunity to do so presents itself. In 1779, Thomas Jefferson said, "Experience [has] shown that, even under the best forms [of government], those entrusted with power have, in time and by slow operations, perverted it into tyranny."

It is also inherent in the nature of Government to concentrate power and to centralize authority as a means of exerting its dominance and increasing its control. The degree of bureaucracy is proportional to the degree of centralization and to the size of Government; that is to say increased bureaucracy is a natural outcome of increased growth in the size of Government. There is also a corollary relationship between size of bureaucracy and degree of corruption, which arises out of the exercise of power and extends itself throughout the system until it becomes pervasive, extending to even the lowest levels. In some countries, these principles have existed for so long they have not only become accepted, but have become an institutionalized way of life.

I was once involved in helping set up an office in a foreign country long dominated by the rule of big Government and its correlatively attending bureaucracy. *After* we had rented the office space we needed, we were shocked to learn it was going to take a minimum of six months to get approval from all of the necessary ministries and agencies to open the office. Of course, this was never mentioned when we were leasing the property. In frustration, we hired a local associate agent of Government (in other words, a lawyer) to guide us through the maze. We then spent two days meeting low level bureaucrats in no less than eleven offices to each of whom we paid small bribes and received stamps of approval (literally) on sheaves of official looking documents. At ten of the stops[6] we also had to pay a small bribe to the policeman assigned to the block where we parked to guard our car and prevent it from being defaced by local ruffians. I later learned this was a street cop's primary source of income since the job paid so little, and the real risk was that if you did not pay the bribe, the protector might himself instigate the vandalism. In the end, and with all of the necessary stamps of approval, we were able to open the office in three days instead of the "customary" six months. The bureaucracy and corruption had become so entrenched as to become the normal and expected way of doing business. We were left with little doubt that the lawyer, the eleven bureaucrats and the ten policemen were pleased to have us operating in their local areas of control.

It makes a great deal of difference whether a given activity is a natural right of The People or merely a privilege granted by Government. For one thing, any privilege granted by Government can also be taken away by that same Government, or any subsequent successor to it. But no Government can legitimately deprive The People of their natural, inherent rights because these are endowed, as the Declaration of Independence says, by the Creator, and thus both preexist and transcend any and all Governments. To be sure, Governments can effectively deny The People their rights, by use of force, but the Declaration has a remedy for that, too. "whenever any Form of Government becomes destructive of these ends, it is the Right of the People to alter or to abolish it, and to institute new Government." it says, and the fact that The People of the American colonies, in spite of the odds, did exactly that means the Right to "alter or abolish" is not a hollow phrase, but a legitimate alternative for any citizenry willing to pledge its "lives, fortunes and sacred honor" to the cause. Indeed, in our own time, the collapse of Communism demonstrated again the power of The People to alter and abolish tyranny. And The People in many of the

---

6. The most important office had an enclosed parking area with an armed guard

long oppressed Arab countries are currently beginning to protest in the attempt to secure their own Freedom.

But first The People must learn to care enough for their Freedom to take action. In America today, the battle to restore Freedom does not (Yet?) require standing in front of tanks or facing Valley Forge-like suffering. Great strides can be made simply through concerted political action. In order for that to happen, however, people must understand what is at stake, and as long as most people define the basic precepts of Freedom as "to go anywhere I want," or "to do whatever I want," they are unlikely to look past the narrow self-interest of receiving one's share of the goodies Uncle Sam the Benevolent Benefactor can hand out. The difference between a true understanding of Rights and a superficial settling for privileges is the difference between individual sovereignty or Government sovereignty over one's life.

JEFFERSON'S HORSE

Let's look at an example. *Freedom To* implies that the State grants The People the privilege to drive. It sets up an entire regulatory bureaucracy, including complex taxation, around this most basic of modern human needs.

Isn't the ability to drive just as important to The People today as riding a horse was two centuries ago? Do you believe that Thomas Jefferson would passively agree that his *right* to ride his horse was in fact a *privilege* granted to him by the State? And would he be willing to be taxed, identified, and licensed for that privilege? Remember, the whole revolution started when the British Parliament decided to impose a rather modest tax on tea.

Neither Jefferson, nor any other American of his day would tolerate a Government that required him to pay a tax in order to receive a license to ride his horse from his home to town. Nor would he countenance a tax on his purchase of the horse itself, or a luxury tax if it happened to be a particularly fine horse. He would most surely revolt if the horse had been further taxed and inspected each year for worthiness to ride, or if he had been forced to pay federal, state, and county taxes to use the public throughways, roads, and bridges. All those taxes are imposed on us today, and to continue the comparison, in Virginia and most other states, Jefferson would have paid an annual tax on the value of the animal as real property, not to mention paying Federal and State taxes on the grain and hay the horse used as fuel.

And we're not through yet. Many accidents, injuries and deaths did and do happen in the course of equine activity, so no doubt, if our present Government's safety rules were applied to his time, Jefferson's horse would have to be ridden at a federally mandated speed, and equipped with a federally mandated saddle and a federally mandated seat belt, in case someone fell off. Then too, riding a horse more resembles operating a motorcycle than an automobile, so the law would also probably require the author of the Virginia Statute on Religious Freedom, in which he spoke of the "impious presumption of legislators," to stuff a federally approved crash helmet over his famous reddish locks.

What would Thomas Jefferson say about all this? We can get a pretty good idea from a letter he wrote to Thomas Cooper in 1802, in which he predicted future happiness for Americans "if they can prevent the government from wasting the labors of the people under the pretense of taking care of them." In a letter to James Madison on January 30, 1787, Jefferson also said, "I hold it, that a little rebellion, now and then, is a good thing, and as necessary in the political world as storms in the physical." Faced with the tax reach of today's bureaucracy, it is interesting to wonder if Jefferson, were he alive today, might believe it is time for a "little rebellion." Regardless, I am completely convinced that he and virtually all the other founders of the republic would believe Liberty is in serious jeopardy in today's America.

In a particularly ominous recent development, Government has begun using its power to control the rules of the road as a form of coercion, punishment and oppression. Government is now taking away the driving privileges of law breakers, even for some infractions that have nothing to do with driving. Because it is only in its fledgling stages, this new found use of law seems innocuous to many, but the fledgling stage is also the precedent-setting stage, and the Government's actions surely contain the potential for abuse and increased control. For most Americans, driving is integrally connected to our most basic needs and pursuit of happiness. If a person cannot drive, his ability to earn a living is severely hampered; his right of free association is curtailed; and in the modern world even his ability to find food and clothing is made precarious.

Thus The People's right to unrestricted Freedom of movement is jeopardized by Government's relegation of driving to a mere privilege instead of a fundamental right, because Government can control, restrict, or even deny a privilege for all sorts of reasons, including "compliance." Under current legal precedents now being set and reinforced, if you do not comply with various dictates of Government, it could result in your losing your driving privilege. Once this precedent is recognized by the courts, it can be applied to enforce almost any edict. If, after all, driving is a privilege, one who is late paying some tax or other, violating a trash recycling regulation, smoking a marijuana cigarette (or in the not-too-distant future, perhaps any cigarette), being late with an alimony payment, or any other shortcoming which, however serious or trivial, has no business being linked to something as fundamental as the right to drive an automobile. Non-compliance is an all-encompassing and *very* slippery slope.

However, if driving is a right rather than a privilege, The People are secure in their mobility. While the distinction may seem subtle to some, the distinction between rights and privileges, when reduced to legal practice, can mean the difference between Liberty and oppression.

This example should serve to remind us that the battle between *Freedom From* and *Freedom To*, and the distinction between rights and privileges, are part and parcel of the battle for Freedom and Liberty. Unfortunately, this is only one minor example: The onslaught is pervasive throughout Government.

FREEDOM FROM

The Forefathers of America recognized and tried to prevent the tendency of Government to gradually usurp power. As they promulgated a new form of Government, they drew from the experiences of the past, and attempted as best they could to place obstacles to the growth of Government power. James Madison said, "There are more instances of the abridgement of the freedom of the people by the gradual and silent encroachment of those in power, than by violent and sudden usurpation."[7]

Our Forefathers believed in a new order. They were not anarchists; they understood that to *secure* the Rights of The People, *governments are instituted*, and that *in order to form a more perfect union*, a rational plan of operations was essential. But they had no illusions that the State and The People would be in perpetual conflict over the issue of sovereignty. To resolve this conflict in favor of Freedom and Liberty, they added to the checks and balances of the Constitution the further protection of a Bill of Rights to expressly limit the powers of Government. Their intent was clear. As stated by Patrick Henry, "The Constitution is not an instrument for the government to restrain the people it is an instrument for the people to restrain the

---

7. Speech at the Virginia Convention to ratify the Federal Constitution (1788-06-06)

government—lest it come to dominate our lives and interests."

They believed Rights belong to The People, that The People may grant Rights to Government, and that all Rights not specifically so granted are retained by The People. They declared that all mankind is endowed with inalienable Rights upon which Government may not tread. They believed that specifically enumerating the powers granted by The People to Government was a primary means of preserving Freedom and Liberty. In a letter to George Washington in 1791, Thomas Jefferson commented specifically on this point when he cited the language of the Tenth Amendment, "The powers not delegated to the United States by the Constitution, nor prohibited by it to the States, are reserved to the States respectively, or to the people," and added, "To take a single step beyond the boundaries thus specially drawn around the powers of Congress, is to take possession of a boundless field of power, no longer susceptible of any definition."

Our Forefathers believed in individual sovereignty—that the individual, and not the Government, should make the choices which affect his life. They would defend the right of the individual to make petty or unwise decisions of his own behalf for they understood that once Government begins to "protect" the individual from his own choices, it will continue to justify the usurpation of powers until only the privileged class and the powerful elite enjoy any measure of real Freedom.

Perhaps the most profound statement by any of the founders on the nature of Government was that stated by Thomas Paine in *Common Sense*:

"Some writers [*he wrote*] have so confounded society with government, as to leave little or no distinction between them; whereas they are not only different, but have different origins. Society is produced by our wants and government by our wickedness; the former promotes our happiness positively by uniting our affections, the latter negatively by restraining our vices. The one encourages intercourse, the other creates distinctions.

"The first is a patron, the last a punisher.

"Society in every state is a blessing, but government, even in its best state, is but a necessary evil; in its worst state an intolerable one: for when we suffer, or are exposed to the same miseries by a government, which we might expect in a country without government, our calamity is heightened by reflecting that we furnish the means by which we suffer.

"Government, like dress, is the badge of lost innocence; the palaces of kings are built upon the ruins of the bowers of paradise. For were the impulses of conscience clear, uniform and irresistibly obeyed, man would need no other law-giver; but that not being the case, he finds it necessary to surrender up a part of his property to furnish means for the protection of the rest; and this he is induced to do by the same prudence which in every other case advises him, out of two evils to choose the least. Wherefore, security being the true design and end of government, it unanswerably follows that whatever form thereof appears most likely to ensure it to us, with least expense and greatest benefit, is preferable to all others."

This is the description of Government that ought to be taught in every classroom in the country, but I doubt it is the one you, or anyone else, has been taught for a very, very long time. Instead, you probably learned that Government is a benevolent benefactor that will protect and take care of its citizens, particularly the weak and needy. It finds, codifies, and doles out Rights in the form of *Freedom To* statements when it suits its purpose and takes them away when it does not.

The evil seen in Government by our Forefathers knows only the bounds of its restriction, and it exists in a constant state of attempting to subvert those restrictions and assume complete and unlimited power. The whole of history, and especially the past 200 years, only serves to prove and strengthen the concepts of Paine, Jefferson, Madison, and the rest.

Government held at least the latent power to dominate every facet of life from the end of the Athenian democracy to the coming of the Enlightenment. In feudal Europe, the King owned all property, and every subject was *subject* to his will and whims. In early modern times, the Divine Right of Kings to rule without regard to the wishes of The People was promulgated. And even when the age of revolution broke out beginning in the late eighteenth century, the results often merely replaced one harsh regime with another. The French Revolution brought on a reign of terror, a stifling bureaucracy, a military dictatorship under Napoleon and an eventual return to monarchy under the Bourbon Restoration. The various Latin American revolutions quickly devolved into bloody attempts by the new leadership to repress The People and to preserve their newfound power. And by the dawn of the twentieth century, the collectivist "isms" —Nazism, Fascism, Totalitarianism, Socialism and Communism—had reaffirmed, as they would again and again, the evils of an unrestricted Government.

America was singularly different, thanks to the intellectual brilliance of Paine, Jefferson, Madison and the other Founders, and the remarkable fact that George Washington had no interest in aggregating all power unto himself, and longed only for retirement to Mount Vernon.

Thus the United States has enjoyed a unique *Freedom From Government*. The question is, can it endure, or has it run its course?

In this book, I hope to examine some of the major factors which will determine how that question is answered. As I write, the nation is experiencing extraordinary economic challenges, which I believe are the result of the subverting and circumventing of restrictions in the

Constitution, and most notably in the Bill of Rights, by people who both believe in and benefit from the expansion of Government at the literal and figurative expense of The People.

They believe in a long list of *Freedom To's*, which they propose to hand out in return for acquiescence to their power grabs. And they have little concern about the *Freedom From* Government that is the only true measure of individual Liberty.

If loss of understanding or clouding of the meaning of the concept of Freedom is any barometer of Government's success in subversion of its restrictions, there may be but precious little time left before it is too late.

This is the burden thrust by time and circumstance on our present generations. Is America to remain a beacon to a world beset with oppression? If so, we must restore the clear understanding of Liberty established by the Founders and preserved by generations of patriots who have sacrificed to defend it. The true and historical meaning of Liberty is worth whatever sacrifice is demanded of us in order that we may fulfill our moral obligation to pass on a better way of life to our descendants and extend the blessings of America across the globe. Nothing less than the flourishing and well- being of humanity are at stake.

CHAPTER 3

THE RIGHT TO ACHIEVE AND THE COLLECTIVE USE OF PRODUCTIVITY

SUPPOSE EVERYONE WHO LIVES ON YOUR block has a say in how the money you earn is to be spent. You are able, industrious, and work very hard. You want to provide for the well-being of your family. You work to save for your children's education and a comfortable retirement for your mother and father. But some who live on the block do not share your drive. Some do not share your ability. Some do not want to work. But in our little thought experiment, everyone on the block has a say in how the fruits of your labor are to be spent.

At a block meeting it is decided that some of your money is to be spent for neighborhood clothes. "But I won't have enough money to help my parents," you protest. They respond that those who do not wish to work need clothes, and surely you can see that their warmth is more important than your parents' comfort. After all, your parents are not cold or poorly clothed.

They have also decided to spend some of your money for food. "But I won't have enough left for my children's education," you protest. They respond that those who do not work need food, and surely you can see that their hunger is more important than your children's education. Only a selfish person would think that their children's education is more important than feeding hungry people.

Your neighbors living on the block concede they do not have the same drive to succeed that you do. But they point out their parents did not teach them the same values which you were taught, so your advantage is unfair. Many also say it is unfair that you have more money than they have. Your wealth, they say, is a direct consequence of your drive to succeed, which they were unfairly denied by their upbringing. You suggest they could correct the inequity of the past by now educating themselves, or by working harder, now that they see the difference it makes. Perhaps we will, they say, but for now, we need food and clothing, and they vote to take even more from your earnings.

This continues until your own financial circumstances become threatened. Since you can no longer provide for your family, your wife takes a job so you can make ends meet. You both continue to work ever harder to earn extra money for the kids' education. But even before your paychecks are deposited to your accounts, the folks on the block find a way to spend much of it. Finally you have had enough. "I won't pay any longer," you protest. The folks on the block respond that we live under the "rule of law." They point out the law says that they have the right to share in the decisions as to how your earnings are spent. And you are told that the Government has used some of your money to hire enforcers to come and take it forcibly if you refuse to pay. In fact, to make it harder for you not to comply with Government wishes, they have told your employers to take a certain amount of your money away from your paychecks. If your employers do not comply with this law they have passed, they will send the enforcers around to see them! You can't even vote to change the laws because those receiving benefit from the money taken from you, continue to support leaders who give them more of your earnings.

In the schools your children are taught to feel guilty about having a greater opportunity, because you are passing your values of education and hard work on to them. And they are taught that Robin Hood was a hero because he "stole from the rich and gave to the poor." They are taught "rule of law" and "majority rule." You note that your children are becoming very confused about the values you have always believed and sought to pass on to them.

You have been alarmed for some time. Now, you are also becoming confused for it seems the system you have so cherished has become stacked against you. And each layer protects and reinforces the next, preventing any meaningful change. The "majority" on your block seem willing to use the "rule of law" as a tool to take what is yours.

You no longer know what to do. Even though you are working harder than ever before, you are told that you and your children will have to accept a lower standard of living. You know that something is dreadfully wrong, but you are unable to pin down the exact nature of the problem. You don't know how to begin to correct the problem because it seems that most of those on the block are in agreement with the system.

And your hopes for the future are growing progressively dim.

You may think this fable is far-fetched, but in fact the arguments the neighbors make are precisely those that people who believe in a collectivist society make in politics. "From each according to his abilities," Karl Marx advocated, "to each according to his needs." But such a system is both morally unacceptable and economically foolish. Think about the collectivist block again. How long could such a system endure? Not very, because once the productive people are financially ruined, it must collapse.

In the Soviet Union, a "block" of hundreds of millions of people were blessed with a huge, fertile heartland, and filled with the greatest abundance of natural resources of any country in the world; it took about seventy years for the system to collapse. The will to succeed was quite literally choked out of people because it became impossible to succeed. Near the end, a man in a Government office noticed that his secretary was stealing paper clips. He confronted her. "Why are you stealing paper clips from the Government?" he asked. "What else is there to steal?" she asked in reply. He was a kindly man (soon after, he defected to the West) and didn't report her. A few months later, she invited him to her shabby apartment to celebrate Christmas. Although frowned upon, small, individual Christmas commemorations were tolerated. The woman had managed to find a scrawny little tabletop Christmas tree, and her boss couldn't repress a smile when he saw that it had been decorated with strings of paper clips. Such is the impoverishment of collectivism.

Today, one decade into the twenty-first century, economic troubles circle the globe, and one country after another is learning that its Government has spent the national wealth and faces bankruptcy. Often, when the Government attempts to scale back the spending in the face of national default, those who only consider the "to-each-according-to-his-needs" side of the equation as being the part that applies to them, foment rioting in the streets to preserve their allotment. Like the greedy people on our mythical block fable, they refuse to understand that always taking from those who have something to take is an unsustainable plan.

But the unworkability of collectivism is only one aspect of the problem. It also has a moral dimension. Slavery is surely immoral, and the productive man on the block has been turned into a veritable slave by his greedy neighbors. He has been robbed of his humanity by being forbidden to make decisions about how to spend his own hard-earned money.

Mankind has a Natural Right to achieve and to benefit from the fruits of his own labor. It is immoral to use force to expropriate the earnings of the individual for the alleged collective good of those un-willing to or less capable of producing.

Man is a caring and giving being who will freely give of his own behalf to the needy and deserving. Americans are a generous people, and the extent of their generosity was particularly notable in early America, as documented by the Frenchman Alexis de Tocqueville on his visit in the 1830s. But when Government uses force to take from those who produce, it does not distribute principally to those who are most deserving of assistance. It inevitably hands out its confiscations on the basis of protecting and preserving its political power. Thus, the bulk of Government handouts go to giant banks and other corpo-rations, to politically powerful labor unions, special interest groups that promote the Government's policies, and to other cronies and hangers-on.

The truly needy generally get lost in the shuffle. The People, the productive people whose taxes finance all of it, react in one of two ways: they may become suspicious of the motives of all of those seeking charity. Or, unsuspecting, they may cut back on charity be-cause Government has already expropriated from their earnings for the express purpose of taking care of those in need. Those in true need are often unable to meet the bureaucratic requirements in a time frame that will give them the assistance they seek (if they can meet the requirements at all). And The People turn a deaf ear of confusion, suspicion and resentment.

And finally, The People are robbed of the feelings of self-esteem and good will that are produced by giving and good works.

When I say it is a *natural right* for man to achieve and benefit from his own productivity, I mean it is something that nature itself demonstrates. Consider the small mammals that must store food for the winter. They must work hard and store even more food than they will need under normal circumstances. Some might store barely enough to survive. But what happens in the exceptionally long and harsh winters?

Those who are more industrious will survive and the others will perish. Indeed, that probably happened long, long ago because the workings of natural selection favored the more industrious, willing, and capable, As example, squirrels are considered some of the most hard-working of all animals, actively storing food for the winter. We might never have seen a squirrel at all if in the primeval forest some were able to use force to steal the food of those who were industrious, and who had provided for the possibility of a hard winter. Sooner or later, natural selection would have resulted in a loss of industrious-ness, and in all likelihood, the species would have perished long ago in some period of global cooling. Both the industrious, who sufficiently accumulated for the winter, and the non-productive who used force to "equalize" the bounty would have starved.

CHAPTER 4

DIVERSITY:
INDIVIDUALISM VS. COLLECTIVISM

NATURE PROMOTES INDIVIDUALISM AND STRIVES FOR diversity and competition as means of strengthening, protecting, and promoting the survival of all species.

Competition vectors the group in a positive direction towards populating its ecological niche, and diversity encourages the expansion of the niche, as well as providing an increased probability that some individuals of the species will survive even dire catastrophes. For instance, because of genetic diversity, a small percentage of individuals in any population will almost always be immune to any given virus. Those surviving individuals often thrive in the aftermath of massive die-off as competition for the same resources has been reduced, and the importance of the contribution of each remaining individual is elevated. Competition is a driving force toward health, strength and adaptability in the population of all species, including humankind.

Conversely, Government strives for homogeneity and conformity with the goal of maintaining the status quo. Diverse interests are more difficult to manipulate and control, and competition leads to the development of independent individuals, interests and power centers, any of which may become a threat to the Government, which demands compliance with its rules and acceptance of its dominance. Government seeks to impose what may be termed "harmonic servitude," which is to say a population that is docile, unquestioning of the omnipotence of the central authority, submissive in accepting its laws and edicts, and that contributes to its growth, its ability to apply force and its perpetuation. The "contribution" is never voluntary but is always coerced or extracted through forcible taxation or service.

This is what Government perceives as order. But note that it is not a *natural* order, because nature seeks precisely the opposite—diversity, experimentation and change. In nature, individuals seek self-perpetuation and exhibit the will to live, but as an organized system, nature is dynamic.

Government, by contrast, seeks to perpetuate the system itself, not the individuals who comprise the system. Thus, it seeks to replace natural dynamism with imposed stasis, and individualism with collectivism. In this very fundamental sense, *Government is unnatural*.

Individualism flourishes on the branches of diversity and competition.

Collectivism infests the branches of homogeneity and conformity. Individualism naturally promotes the well-being and strength of The People. Collectivism forcibly promotes the strength and dominance of Government over The People. Individualism appeals to reason and rationality to achieve accomplishments.

Government applies force, fear, and intimidation to achieve compliance and to maintain the status quo.

The concepts of individualism and collectivism are antithetical to one another. The stark example of how each fared in the twentieth century should provide a clear indication of which is better for humanity. The experiments in various forms of collectivism have failed in chaos, misery, and destruction time and again. Yet worldwide

Government propaganda has been successful in obfuscating the true cause of failure, and like a phoenix, collectivism arises from the ashes of its last destruction to convince new victims of the virtues of self-sacrifice to the group, the selfishness of any who do not agree, and that Government is a benevolent entity necessary for preserving order and taking care of The People. While The People equate "order" with security, Government's pursuit of "order" is instead, a function of its predilection toward harmonic servitude.

Individual sovereignty, rooted in nature, is a cornerstone of Freedom and Liberty and promotes happiness, progress and prosperity by encouraging the economic well-being of all of The People. Government sovereignty is the pathway to oppression and servitude and promotes the interests of the elite few at the expense of The People and in particular those whose individual attributes encourage them to be the most prolific producers in any given society.

TOLERANCE

Tolerance is the operating system necessary for running the diversity program. As such, it is a veritable anchor of Freedom and Liberty. It is predicated upon Freedom of thought and upon the sovereignty of the individual who is imbued with autonomy. Tolerance incorporates recognition of human fallibility and restraint of power. It promotes open-mindedness, philosophical modesty, reason, receptivity, understanding, equity, impartiality, justice, cooperation and dialogue; and tolerance is practiced whenever an individual restrains from negating the action of others with whom they disagree.

Intolerance is practiced through prohibiting, regulating, restricting or negating the action of others through force, in order to impose a perceived moral imperative or simply in the pursuit of amoral political self-interest.

Tolerance offers vigor to the myriad benefits society derives from the intermixing, exploration and integration of diversity in all things. In so doing, it is one of the driving forces of discovery, exploration, and advancement. It encourages autonomous individuals to explore wider latitudes of possibilities.

Intolerance creates barriers which *compartmentalize*, rather than *integrate* diversity. It hampers autonomous individual exploration and action, and utilizes the force of Government to prohibit, tax or regulate such activity for the purpose of maintaining the status quo, often under the guise of some societal moral imperative of security, or of preserving order. Forcible homogenization by Government is antithetical to the benefits of intermixing derived from tolerance and destroys the societal benefit produced from the natural integration of diversity.

The need for tolerance arises out of diversity, and likely arose from early man's need for cooperative achievement. There is synergy in working together whereby a handful of individuals can accomplish things impossible to the same number working alone. Maintaining individualism and autonomy, yet benefiting from cooperative achievement, requires some degree of tolerance.

Among the classical Greeks, Socrates sought truth through dialogue and encouraged questioners to pursue differences with pedagogical emphasis on open-mindedness. While tolerance had some parallels within Stoicism and was extolled as a virtue of power among some Romans, it achieved little practical application during the centuries of the Empire, which never incorporated respect for autonomy.

Various religions struggled with the concept of tolerance, attempting to incorporate it into other virtues such as love and forgiveness on the one hand, but on the other often granting a license to use force to gain converts, save souls, or win territory.

Considering the three great monotheistic religions, we find that

each of them endured a time, in their earliest days, when internal disagreements escalated into serious disputes marked by intolerance. The
Hebrew Bible records a series of such disputes, beginning with the
dispute between Moses and Aaron; early Christianity had numerous
fissures, Arianism and Pelagianism being two of the major early ones,
which were ultimately crushed and declared to be heresies—surely a
victory for intolerance. In the case of Islam, the great split, occurring
in the first generation after Mohammad, between Sunni and Shi'a, has
yet to be resolved, or ameliorated by a spirit of tolerance.

In addition to these doctrinal disputes, a consistent pattern seems
to have developed in that whenever a religion became coterminous
with a Government, the trend toward violence and intolerance became
exacerbated. Thus the ancient Israelites massacred the Canaanites; the
Muslim irruption from Arabia in the seventh century swept south-
western Asia, northern Africa, and the Balkan and Iberian peninsulas
in its vast and bloody conquest. And Christianity, having become a
state religion throughout most of Europe, authorized the series of crusades to recover its Holy Land from the Muslims and Jews, to which
it was equally holy. Nor did the popes of the middle ages refrain from
taking sides in the intra-Christendom warfare that plagued medieval
and early modern Europe, although, to be fair, they often attempted to
mediate between warring kings in the interest of peace as well.

In Europe in the fifteenth and sixteenth centuries, new ideas on virtually every imaginable aspect of culture, art, science and philosophy
emerged. Many of these new ideas favored the concept of tolerance,
in particular the writings of humanists such as Erasmus (1466-1536),
De Las Casas (1484-1566), and Montaigne (1533-1592). These and
other thinkers emphasized the role of reason as superior to the pas-
sive acceptance of dogma, and although they sparked a reaction of
intolerance, notably the Inquisition, the genie was, so to speak, out
of the bottle, and with the coming of the Reformation beginning in

1517, the power of the Church of Rome to crush heterodox Christian views was forever lost. Protestant and Catholic today may have their differences, but they mostly tolerate one another with generally commendable ecumenicism.

By the seventeenth century, both religious and secular philosophers were making durable cases for the value of diversity in human thought and opinion. Religious wars and persecutions were hardly over, but the tide of history had been firmly pointed toward a greatly enhanced view of tolerance. It was a time of turmoil, upheaval and flowering of new thought. The country of Holland was deeply engaged in trade and was thereby immersed in the intermixing of cultures. With a societal penchant toward cultural openness, and in the tradition of the celebrated humanist Erasmus, himself a Dutchman, Holland arose as an island of refuge and tolerance for some of the great thinkers of the day. Each of the three seventeenth century writings considered today as most important on the subject of tolerance were written in Holland by men who sheltered there including Baruch de Spinoza's *Tractatus Theologico-Politicuss* (1670); John Locke's *A Letter Concerning Toleration* (1689); and Pierre Bayle's *Commentaire Philosophique* (1686). It is fitting that the Dutch have continued their tradition of tolerance, and compared to the rest of Europe, Holland has remained a haven of open-mindedness, Individual Freedom and autonomy to this day.

Spinoza championed Freedom of thought, and is most important for separating religious and political authority arguing that it was futile for the State to pursue the restriction of thought, and that it should only concern itself with actions. Bayle attempted to decouple religion and tolerance in a manner that would even include nonbelievers, arguing that practical reason could reveal moral truths which deserved equal respect with religious truths. However, it was Locke's iconic *Letter Concerning Toleration* which was to have the greatest societal impact, both of the day and into the future.

Locke spoke directly to the struggle between political and religious authority. He believed that, "While it is the duty of the state to secure the 'civil interests' of its citizens, the 'care of the soul' cannot be its business, it being a matter between the individual and God to whom alone one is responsible in this regard. Hence there is a God-given, inalienable right to the free exercise of religion."[8] However, Locke did believe that some religion in the political realm was necessary for stability.

A continued flowering of the concept of toleration occurred in the eighteenth century, with the writings of Voltaire, Montesquieu, Thomas Paine and Thomas Jefferson. The political and religious began to find separation and to decouple into the thinking that would find expression in the important documents of the American Revolution.

Montesquieu, in his *Persian Letters* (1721) and *On the Spirit of Laws* (1748) supported religious pluralism and "argues for the toleration of different religions for the purpose of preserving political unity and peace." Voltaire was concerned with religious intolerance and both the injustice and warfare it produced, and was a champion of improving the conditions of the incarcerated. In his *Philosophical Dictionary* (1764) he wrote of the French religious conflicts:

> "This horrible discord, which has lasted for so many centuries, is a very striking lesson that we should pardon each other's errors; discord is the great ill of mankind; and tolerance is the only remedy for it."[9]

Thomas Paine was highly critical of institutionalized religion and promoted separation of church and State, when he says in *The Rights of Man* (1791), "Persecution is not an original feature in any religion; but it is always the strongly marked feature of all religions established

8. Stanford Encyclopedia of Philosophy, Toleration, 3. Paragraph 9
9. Stanford Encyclopedia of Philosophy, Toleration, 3. Paragraph 11

by law. Take away the law- establishment, and every religion re-assumes its original benignity." He also stressed the importance of autonomous reason, writing, "I have always strenuously supported the right of every man to his own opinion, however different that opinion might be to mine. He who denies another this right makes a slave of himself to his present opinion, because he precludes himself the right of changing it."

Both Jefferson and Paine drew beneficially from Locke and Montesquieu. Their major divergence was to separate religion and politics into a new concept of how humanity can best govern itself. Thomas Jefferson and James Madison purposefully incorporated ideas of tolerance into the basic documents underpinning Freedom in the founding of America. In his draft of the Kentucky Resolutions in 1798, Jefferson analyzed the First Amendment, stating that it:

"...expressly declares that 'Congress shall make no law re-specting an establishment of religion, or prohibiting the free exercise thereof, or abridging the freedom of speech, or of the press,' thereby guarding in the same sentence and under the same words, the freedom of religion, of speech, and of the press; insomuch that whatever violates either throws down the sanctuary which covers the others."

Jefferson incorporated a theory of tolerance into a political theory with practical application. It is a theory of Freedom and Liberty that stresses sovereignty and autonomy of the individual, with tolerance as a necessary and practical restraint on Government action. These ideas are infused in the American Constitution and Bill of Rights, which are some of the most powerful documents ever written, justifying Freedom of The People from their own Government.

In this author's opinion, some of the greatest writings on Freedom of the nineteenth century are by the gifted philosopher John Stuart

Mill. *On Liberty* (1859) stands as a seminal work on the political concept of tolerance. Instead of focusing on religious questions, Mill stresses tolerance as necessary to resolve irreconcilable cultural and philosophical differences.

Mill believed that, "the only purpose for which power can rightfully be exercised over any member of a civilized community, against his will, is to prevent harm to others." Moreover, his argument that Government has no authority to restrict or regulate the private lives of The People was not simply a moral position; he asserted that society as a whole benefits when diverse individual pursuits are unfettered. When tolerance prevails, The People are happier than they would be when their private differences are not respected. In addition, Mill noted that when freedom of thought is restricted, the development of knowledge is thwarted. His general approach toward tolerance was thus *utilitarian* in that it provides benefits to the broad spectrum of society, rather than to an elite few.

The subject of tolerance can lead to various conundrums, notably the question of whether one ought to be tolerant of intolerance. Most of the classical thinkers on tolerance concluded that the intolerant cannot be tolerated, and they did so with an awareness of the underlying principles that view tolerance in the context of supporting individual autonomy. In the twentieth century, it became fashionable to distort the underlying concept and to simply label those in disagreement as *intolerant*. In this manner, tolerance becomes surreptitiously converted into a tool of the truly intolerant and/or manipulators who are trying to promote political agendas. They perceive tolerance as a license and as a point of agreement, proclaiming those who disagree with their views as being intolerant. They then justify using the force of Government against those they have declared intolerant as an imperious means to impose their viewpoint.

This is a perversion of the fundamental principles of toleration.

Tolerance implies "disagreement." By definition, tolerance is restraint from negating the actions of those with whom you disagree. There is no implicit license, and to term those in disagreement as intolerant is an absurd transmogrifying of any accepted definition of political tolerance.

Tolerance does not demand that we refrain from making judgments but rather that we restrain from overt action against others with whom we disagree.

Relativists and skeptics believe we must be tolerant of other viewpoints because all viewpoints, being relative, are equally valid; they deny the existence of any transcendent Truth. Mill views the issue in a more enlightening way, believing the "point is not that there is no truth but, rather, that toleration is required for us to come to know the truth."

Tolerance is a commitment to the value of human autonomy and the pluralism of points of view, not a commitment to relativism.

There has been a trend developing in the twentieth century that should be of grave concern to those who love Freedom. It is an attack by collectivists on the American Constitution's First Amendment right of free speech. The threat arises from the claim that speech can cause harm.

In discussing this particular topic, I am not suggesting denigrating politeness. Politeness is a virtue to be much admired and sought after. It is, in many ways the natural vehicle of tolerance. But there is a trend toward straitjacketing ordinary human expression, limiting what may be uttered in the classroom, at the workplace, or on the airwaves to that which is considered "politically correct."

This trend is often promulgated against political talk radio, certain cable television channels and the Internet, and claims that passionate speech might incite violence, or that it might cause psychological harm to some group favored by the rule-makers. It may also be combined with the issue of "security" to mount a call for regulation of the Internet. Government will always fear free speech and any message it cannot control, either overtly or surreptitiously. The modern media, especially through the Internet, offers the first uncensored means for an unapproved and independent message to reach a large audience in many generations. It is therefore, and no doubt will continue to be, subject to a growing chorus of calumniating attacks in an attempt to achieve Government regulation. One must tolerate the attacks, but resist at all costs the regulation.

Once upon a time, it was religious authorities who sought to prevent the free discussion of ideas they considered immoral or blasphemous. People who thought of themselves as liberals objected, and American society has largely accepted their notion that the right of free speech largely trumps such considerations. But today we have the phenomenon that the same person who will loudly defend the First Amendment rights of a pornographer is perfectly willing to prevent an Army recruiter from setting up shop on a college campus, or to countenance the firing of a political commentator who strays from the politically correct line. I fear Thomas Payne must be rolling over in his grave at the thought that America would attempt to restrict passionate speech. Or how about Patrick Henry's now iconic and decidedly inflammatory speech in which he cried, "Give me Liberty or give me death!"? Was it not incendiary? Indeed.

One senses a strong whiff of hypocrisy in modern political correctness, but hypocrisy is the antithesis of tolerance, which I repeat, implies disapproval. A great many people, I fear, go about begging society to tolerate those things of which they approve, while not lifting a finger for those to which they object, but this kind of tolerance is a sham.

As a practical matter we must restrain ourselves from using force against those with whom we disagree, lest the precedent be used to rob us of our Freedom. If I join with others to take away your right to protect yourself and your family, and others join together to take away my right to assembly or privacy, and still others take away both of our right to freely express our ideas, then a point will soon be approached where individuals have no rights, and The People are forced to live under whatever privileges Government grants us. Intolerance puts all the rights guaranteed in America's founding documents in jeopardy: our Freedom of thought, our Freedom of speech, our Freedom of movement and our Freedom of action. Because it is the only possible operating system for diversity, tolerance is not only crucial to the flourishing of society, it is quite literally *the price we have to pay for Freedom.*

CHAPTER 5

THE RISE AND FALL OF FREEDOM

IT IS A CENTRAL CONTENTION OF this book that Freedom is to be sought based not only on self-evident justification, nor only on moral grounds, but also on the practical, utilitarian principle that it is the single most important driving force that leads to the progress and prosperity of the human species. From the Stone Age to the present day, history may be seen as a succession of brief periods of progress and prosperity stimulated by an increase in Freedom, which unleashes the power of achievement of the individual, thereby fostering greater advancement in every field of human endeavor. Through greater economic, philosophical and scientific advancement, the individual is offered wider latitude of choices, which creates synergy and stimulates even greater achievement and a flourishing of humanity. Periods of Freedom are followed by much longer periods of decline, generally initiated by increased Government oppression and taxation that usher in new eras of reduced prosperity, increased misery, and little progress of any sort. There is a corollary relationship between the degree of Freedom or oppression, and human achievement.

These cycles are not natural phenomena, or a function of the cosmic laws of the universe; they are the result of human action that is either amplified by Freedom or suppressed by oppression. Freedom creates among individual men and women—who may be inspired by their environment, by chance, by calculation or by ideas formed in a particular person's mind—the ability to take action by pursuing their chosen course toward achievement. Oppression cripples the individual's ability to take action or innovate, and achievement is stultified.

Freedom has been fleeting throughout history, but almost all of the progress of humanity has occurred in those brief moments in which the The People have been free to pursue their own destiny.

The world does not move in unison through these cycles, of course; some areas may be advancing in achievement while others are regressing depending on the degree of Freedom accorded The People of the various countries. Yet today every part of the world seems to influence every other, by example at least, if not by direct interaction. This was also true of the known world in ancient times, even with slow communications. Oppressive Governments have always tried to isolate their people and monopolize knowledge, which has become increasingly difficult in today's global community. Even so, the vast majority of humans have lived, and continue to live, under the yolk of Government oppression. Just as their ancestors did, they live and die in bondage to an elite few, and are effectively thwarted in their ability to significantly improve their own circumstances or contribute to human achievement.

Nonetheless, within Western civilization, we can observe, at a minimum, the following key moments when the cycle turned dramatically:

The "invention" of democracy in late sixth century BC, Athens spurred the flowering of the classical civilizations of Greece and Rome.

As the days of the Roman Empire advanced, corruption, debasement of the currency, heavy taxation and overreaching by Government in both civil and military affairs eventually sapped the resources of the Empire, constricted the Freedom of action of its people, and obliterated the gap between the standard of living within the Empire and the rest of the world. As a result, the western half of the Empire collapsed in the fifth century AD, and although the eastern half lived on, it ceased to be a force for progress and advancement, and became an effete, stultified society.

After more than one-half millennium of stagnation and misery, which are properly called the Dark Ages, Freedom began to reawaken in medieval times as small pockets of civilization cast off oppression. In Northern Italy, a remarkable development, which can be considered the birth of capitalism occurred; private money began to be invested in projects such as trade and manufacturing. *For the first time in a millennium, wealth became separated from Government, and individuals began to develop and pursue their own ideas.* This activity led to the unprecedented artistic explosion of the Renaissance, the Age of Discovery, the Protestant Reformation and the Enlightenment—all of which furthered individual Liberty in significant ways and led to the American concept of representative Government, which spread to other nations throughout western civilization and beyond.

We will examine some of this history in more detail in the next few chapters, but one of the questions of this book will be to consider where we are in the present moment with regard to the cycles which the above analysis suggests. Beginning with the premise that Freedom is good, both in and of itself and because of the material, intellectual, artistic and other benefits it brings to The People, I will attempt to put forward a program for extending—hopefully indefinitely the cycle of Freedom upon which we precariously ride in the early twenty-first century.

What forces threaten to turn the tide and place us on the road to another modern day Dark Age? What actions must we take to preserve the vision of Freedom that inspired the founders of America, which they so eloquently expressed in documents such as the Declaration of Independence, the Constitution and the Bill of Rights?

Let's take a brief look at the rise and fall of some of the previous cycles.

FREEDOM AND ACHIEVEMENT IN ANCIENT GREECE

The Athenian democracy lasted for a little less than 200 years, from its founding in 510 BC, in the wake of a losing war against Sparta, to its conquest by Philip of Macedon (with his son, Alexander commanding the left wing) in the battle of Chaeronea in 338 BC.

When the Spartan army marched out of Athens in 510, the old aristocratic leadership of the city was in a shambles, and a man named Cleisthenes won the support of The People by promising a new kind of Government in which all adult male citizens were eligible to vote, serve on juries and attend the Assembly, and all but the poorest class could actually serve in public office, such as the Council of 500, which had previously been composed exclusively of aristocrats.

The first order of business was to provide for the common defense because the other states in the area knew of Athens' weakness at the time and several figured they were ripe for conquest. It may have looked that way, but looks were deceiving, and the Athenians defeated all invaders, leading the historian Herodotus, writing decades later, to say that the Athenians had previously been, "willing cowards, like slaves working for a master, but when they became free, each man was eager to achieve honor for himself."

Some measure of security was established. Athens was never completely free of the need for a strong defense; the Persians were a constant threat, and other Greek cities would challenge Athens from time to time, particularly as the city grew ever richer. The Athenians began to refine their democratic institutions. It was of critical importance that their leaders at this formative time were men truly dedicated to The People and not motivated by the opportunity for personal aggrandizement and power. As in the case of George Washington, men like Cleisthenes and, in the next generation, Cimon and Pericles, had a knack for leading without tyrannizing.

Pericles, in particular, is remembered as an outstanding example of democratic leadership. For more than thirty years, he was the most prominent man in the city, demonstrating exceptional talent as a military strategist, diplomat, orator and manager of public works, among other things. Another man, similarly endowed with ability, might well have aggrandized power unto himself and become a tyrant. But through a combination of his own beliefs and the political mores of The People of Athens, all the available evidence is that Pericles (like Washington) never succumbed to that temptation. Although he enriched the city, he never enriched himself at the city's expense. There was always opposition to the policies and actions he proposed, and no charge is known of his having suppressed it by any means other than the power of his arguments and the regard in which he was held. He advised the development of what was called an empire, but only to the point that it served to protect Athens from aggression and piracy. Beyond that, he counseled restraint. When an opportunity arose to build an Athenian colony in southern Italy, he instead proposed a Hellenic colony—that is, a colony from which all Greek cities could benefit.

Pericles's devotion to democracy is particularly captured in a speech known as the "Funeral Oration." This remarkable wartime speech honoring the city's fallen soldiers, has been compared to Lincoln's Gettysburg Address because Pericles took the opportunity to remind his audience of the nature of the Government for which the heroes had died, and the living, meaning those in the audience, fought on.

"Our city," he said, "is called a democracy because it is governed by the many, not the few. In the realm of private disputes, everyone is equal before the law, but when it is a matter of public honors, each man is preferred not on the basis of his class but of his good reputation and his merit."1 He also gave a strong defense of citizen involvement in governmental decision-making. "… even those who turn their attention chiefly to their own affairs do not lack judgment about politics," he said.

Athens grew rich through the commerce of her empire, held together (like the British Empire millennia later), by a powerful Navy, and Pericles, rather than use this wealth to build himself palaces, spent it on public art and architecture.

He decorated a hill overlooking Athens, the Acropolis, with some of the most magnificent buildings of history, including the Parthenon. The design of the Parthenon included resplendent friezes depicting scenes designed to make Athenians proud of their achievements in democracy and Freedom. In the center of the building, the architect, Phidias constructed a magnificent forty-foot high statue of Athena, the city's namesake. Her garments were of pure gold, and some suspicious critics accused Phidias and Pericles of having taken a share of the gold for themselves. But Pericles had ordered Phidias to construct the statue in such a way that the gold was removable, so if it were ever needed in an emergency by The People, it could be taken down and melted. To respond to the spurious charge of skimming profits from the construction, they simply removed and weighed the gold, finding every ounce accounted for. Seldom in history has the charge of graft been more convincingly refuted by a politician.

Following Pericles's death in 429 BC, the Athenian democracy continued albeit under less vigorous leadership for almost another century before the Macedonian conquest. The prime achievements of the era rest securely among the greatest of all time. To the architectural wonders of Phidias must be added the veritable invention of theater: the tragedians Aeschylus (525–456), Sophocles (495-406) and Euripides (480–406), and the comedian Aristophanes (446-388) were all contemporaries of Pericles. Pioneers in modern philosophy, Socrates was born when Pericles was twenty-six, Plato when Socrates was forty-one and Aristotle when Plato was forty-four. Aristotle, one of the most important founders of Western philosophy, was famously the tutor of the boy Alexander the Great, son of Phillip of Macedon and conqueror of all Greece, including Athens, and later much of the known world.

FREEDOM AND ACHIEVEMENT IN ANCIENT ROME

At the same time, the Athenian democracy was reaching its apogee, important developments were underway on the Italian peninsula. There, for centuries, the city-state of Rome had been expanding into the territory surrounding the city, at the expense of the Latin, Etruscan, and Sabine people, as well as other smaller tribes.

Early Rome was a monarchy in that it had a king, but it also retained a remnant of its old tribal days; the Senate. Primitive tribes, ancient as well as present day, are often governed in large part by a council of elders; and as Rome grew in size and power, this system became formalized in the Senate, a word which originally meant "old men."3 In the early system, membership in the Senate was inherited and limited to the most influential and ancient families. In political terms, it was an oligarchy.

The result was ongoing tension between the Senate and the King, which was resolved in 508 BC, when the last King was overthrown and the Roman Republic established. Still, The People (*Plebs* in Latin) were accorded little Freedom, and languished under the oppression of the oligarchic aristocracy as much as they had during the days of the old kingdom. The struggle between the Senatorial families and the plebs broke out in open revolt as early as 494 BC when the plebs, led by factions representing the peasantry, artisans, merchants and immigrants won the first of a long series of concessions that expanded their Freedoms. Through their efforts, they gained a role in the Government through the establishment of the office of Tribune and the founding of the *Concilium Plebis*, which means Assembly of the People. Of perhaps even more importance, the plebs won the right to engage in commercial activity. These concessions were a start, but the plebs needed to do more to secure their Freedom. In 451 BC, work began on the development of the famous Law of the Twelve Tables, which would become the permanent foundation of Roman law, a sort of primitive constitution. The men who wrote the Twelve Tables were diligent in their work, even visiting Athens to research ideas.

Warfare dominated the next several centuries of Roman history, much of which is obscure. There was a great invasion of the Italian peninsula by the Gauls in 390, ongoing contention with the post-Alexandrian power of Macedon, and of course the great series of wars with Carthage called the Punic Wars, which began in 264 BC and ultimately ended in complete victory for Rome in 146 BC. The destruction of Carthage was so thorough as to literally wipe the city from the face of the earth as well. Early modern historians introduced the notion that the Romans plowed the city and sowed it with salt, although this is probably merely a metaphor. Today, the site of the ancient city lies slightly southeast of Tunis, the capital of the modern nation of Tunisia, where in 2011 a new chapter in the struggle for Freedom of The People has erupted.

War is seldom the ally of Freedom, but during the war-filled century and a half following the adoption of the Twelve Tables, The People of Rome gradually gained more rights until in 287 BC, the acts of the *Concilium Plebis* were given the force of law, a moment which the historian Donald R. Dudley calls 'the high water mark of the Roman Republic."[10] If that is true, it must mean that things went downhill after that. Indeed, they did, first a a result of the Punic Wars, and then by a process familiar to those who have studied any number of popular revolutions of more modern times—the more the leaders ceased to be the revolutionaries and assumed the role of Government, the more they became corrupted by power and turned from Freedom to coercion. Like France in the 1790s, although over a more pro-tracted period of time, Rome in the last two centuries of the Republic experienced the plagues of demagoguery, state terrorism, excessive taxation, repression and tyranny. Leaders like the Gracchus broth-ers, Caius Marius and Lucius Cornelius Sulla all came to power with grand and popular schemes, and each took some actions which may be considered positive. But each of them in the end became dictators, not just in the old, technical Roman sense of the word, but in the modern pejorative sense as well. In the end, all that really mattered was who controlled the most powerful and most strategically located legions.

The history of the final decades of the Republic is fascinating read-ing, as centuries of writers of history and historical fiction (Shakespeare, for example) have amply demonstrated. The murder of Julius Caesar is surely one of the most dramatic moments in all history. Here, we can only look at those troubled times and ask what was the condition of Freedom? The answer is that it was not healthy. The commercial and political Freedom which had theretofore sustained the Republic col-lapsed into an anarchy, as gangs associated with one or another should-be military dictators frustrated any semblance of Freedom to live one's life in accordance with one's personal values and talents.

That being the case, it is not hard to understand why, by the end of the Battle of Actium, when Crassus, Pompey, Caesar, Lepidus and Mark Antony were counted among the dead, and only Octavian remained, The People breathed a collective sigh of relief we might

10. Dudley, Donald R., *The Civilization of Rome*, 1960

paraphrase today as, "Thank God that's over." The Senate promptly bestowed on Octavian the name Augustus Caesar. Both People and Senate would willingly have made him King, but he declined, and accepted only the title of *Princeps*, or "First Citizen." The institutions of the Republic remained in place, but for the remaining forty years of his life, the First Citizen made all the important decisions.

In his popular book, *The 100,*[11] author Michael H. Hart attempted to name and rank his choices of the one hundred most influential people of all time. He ranks Augustus nineteenth, possibly too low given his historical role, However, I think the most interesting thing he says about Augustus is found in his discussion of George Washington, whom he ranks (definitely too low, in my view) twenty-seventh.

Speaking of Washington, Hart observes that he is "the American political figure who roughly corresponds to Augustus Caesar." Many people have been called "The George Washington" of their country, and while few have truly deserved the comparison, that between Washington and Augustus is apt in that both regarded leadership as service and not glory. Both could have assumed the role of dictator, but neither did.

Augustus had no Jefferson or Madison to expound the theories and draft the rules of the new Roman nation that he erected from the ashes of the Old Republic. The omission is unfortunate, because in all the centuries that the Roman Empire endured after Augustus, it never satisfactorily solved the problem of succession, and as a result, the Freedom of the People of Rome vacillated with the whim and competence of the Emperor. Like Washington, Augustus set an extraordinary example; lacking the firm framework of a Constitution to guide them, his successors did not always follow the example. From the brilliant literary achievements of Virgil, Horace, Ovid and many others, to the

---

11. Michael H. Hart *The 100*, 1978. Hart was forced to revise his list following the collapse of Communism in the early 1990s, downgrading Lenin, Stalin and others, but, interestingly, not Marx.

spectacular achievements of Roman engineers with their construction of roads and aqueducts, to the *Pax Romana* itself, few epochs in history can match the early decades of the Empire in political, artistic or technological progress, nor in widespread and increasingly diverse prosperity. A modern American or European transported to those times would complain about a great deal, but few citizens of any previous nation (save Athens during its height), nor of most subsequent nations even to this day, would join in the complaint. At its height, the Roman Empire could and did provide an exceptional level of Freedom and human achievement.

It was not always at its best, however. Evil and even deranged Emperors—Caligula, Nero and their ilk—demonstrated again and again the fragility of the blessings of civilization. But there were good times, too, notably the years AD 96 to AD 180 which was and is remembered as the period of the Five Good Emperors (Nerva, Trajan, Hadrian, Antoninus Pius and Marcus Aurelius).

During this period, the succession was accomplished by a system wherein the Emperor selected his successor and then formally adopted him as his son.

The first four of the Five Good Emperors chose their successors wisely, but Marcus Aurelius, otherwise a praiseworthy leader who would be remembered as a great stoic philosopher even if he had never become Emperor, did not. He had a natural son, Commodus, from whose troubled reign the true centuries-long decline and fall of the Roman Empire can be said to date. Writing in the following century, Dio Cassius, said the history of Rome, "... now descends from a kingdom of gold to one of iron and rust, as affairs did for the Romans of that day." Commodus raised taxes, wasted the Treasury on unsustainable handouts and gladiatorial contests, and—rejecting completely his father's stoic philosophy—engaged in megalomania to the extent of renaming all twelve months of the year after himself. He had twelve names, altogether. The Empire was never again the same, and The People never again as free.

FREEDOM AND ACHIEVEMENT IN THE EARLY MIDDLE AGES

The last western Roman Emperor, a boy named Romulus Augustus, was deposed by the German leader Odoacer in 476, marking the beginning of the Dark Ages. In most of the Western Roman Empire, few people noticed, Romulus and his predecessors having exercised no recognizable authority for decades. The economy had collapsed, and a severe and brutal existence would ensue for centuries.

The citizens of Rome attained lofty accomplishment in most fields of human endeavor, such as engineering, art, and architecture. Evidence of their achievements are still littered throughout the old Empire. To give just one example, there was the old Roman road system—roughly 250,000 miles of improved roads at the height of the Empire, about 50,000 of them actually paved. They would still be the best roads in all of Europe a millennium after the Empire was gone, and their very existence must have caused at least a few thoughtful medieval nobles, or peasants for that matter, pause and wonder about who had built them, and why no one could build such a thing in their time.

In the far southeast corner of the old Empire, far out in the desert past the last road, there was born less than a century after the short reign of Romulus Augustus, a boy who was destined to have an impact on the world that some have judged to have been greater than any Roman emperor. Michael Hart and many others indeed have judged him to have been one of the most influential human beings in all history. This was Mohammed (570-632), founder of both a religion and an empire.

Like Europe, the part of the world we now call the Middle East was experiencing a post-Roman dark age of its own, and Mohammed's army of followers, having conquered the Arabian Peninsula, quickly moved out in all directions. By the year AD 750, they ruled an enormous territory that stretched from western India westward across North Africa, and crossing the Straits of Gibraltar, to the borders of France. And once the fighting stopped, they ruled it very well for several centuries. Two centers, known as Caliphates, would develop. The Abbasids built a great city on the Tigris River and named it Baghdad, in the process chasing out their rivals, the Umayyads, who ultimately built a capital in the land they called Al-Andalus, and we call Spain. Though rivals, the two Caliphates were so distant geographically that they had little actual conflict, or even contact. Given the times, both provided remarkable Freedom for The People of their lands. Christians and Jews (although not pagans) were allowed to keep and practice their faith simply by paying a tax, which seems to have been quite affordable. Or they could convert and be free of the tax altogether. If we compare the way the two faiths were treated with the way Jews were treated in contemporary Europe, there can be no doubt that in that time the Muslim world had Christendom beaten hands down when it came to tolerance.

Both Baghdad and the Umayyad capital of Cordoba grew into renowned centers of learning and scholarship, and between them are largely responsible for the survival of classical Greek and Roman learning. Under the enlightened rule of Abd al-Rahman III (912–961), Islamic Spain flourished and Cordoba became one of the most important centers of learning and achievement of its time. A vast library was created that began importing books from all over the world, and scholars were recruited through offerings of patronage. Tolerance promoted the mixing of cultures, and the infrastructure of knowledge and achievement soon attracted historians, poets, philosophers and musicians that established an intellectual tradition lasting hundreds of years. Great advancements were made in the fields of geography, botany, medicine, surgery and education. Our knowledge today of Plato, Aristotle and virtually all the other great thinkers of the ancient world would be immeasurably poorer were it not for the careful and diligent scholars of the early Islamic world. This is even more remarkable in that only a small fraction of the works so painstakingly assembled and translated were to survive, as the libraries were burned by less tolerant successors.

The Umayyads, or Moors (so called because they came into Spain from Morocco) ran such a rich and vibrant, learned and tolerant country that it earned the sobriquet "Ornament of the World," a phrase coined by a tenth century German nun named Hroswitha[12], who had the run of the court of Otto I, and so came into conversation with diplomats, many of them Christians, who represented Cordoba at the German court in Saxony.

As noted in the previous chapter, "tolerance" is crucial for maintaining Freedom, and thereby, the achievement of humanity. But it is difficult, given the nature of our times not to note, and lament the passing of a time and place when adherents of Islam ran not only the most advanced country in Europe, but also flourished as the most tolerant. One further example will have to suffice as evidence.[13]

Sometime around the year AD 940, a boy was born, in his own later words, to "poor and humble parents" somewhere in the south of France. His father may have been a servant at the Abbey of St. Geraud. In any event, it was obvious early that the boy, who was named Gerbert, had uncommon intellectual gifts. The monks of St. Geraud took him under their wing, taught him all they could, and eventually brought him to the Caliphate of Cordoba, where he blossomed

---

12. Hroswitha was also an accomplished poet and playwright whose remarkable life is worthy of celebration, and is at least to some extent celebrated. Every year, in her hometown of Gandersheim, the Hroswitha Prize is awarded to female writers.

13. Readers who wish a more detailed history of Moorish Spain can find it in *The Ornament of the World*, by Maria Rosa Menocal, 2002.

into perhaps the most learned scholar in Europe. He was counselor to Holy Roman Emperors Otto II and Otto III, and eventually was elected Pope as Sylvester II. Along the way, he played a key role in bringing Arabic numerals into use (replacing Roman numerals) in Christian Europe, and fostered the growth of many arts and sciences. He also made enemies; so advanced was his thinking that some people couldn't believe he was not under the power of the devil.

Gerbert was the most prominent of many European scholars who trained at Cordoba, and the education they brought back played a key role in bringing the continent out of the Dark Ages, and on the path to the Renaissance. But the Caliphate's days as a bastion of Freedom and tolerance were numbered.

Umayyad rule declined after 1009 and ended in 1031 under pressure from more extreme Muslim sects associated with the Fatimid dynasty which, ruling from Cairo, had challenged both the Umayyads in the west and the liberal-leaning Abbasids in Baghdad. After a period of confusion and religious confrontation, a new dynasty was established in Spain by the Almoravids, who were believers in only their strict interpretation of the Koran.

FREEDOM AND ACHIEVEMENT IN THE HIGH AND LATE MIDDLE AGES

The Ornament of the World had fallen from its branch of tolerance and shattered. But the shards would prove invaluable. Most of them would land in Europe where they would become key pieces in building something entirely new, which today we call the private sector. Pericles believed in Freedom, but he intertwined Freedom with participation in Government. In the very same passage quoted earlier from the Funeral Oration, he said of the Athenians, "We alone regard the man who takes no part in politics not as someone who minds his own business, but as useless." Two millennia later, the world would finally be ready to learn that men who minded their own business could be very useful indeed, and could bring about levels of achievement and prosperity never before imagined. Their achievements were, in the modern sense, *viral*, spreading throughout society impelled by an invisible hand more powerful in its way than the hand of Government could ever be.

But that is getting ahead of the story. First, backward, poverty-stricken, bickering Europe had to pick up the shards and put them to some use. In his 1997 *book The Measure of Reality*, Professor Alfred W. Crosby of the University of Texas has devoted his career to the study of why Europe came to dominate the world, and it is a great tragedy that his writings have been eclipsed by the ideologically-driven ideas of Jared Diamond, the author of *Guns, Germs, and Steel*.

Crosby speaks of what he calls the "New Model" of viewing reality, which came to fruition in the late Middle Ages. This new model was "distinctive in its growing emphasis on precision, quantification of physical phenomena, and mathematics," and "the individuals chiefly responsible" were led by a "cultural avant-garde ... who spent their working hours in one of two centers; the university and the marketplace."

This combination of academic and commercial energy was new, and its results spectacular. Crosby zeroes in on the half-century between 1275 and 1325 as the point where things reached a sort of critical mass. In those brief fifty years, the first known cannon, mechanical clock, *Portolano* marine chart, perspective painting, modern musical notation and double-entry bookkeeping all appeared, he says. Thus did art, science, business, war and virtually every other aspect of European society come to be different from anything that had preceded it or any other society on earth at the time.

And, with the exception of the cannon, all those items found their greatest applications in the lives of people minding their own business. This implied the Freedom to engage in business, and that Freedom could be found in Europe as nowhere else on earth, precisely because Europe was a confused agglomeration of competing countries, making it easy for an entrepreneur to escape the clutches of Government by simply taking his operation over the mountain, or across the river to another jurisdiction. Nothing nearly so easy was possible in China or the Muslim world. Thus, the shard of Arabic numerals became, in European hands, one of the cornerstones of commerce, although author Jack Weatherford8 notes that, "Most Governments refused to accept the use of Arabic numerals for official purposes."

But "Merchants ... needed a practical means of calculation, even if it lacked the prestige of classical Roman numerals, and they immediately began using the new numerical system." Moreover, they improved on it. "When merchants noted an overweight or underweight item" Weatherford continues, "they marked it with a plus sign or a minus sign. These signs soon became the symbols for addition and subtraction, and, eventually, for positive and negative numbers."

As with numbers, so with letters. In the universities, scholars developed a little used idea into a comprehensive system: alphabetization. Here again, we can see that Crosby's New Model brought speed and efficiency never before possible.[14] Nor were advances confined to the "white collar" world of reading, writing and arithmetic. It was during this same period that farmers first developed a horse harness that didn't strangle the horse by pulling against its throat; the New Model transferred the weight to the horse's shoulders, greatly increasing its effective strength when pulling any sort of burden. Another agricultural advance of great importance was the invention of the moldboard plow, a great improvement over the scratch plows of the Roman era.

---

14. In the case of libraries, for example, the most popular previous system was to catalogue books by their importance, with the Bible first, and so on. Imagine trying to find this book, or any of those referenced in it, under such a system.

Again, advances like Arabic numerals, alphabetization, the shoulder harness and the moldboard plow are notable in that their principal advantage lay not in massive public infrastructure like Roman roads and aqueducts, but in the individualized private concerns of traders and farmers. And as individuals increasingly prospered, they found themselves able to hire others and to build on their newfound prosperity.

As the ability of and opportunities for people engaged in commerce increased, so did their wealth, and to accommodate this new wealth, new financial institutions came into being. Kings had always needed ways to finance their operations, given the irregularity of their income and the vulnerability of their treasuries. In the year 1100, the English King William II and his younger brother (and heir) Henry were out hunting when a (stray?) arrow killed the King. No contemporary source or subsequent historian has ever been able to make a fratricide case against Henry, but it is clearly recorded that his immediate reaction was to ride pell-mell to Winchester where the treasury was stored.

Clearly someone needed to invent the bank, and kings increasingly began turning to the Knights Templar, whose vast fortune, derived from the Crusades, was safely ensconced on the island of Malta. The Templars became the Bank of Europe, a designation both lucrative and dangerous. In 1295, the French King Philip the Fair got angry at the Templars and withdrew his holdings. Then he went after the rest of their vast holdings, eventually cutting a deal with the Pope, who abolished the order and split the loot with Philip. In 1314, the last two Templar leaders were burned at the stake in Paris. The Templars had been reduced to fodder for twenty-first century novels and movie thrillers.

But none of that obviated the need for a bank. Or banks, actually. Since no one at the time had enough resources to replace the Templars *en toto*, and since the growing wealth of the private sector was as vulnerable as that of kings, banks developed in the private sector, first in northern Italy. There had never been anything like these private banks anywhere in the world, and unlike the Templars, they were motivated by a desire to provide innovative ways to serve their private clients. To give just one example, they came up with the bill of exchange, a written document that was, as long as you could trust the bank anyway, literally as good as gold, less a small fee for the banker, of course. "The new Italian bank money," Weatherford writes, "boosted commerce by making it transpire much faster."

In 1338, a shipment of coins required three weeks to wend its way from Rouen in the north of France, to Avignon in the south, a distance of just over four hundred miles, and the shipment faced the hazard of being lost, stolen by robbers, or pilfered by the very people hired to transport it. By contrast, a bill of exchange could be sent in a mere eight days, and if it was stolen, the thief could not redeem it….Bills of exchange helped to free money from its spatial limitations.[15]

As the velocity of monetary exchange increased and spatial limitations were overcome, the pool of potential investment capital was vastly expanded. Where private capital had previously been mostly localized, it was now free to pursue prosperity across new geographical and metaphorical horizons.

The advantages of this new money on land were often amplified when it went to sea. The great voyages of discovery may have been financed by royals like Portugal's Prince Henry the Navigator and Spain's Ferdinand and Isabella, but it was private traders from England, the Netherlands, and elsewhere, organized and financed by private companies such as the East and West India Companies that made the new discoveries profitable.

The new private sector economy was a corollary outgrowth of individuals gaining more Freedom. For the first time, it was possible for commoners to become prosperous, even wealthy, even

15. Jack Weatherford, *The History of Money*

fabulously wealthy, like the Medici family of Florence and the Fuggers of Augsburg, and in the few remaining centuries when it mattered, some were even able to achieve titles and nobility. But the new Freedom was more than just monetary. The new wealth was spent on things like art, inspiring the splendor of the Renaissance.[16] Science benefited from the new Freedom as much as art. When Isaac Newton (1643–1727) said that if he had seen farther, it was by standing on the shoulders of giants, he meant not only ancients like Archimedes, Pythagoras and Aristotle, but also those whose work was included in Crosby's New Model: men like Roger Bacon, William of Ockham and Nicole Oresme, as well as Copernicus and Galileo. Literature also thrived in the wake of the new Freedom—the dramas of the Elizabethan masters including Christopher Marlowe, Ben Jonson, and, preeminently, William Shakespeare being the prime examples, notable both for their quality and their humanism.

Free people had new thoughts about religion and philosophy as well. Christians in Europe wanted, first of all, to be able to read the Bible for themselves. The invention of modern printing, with movable type, by Johann Gutenberg in the 1440s had made possible the printing of books, including Bibles, in quantity for the first time, but that only helped if you could read Latin. The translation of the Bible into the vernacular languages of Europe was both a precursor and a consequence of the Protestant Reformation of the early seventeenth century. But the demand for the product was surely a consequence of the new sense of Freedom and individualism that led directly to the reform of philosophy we call *The Enlightenment*, and the reform of Government sparked by the American Revolution and its aftermath.

---

16. Renaissance art was not just another wave of good painters, sculptors and architects. It represented new science, such as in anatomy and the revolutionary physics of perspective, as well as a new philosophy. When Michelangelo painted the hand of God reaching out to touch the hand of Adam on the ceiling of the Sistine Chapel, he was saying something utterly new about the position of man in the universe, an elevation of the status of humanity utterly impossible to have been expressed a few centuries earlier.

During the Enlightenment, Freedom as the driving force for human achievement was about to see a reinvigoration not achieved since the time of Pericles in ancient Athens, and this was only a precursor of even greater achievement that was to arise out of that little "rebellion across the pond" in America.

———— **CHAPTER 6** ————

THE DYNAMICS OF CHANGE IN SOCIETY

THERE IS A COROLLARY RELATIONSHIP BETWEEN the advancement and
well-being of mankind and the amount of Freedom accorded the individual. From Protagoras to the present day, many of the truly great
thinkers and philosophers have extolled the virtues and importance of
the individual. The subject has been most often approached from the
viewpoint of morality with the well-being of society when free and
the agony of society when oppressed offered as philosophical proofs.
The last chapter presented an historical overview of the rise and fall of
Freedom through history showing its importance to human achievement. But a poignant question remains. Why? Why has society so
benefitted from Freedom of the individual? What has caused the endeavors of mankind to flourish in the brief periods of history where
the individual has cast off the oppression of the State? I believe that
the answer lies in the nature and dynamics of how change takes place.
In this chapter I propose a theory that will embrace and reinforce our
Forefathers' belief in a relationship between the biological nature of
man, and how he governs himself.

Some aspects of change take place differently for humans than for other species, and it is through these differences that people have developed the ability to alter their world on a scope and in a time frame unparalleled by any other living creature on earth. These differences amplify the potential contribution of each unique individual in a manner not possible in the rest of the animal kingdom. It is in this difference that the corollary between individual Freedom and the ability to effect change exists. Let us now consider the dynamic forces of change in any species and the specific relationship of man to change. In so doing, we will see *why* the success of mankind depends upon his ability to exist and create in conditions where his personal Freedom is maximized.

Prior to the Enlightenment, most scientists still accepted Aristotle's concept of *scala naturae* in which all living creatures were classified by an ideal pyramid with simplest animals occupying the bottom and progressing upward through complexity with human beings occupying the top. Most western, religious beliefs were anthropocentric, and taught that all creatures were created by God to serve man.

Jean-Baptiste Lamark (1744–1829) is generally recognized as originating the first complex theory of evolution. He believed that through time all creatures trend toward greater perfection, as observed in that body changes and behaviors can be transmitted from generation to generation. The science of animal breeding depends on this process, although, of course in this case it is not a natural process, but rather one directed by what might be termed "intelligent design."

Charles Darwin (1809–1882) proposed what is recognized today as the explanation of the diversity of life with his publication of *On the Origin of Species* in 1859. It holds that all species have evolved over time through a process he termed "natural selection." It caused a furor among many in the religious community who viewed it as a direct attack on some of their fundamental beliefs, but that debate is outside the scope of this book, so I will simply note that many, perhaps most, religious groups have incorporated an accommodation of at least some aspects of evolution into their beliefs. The overall point is that most of the animal kingdom is inexorably tied to only one means of achieving cumulative change—genetically unique individuals capable of successfully passing on their acquired characteristics.

Genetic change occurs in human beings, too. However, they have an additional avenue; they can disseminate and pass on change nongenetically through their ability to *communicate*. This means change can also be passed on to contemporaries *ubiquitously*, instead of only to genetic descendants, and in a collapsed time frame.[17] We shall also see that superseding the need for genetic change also increases the probability that some aspects of change can be harmful for our species.

There are many theories and much disagreement as to what constitutes the most important characteristic elevating humans to the top of Aristotle's pyramid. I personally believe it is human beings' *ability to integrate complex concepts*, two of the highest expressions of which are reason and language. And I believe the rarest and most valuable commodity of humankind is original thought.

As a simple example of integrating complex concepts, let's use language and consider the sentence, "We went to town." From that handful of words, some of the implied concepts are: *self, other, togetherness, place* (here or originating), and *place* (other destination). Also implied are *conveyance*, which can be accomplished by any vast number of means from walking to airplanes dependent on the complexities of distance, terrain, and available means; Also implied are the concepts of *present, past,* and *town*. A description of the complexity of "town" as a concept could far exceed the pages of this manuscript with sensory phenomena such as typical sounds like dogs barking or emergency vehicle sirens, to complex smells from the appetizing bakery or the noxious sewer, to construction from curbs to skyscrapers.

---

17. Or, for that matter, an *extended* time frame. The rediscovery of Aristotle's writings in the late Middle Ages helped spark the Renaissance almost a millennium after the great philosopher's death. No such delayed influence is possible through genetics.

Also consider the differences in all of the above characteristics if the towns were Houston, or Hong Kong, or Dixville Notch, New Hampshire! The point is that with just four simple words, humans can convey an enormous amount of complex information, the understanding (or misunderstanding) of which is filtered and interpreted on the basis of what the hearer already knows about the subject. For instance, the meaning from context will depend on such variables as whether it applies to a just completed trip in a 2006 Jeep Cherokee into a small, nearby rural town, or if the speaker were referring to a past event that took place decades previously. Think how much that could change the concept of town.

The ability to abstractly integrate complex concepts through reason is the highest expression of human advancement, and use of the ability to reason is the most moral of all human endeavors. Foregoing reason turns humans into automatons influenced by the direction of others, which abdicates individual responsibility to make correct choices to the best of one's ability.

All individuals are unique; since the mapping of the human genome, we understand that truth in its ultimate, biological sense. But even before modern science came up with the technical explanation, it was a demonstrable fact. The American novelist John Dos Passos made a particularly succinct statement of human uniqueness in his 1960 novel *Mid-Century*. "We none of us smell alike," he wrote. "That is how bloodhounds earn their kennel rations. The bloodhound can tell."[18]

But while all are unique, some kinds of uniqueness are particularly noteworthy, for example, the ability for *purely original thought*, which is to say the ability of a small number of humans to reason out in the

18.Dos Passos is an excellent example of modern cultural bias. He was a Communist as a young man, and the novels he wrote during that period of his life are still featured in many university courses. But his work after he abandoned Communism and became a conservative, including the excellent *Mid-Century*, are ignored by the left-leaning intelligentsia.

abstract something previously unknown or which has not previously occurred. Einstein's thought experiments are an iconic example. I do not wish to confuse this meaning with a thought that might be original to any particular individual, but which is already known to the species which happens all the time. I am distinguishing purely original thought as that outside of what is known, or at least known to be known.

The ability to integrate complex concepts also enhances discovery and comparative observation. Being capable of observing causal chains among events or of understanding benefits or detriments are powerful advantages. Much of what we know in the world has been discovered through serendipity wherein the importance of a bit of knowledge gained by chance occurrence is recognized by someone engaged in, or observing, an event. Weed trimmers were invented by a man viewing spinning nylon bristles in a car wash. Velcro was invented by the curiosity of a Swiss mountaineer when he and his dog became covered with burrs while on a hike. Serendipity aside, however, the striking complexity of human thought is revealed in these seemingly trivial examples: "Gee, I wonder if it would be possible to create an artificial bur that would allow a person to stick things together when he wanted to, instead of when he doesn't want to." That is an immensely complex thought sequence, and utterly human.

Not only the human abilities to create and discover, but also those to disseminate, interchange, and store knowledge are enhanced by the ability to integrate complex concepts. Today, the power that concept integration unleashes has developed to the point of enabling an individual to radically affect the lives of the entire species in his own lifetime! (For good or bad.) This has primarily been reflected in man's development and dissemination of technology. Absent technology, humans would still be subsisting in crudely fortified caves and hovels hoping to avoid predators.

Such crude fortifications, and the tools used to build them, indeed represent the beginnings of technology, and various animal species have evolved to the point of beginning to change their environment: the beaver in his moated home, the wasp in his self-made mud tunnel. Some animals, such as elephants, are also believed to have the ability to retain long-term memories, but it is difficult to quantify or compare this ability. Humans have the advantage of the ability to reason, but they also have the resulting advanced technology, which allows them to store knowledge and transmit it far into the future, even past their own lifetimes. The original ideas of, say, Aristotle or Newton, initially combined with no more complex technology than writing, still influence people today.

Thinking is an individual, not a collective, activity. It follows that the more and varied opportunities people have, the wider-ranging will be their thoughts. You may object to this idea. You may say that when people come together and share their thoughts, they stimulate one another and produce more advanced thoughts. This can be true, but it is only true to the extent the individuals in the group have thoughts that are different from one another, and the uniqueness of individuals is only partially genetic. The remainder (No one knows how much; In *The Bell Curve*, authors Richard Herrnstein and Charles Murray found expert estimates of intelligence ranging from 40 to 80 percent genetic.)[19] must be due to environmental factors, and the variety of such factors is clearly a function of individual Freedom. Thus in the process of "group thought," the potential importance of each *individual* is vastly amplified in an environment of diversity as opposed to collectivism. By collapsing the time frame for change and by being able to effect environmental as well as genetic change throughout the species, the volume of change is greatly augmented. But enforced conformity to a collective norm will diminish the advantage. This is the answer to why The People flourish in all fields of endeavor when

19. Herrnstein and Murray, *The Bell Curve*, The Free Press, 1994, page 298.

allowed to operate under the tenets of Freedom and Liberty and also why progress is thwarted by oppression of the State.

UNIQUE HUMANS AND CHANGE

For our purposes, most major change in man's history can be condensed into only three categories of unique individuals: conquerors, scientists/inventors and philosophers. Some may fit more than one group such as conqueror-philosopher or philosopher-scientist, but as shown by Michael H. Hart in his book, *The 100*, almost all of the major change in the history of mankind can be attributed to a very small number of unique individuals. Even if you disagree with the order of Hart's ranking (as I do), the concept of a handful of individuals disproportionately influencing history is compelling, as the achievements of each are highlighted.

Some of you may object that I do not include artists as a category of those causing major change. While such a case could be made, I agree with Hart, who says "In general, literary and artistic figures have had comparatively little influence on human history." Hart includes five artists on his list of the one hundred most influential people of all time, with Shakespeare foremost at number thirty-six.

It may be that Hart and I underestimate the impact of artists on history, but the problem is that the impact individual artists have is virtually impossible to quantify. I have already mentioned the great achievement of Pericles' sculptor and architect Phidias in building the Parthenon. This sublime work of art no doubt had an impact on Athenian life and politics, but how is one to say how much?

You still may argue that great art is an end in itself, independent of politics or economics. That may very well be true, but it is not the topic of this book.

CONQUERORS

A significant part of recorded history has been shaped by men whose goal was to conquer and rule mankind. Probably the most famous and successful was Aristotle's pupil, Alexander the Great. Some others whose names and degree of success are familiar include, in chronological order, Cyrus the Great, Hannibal, Attila, William the Conqueror, Genghis Kahn, 'Umar ibn al-Khattab, Ivan the Terrible, Napoleon Bonaparte and Adolf Hitler. The conquests of these men, whether temporary or enduring and for better or worse, brought dramatic change to the lives of millions—some (the conquered) directly, and others as a result of the historic forces unleashed by their actions. William the Conqueror, for example, whose territorial acquisitions are modest compared with others on the list, had an enormous impact on subsequent history by bringing England into intimate contact with France and the rest of the European continent. Hart and other historians believe that if William had not conquered England, the British Isles would have remained part of the Scandinavian world, peripheral to the affairs of Europe—a very great change indeed.

The phenomenal increase in population and the "shrinking" of the world through instant communication and travel will make it difficult for a modern day conqueror to subjugate large parts of the world. It is far more likely that mankind will continue to be enslaved by their own Governments. However, old-fashioned conquest is a possibility that must not be dismissed completely. With history as our guide, it is probable that the use of force to conquer will continue to be applied along the ethno-religious or ideological groupings of modern mankind. But should a unique individual with the proper mix of charisma, leadership, and ambition appear again in our world, the potential for conflict is real. The mitigating factor that any potential conqueror would now face in subjugating the entire world is that humans have become so efficient at killing through technology. An all-out war utilizing nuclear technology could bring about the destruction of all mankind, and so global war on the scale we have previously known must of necessity be a part of man's past. Though there are those who argue that conquerors have brought about positive change, I believe that there is a far more compelling case for the use of reason than force. Freedom is a precarious commodity afforded to the vanquished only by the good will of the conqueror, and Government dominance over their lives is increased, which brings about long-term economic decline.

SCIENTISTS AND INVENTORS

The contributions of scientists and inventors touch virtually every aspect of our existence. Advances in medicine alone have given humankind a longer lifespan and provided the weaponry, so to speak, which allows us to at least hold our own in the never-ending battle with the micro-world of pathogens, which wiped swaths of death across whole continents in past centuries; the Black Plague of 1348–50 reduced the population of Europe by one-third or more. Science has made it possible for us to communicate with one another across space and time, and to transport ourselves and our things from one end of the earth to the other—even to outer space. If we stay at home, we can live in comfortably heated and air-conditioned homes and enjoy pleasures and entertainments literally unimaginable to previous generations. This lifestyle, which we now take for granted, is the gift of science and technology, without which we would still be engaged in the struggle for mere subsistence that dominated the days of our forebearers. We can also use our spare time to study, think, learn and create. There's no assurance, of course, that a given person will use his or her time wisely; much of it is wasted in frivolity to be sure. But the total experience surely means progress, however defined.

Without the accomplishments of the scientists and inventors—individual humans thinking their individual thoughts—The People would still be drinking the same tainted water and suffering from the same malnutrition and disease as did their ancestors. They would still travel no faster than a horse can run—not that fast, actually, because the domestication of the horse itself can be counted as a significant early achievement of a Stone Age proto-scientist.[20] Try to maintain this perspective as we consider the contribution of the scientist/inventor. They were amazing men.

The accomplishments of scientists and Inventors are generally tangible, making many of these men easy to identify. Benjamin Franklin, for instance, was one of the truly great minds from our past. He would be categorized as scientist, inventor, politician and philosopher. He was called the "Father of Electricity," and much of the early knowledge of electricity, such as positive and negative charge, came from his fertile mind. His inventions are too numerous to mention, but many had a major impact upon The People of his day. Franklin's *Poor Richard's Almanac*, his contribution to the U.S. Constitution, and his political activities would place him in the category of Philosopher. An argument could even be made that Franklin was a military leader in that he directed part of America's war effort while in France.

The individual whose achievements have arguably had the greatest

20. One of the most absurd arguments by Jared Diamond in his flawed, but enormously popular book *Guns, Germs and Steel*, is that zebras are impossible to domesticate, being much more vicious than horses, thus diminishing the achievement of Eurasian horse-domesticators and excusing their African contemporaries for not having done likewise with their native equids. But of course Diamond cannot possibly know the relative dangerousness of the multimillennial ancestors of horses and zebras, as they were when the horse was being domesticated. Diamond does admit that Baron Walter Rothschild (1868-1937) "drove through London in a carriage pulled by zebras," but he dismisses Rothschild as "eccentric," when in fact he was a trained zoologist, and if having a stable of zebras which were regularly hitched to a carriage and driven even to Buckingham Palace doesn't constitute domestication, I can't imagine what does. Diamond's whole effort in *Guns, Germs and Steel* is to account for European domination of the modern world without giving any credit whatsoever to any individual Europeans, and it is that prejudice against the achievements of individual human beings that discredits his book.

effect on all of humanity is Sir Isaac Newton (1642–1727). Born in the first year of the English Civil War, he rose to prominence during the liberal times of the Stuart Restoration, and continued his remarkable career well into the succeeding Hanoverian dynasty. While still in his twenties, he proposed the scientific theories which revolutionized the world. His contributions to physics, optics, astronomy, and mathematics are known and used by all educated men today. No other individual (save possibly Leonardo Da Vinci) has even come close to Newton's impact on our fundamental understanding of our world and our technology. Newton was also devoutly religious, but his religious views were decidedly unorthodox. Had he lived earlier (or elsewhere) he might have been persecuted, even tortured or burned at the stake as a heretic, and his scientific writings, like those of Gerbert, denounced as the work of the devil. But Newton lived in the Age of Enlightenment, and his career lends considerable support to the theory that the individual must be Free for the betterment of mankind. Had Newton's work been suppressed, the technological marvels, resulting from his insight into physics and mathematics, might not now exist.

By the same token, had Newton lived in twentieth century Russia, he might have ended up in the Gulag, or been assigned to a collectivist farm, the fate of countless men of ability and intelligence. In either case, the loss to the advancement of humanity would be without question. **Collectivism quenches the guiding light of the brightest and best individuals.**

In comparing individual scientist/inventors and conquerors, it is fair to say that intellect is the general unifying characteristic of the former, while among the latter, willfulness and aggressiveness come to the fore. One can scarcely imagine a greater contrast than that between, say, the gentle Franklin and someone like the illiterate Attila the Hun, whose rise to power depended upon his charisma, his skill as a warrior, his ferocity, and his ruthlessness

Some other important scientist/inventors are (in alphabetical order): Francis Bacon, Nils Bohr, Copernicus, Marie Curie, Charles Darwin, Thomas Edison, Albert Einstein, Michael Faraday, Galileo Galilei, Johann Gutenberg, Stephen Hawking, Werner Heisenberg, Antony van Leeuwenhoek, Joseph Lister, Ts'ai Lun, Guglielmo Marconi, Gregor Mendel, James Clerk Maxwell, William of Ockham, Louis Pasteur, Nikola Tesla, and Leonardo da Vinci. These unique individuals made far-reaching contributions in the field of science and in practical inventions which affect the everyday lives of mankind. *Much of the understanding of our world is a product of the work of this short list of these individuals.*

This is not to say that many others have not contributed. On the contrary, every moment of each day it is likely that a bright mind somewhere is filled with unique insight that contributes to the accomplishments of mankind. However, the achievements of the handful of individuals listed above lift them to a level far above that of the small daily discovery. We cannot accurately measure the enormous benefit to mankind provided by this group of unique individuals in our species, but it has literally transformed almost every aspect of our lives.

PHILOSOPHERS
(INCLUDING MYSTICS AND POLITICIANS)

While scientists and inventors have had the greatest impact upon the physical condition and the alteration of man's environment through technology, it is the philosophers who have had the greatest impact upon his thinking, his social condition, his mores, his values *and his conflicts*. Thus, philosophers have had an overall impact on our lives equal to, or even possibly surpassing, that of scientists/inventors. It is also the philosophers who have had the greatest detrimental impact, as well as the most positive. This would seem a paradox; yet the ideas put forth by various philosophers have benefitted or harmed mankind, depending on their nature, and not infrequently as a result of often bloody conflict associated with their promulgation. The competition of these ideas has caused more warfare, intolerance, hatred, death, destruction, poverty, and misery than any other driving force. By the same token, they produced the Sophist movement, the Enlightenment, the American, French, and other Revolutions, and eras of greatest advancement in man's history. It is here, more than in any other arena, that the forces of collectivism, authoritarian rule and force and fear, battle the forces of Freedom, Liberty, logic and reason.

The proposition that philosophers have been of equal or greater consequence than scientist/inventors rests on the fact that while the latter have given us knowledge and the capability of technology, it is in the arena of philosophy that mankind decides whether to embrace or reject such advances. Consider the present day debate on the use of nuclear reactors to produce electricity. Knowledge and the instruments of that knowledge (technology) are tools to be utilized or rejected for the betterment or detriment of mankind. It is philosophy which makes those ultimate determinations. Will knowledge of nuclear physics be used to build bombs or produce electricity (Or both? Or neither? If a byproduct of modern technology is the destruction of the rain forests of our planet, will we continue to use that technology? How do we weigh the relative benefits and dangers of a given technological achievement? If French scientists have developed a pill which allows a woman to abort a fetus, is it a legitimate use of Government to prevent her from using it on moral grounds? Or to *force* her to use it? Who will make the determination? Government? The Individual? These are some of the questions of philosophy that our era is struggling with, the consequences of which have a direct impact on Freedom.

Another question is that of war and peace. War is occasionally the result of the megalomania of a leader with the resources to wage it.

Other wars have been the result of competition for resources or territorial rights. And of course, wars are sometimes started by people seeking to break the shackles of oppression and win their rightful Liberty. But much organized warfare has historically been rooted in the intolerance of differing philosophical (particularly religious and ideological) viewpoints, and has been used to impose a particular viewpoint upon a population of nonbelievers. The world may never be entirely free of war, and as long as mankind continues to teach philosophical intolerance, the sum of war-borne death, destruction, and misery will continue unabated. The Crusaders, the sectarian zealots who prosecuted the bloody Thirty Years War, the fanatical Communist, Fascist and Nazi ideologues, the jihadists, all believe that adherence to their views compels them to reject tolerance of others who ask only to be left in peace.

But among the philosophers themselves, few have advocated war for their principles, and most have been decidedly peaceful. Who are some of these unique individual philosophers whose ideas have shaped the history of mankind? Though I am sure there are omissions, here is a partial list in alphabetical order: St. Thomas Aquinas, Aristotle, St. Augustine, Marcus Aurelius, Avicenna, Cesare Beccaria, Jean Jacques Burlamaqui, Jesus Christ, Confucius, Democritus, Rene' Descartes, Mohandas Gandhi, Friedrich Hayek, Thomas Jefferson, Immanuel Kant, John Maynard Keynes, John Locke, Martin Luther, Niccolò Machiavelli, James Madison, Mahavira, Thomas Malthus, Mani, Karl Marx, Mencius, John Stewart Mill, Ludwig von Mises, Charles de Secondat Montesquieu, Moses, Muhammad, Thomas Paine, Plato, Protagoras (of Abdera), Ayn Rand, Jean-Jacques Rousseau, Saul of Tarsus (St. Paul), Prince Siddhartha (Gautama Buddha), Adam Smith, Socrates, Lao Tzu, Sun Tzu, Voltaire, Zeno and Zoroaster.

HAD THEIR ACHIEVEMENT BEEN OBSTRUCTED

A point of consideration for anyone contemplating the theory of change determined by the unique individual: Remove these three groupings of unique individuals and their ideas and the impact of those ideas from history and see what is left! And a closer examination of the list shows that a disproportionate number of these icons lived in times and places of relative Freedom.[21] By correlating achievement with the size of Government and the prevalent political doctrines in the varied ages and countries in which they lived, we can reasonably assess which political doctrines have worked to man's benefit and which have worked to his detriment.

Two central observations from comparison of the previous lists are these: A disproportionate number of these men and women came from Europe and America, and there is a disproportionate concentration of them in specific historical periods. Prior to the second century BC and during and after the sixteenth century AD, we find a greater concentration of our unique individuals and the greatest degree of positive change.

Equally revealing is looking not only at the Age in which these unique individuals lived, but also at whether their impact was beneficial or detrimental to the future of mankind, and the amount of Government control to which they were subjected in the various countries where they lived. The historical record is quite compelling.

When humans are afforded the intellectual and philosophical

---

21. Consider the case of the German Werner Heisenberg (1901-1976). He became one of the world's most renowned physicists during the liberal, although chaotic, times of the Weimar Republic in the 1920s, and it is significant that his Nobel Prize for the creation of Quantum Mechanics came in 1932, the year before the Nazi takeover. Hitler assigned him to develop an atomic bomb for the Reich, but Heisenberg deliberately stalled the project because of his disapproval of Nazism. (See Thomas Powers, *Heisenberg's War*, .Da Capo Press, 2000). Under Freedom, Heisenberg produced one of the seminal ideas of modern physics, the Uncertainty Principle. Under totalitarianism, his achievement (albeit monumental) is merely negative—he managed not to do something bad.

Freedom to constantly probe the limits of what is known and to challenge the accepted truth, they can achieve great things. To impede the widest possible latitude of thought and experimentation of men like Aristotle or Newton is to literally obstruct the progress of humanity. Because of the phenomenal achievements of the men and women listed in this chapter, the potential loss is easy to see, but *the principle is the same for all people.*

The importance of the cumulative effect of less spectacular or far-reaching innovation by all of those capable of some degree of original thought, is crucial to the advancement of our species. Whether in the field of science or philosophy, *the rarest and most valuable commodity of humankind is original thought.*

There can be a reasonable difference of opinion as to whether it is the philosophers, conquerors, or scientists/inventors who have had the greater impact upon mankind. But any disagreement as to whose contribution is greater cannot obviate the point that achievement takes place due to the ideas and actions of unique individuals. Even recognizing the potential for synergy through collaboration, the original thoughts of each participant are still uniquely individual and provide the fuel for the collaborative effort. The advancement of humankind has been made possible because the change brought about by each of them individually did not have to be passed on genetically, as it does in all other species.

Because this view challenges the collectivist paradigm of modern political correctness, it has been challenged by the contrary idea expressed, among many others, by Diamond. This view denigrates the achievements of individuals and attempts to explain history and change as the result of impersonal factors. Diamond's answer to the question of why Europe and Asia developed high civilizations and Africa and pre-Columbian America did not comes down to nothing more or less than the fact that it is a very long distance from Dublin to Vladivostok. It is hard to imagine a more absurd proposition, but precisely because it is anti-Freedom, and indeed, anti-human, it has found much favor among the intelligentsia of the modern world.

The failure to recognize and respect the role of the individual in driving change and progress is the hallmark of the various collectivist ideologies which promote Government intervention in the free market and State control of almost every facet of man's existence.

Most of those societies that readily embraced these anti-individual concepts descended into economic collapse and chaos in less than one century. Thus far, America has only partially embraced this evil philosophy, but has begun down the same path of decline. Yet the speed at which we are rushing toward our own ruin is increasing by the moment, as the power of Government grows and extends its cancerous tendrils throughout the flesh of society once more. Not even the stark examples of chaos and misery in the collapsing, collectivist States of the late twentieth century dampens the zeal of those who believe that Government is the answer to our problems. The personal power they derive from association with their beloved State has blinded them to the obvious realities of ruin to which they are leading America, just as many of the power elite of Communism refuse to accept that it was their failed policies which caused the collapse of the Soviet Empire.

The theory of change as the result of human action spurred by uniquely talented individuals is central to the difference between a Freedom-affirming or Freedom- denying view of the world. In addition, it highlights a seldom-recognized difference between the two visions of how the world ought to operate.

Because, as this chapter has argued, if change is a derivative of Freedom, then a Free world is *dynamic*. By contrast, a collectivist world is *static*. The socialist intellectual believes he has envisioned the perfect world, which if he can put it into place represents the end of history and progress. Marx states as much explicitly. The

Freedom-seeker, however, understands that the static world is not only undesirable, but ultimately impossible, and further that it is in continual improvement that man's destiny lies. Not all change is good, but progress is real, and it is in the Freedom to dynamically pursue creativity and the development of science and philosophy that the future advancement of the human race is to be found.

PART II. THE HISTORY
OF FREEDOM

★ ★ ★

CHAPTER 7

ANCIENT GREECE AND THE
POWER OF THE INDIVIDUAL

IN A TIME WHEN MOST OF the world was ruled by despots, tyrants and barbarians, the Greeks built a State unlike anything the world had ever known. They changed the basic relationship between The People and their Government. This fostered an unprecedented advancement in all fields of human endeavor, including the arts, mathematics, architecture, science, technology, and philosophy in a time frame and scale that is still breathtaking to contemplate. What stimulated this flowering of culture? By changing the basic condition of man's relationship to the State from one of "being ruled" to one of "participation," the ancient Greeks unleashed the power of the individual. Liberated to make choices based on their own individual circumstances, rather than simply accepting the edicts of the State, the ancient Greeks responded by creating ideas about art, science and philosophy, many of which have endured for two and a half millennia. They built a culture that valued knowledge and reason, and stressed both the contribution and responsibility of each individual; the result, by any standard, was magnificent.

Though most early cultures leaned toward group authority (i.e.

oligarchy) at the expense of the individual, there is no reason to believe that the timeless question of State authority versus individual rights did not appear even before the time of classical Greece. It should also be noted that the groupings of ancient man were less organized, less intrusive, and less demanding than the omnipotent, monolithic State of today. In general, People were free to leave the group and seek their destiny elsewhere; this was certainly true in the principal Greek city-states of antiquity. The group occasionally "ostracized" the individual as a form of punishment meaning that they were expelled from the group for a certain period of time. From the early mists of Greek history, a long cultural tradition had evolved in which all rights arose from the State, although there was never a unified Greece in ancient times. Each individual State endowed status, granted privileges, and used force to command obedience as a price of inclusion in the group. The People were expected to obey authority, and the State used force and fear to control society. This system was reinforced through dogma, doctrine, and tradition. But during the fifth century BC this system came into question. At the same time, by coincidence or synergy, literacy rates grew enormously; as a result, we have an historical record of the earliest beginnings of the recognition of the importance of concepts such as the individual, democracy, and Freedom.

It is also noteworthy to understand what caused the classical Greek thinkers and philosophers to reject the dogma of the past and to seek a more enlightened explanation for the relationship of man to politics. As the Greeks were the first people to think seriously about this question, they obviously had no framework within which to operate. As a result, they arrived at quite disparate answers; moreover, because there were many Greek states, a wide range of systems was implemented. Some worked reasonably well in some respects but not others. Authoritarian Sparta, for example, was strong militarily, but produced virtually no artists or philosophers whatsoever. Corinth was a great trading, shipbuilding and manufacturing city, but was such a failure at diplomacy and war that she seemed to always be on the wrong side of the battle.

It was Athens where The People gained the most Freedom during the classical period, and it is hardly coincidental that Athens was by far the most successful of the Greek cities in most areas of endeavor. Whether in art, war, trade, diplomacy, prosperity or intellectual achievement, The People of Athens—were making their public decisions by direct democracy in the Agora—where every citizen had a right to speak as well as a vote, where every voter was a leader and an example for Freedom-loving thinkers from that day to this.

As history has repeatedly demonstrated since that time, Centralized Government is fatally flawed. Bureaucracy hampers progress and productivity. Power corrupts.

Power brokering, nepotism, and corruption in Government grow in proportion to the amount of central control, the size of the bureaucracy, and the amount of authoritarian rule forced upon The People.

How does one judge the success of a society? By its wealth, intellectual life, physical health, tolerance and charity, military power, ability to get along with other nations? My purpose in this book is to suggest that the answer is measured by the extent that The People who live in it enjoy individual Freedom. But I would further maintain that all the other possibilities mentioned are relevant because they flow in proportion to the amount of Freedom. In Greece, and especially Athens in the fifth century BC, we find the first historical example of the benefits that Freedom can yield to society.

Let us now consider a few of the men whose ideas contributed to what has been aptly called "the glory that was Greece," and whose thinking has inspired men ever since.

Among the earliest Greek thinkers to consider the relationship between the individual and the State, several merit special attention.

LYCURGUS (800 BC – 730 BC)

The early life of Lycurgus has been lost to history, as we have no reliable accounts of his youth. He appears in maturity and is known as the most important figure in the reconstruction of the Dorian State of Sparta.

Lycurgus established an oral constitution known as the Great Rhetra that instituted one of the first instances of direct democracy through monthly votes by the heads of the various families. The meetings took place in a prescribed place where they had to stand as a means of keeping the meetings brief, and were limited to a yes or no vote on proposals put before them by the ephors, which was a body of five men elected annually by the assembly and sharing power with the kings; by the Spartan Senate which consisted of thirty men; twenty-eight of age sixty or greater plus the two rival Kings, or by the Kings.

Citizens were required to perform military service as part of a standing army, and their lives would be considered very harsh and austere by today's standards. But the changes laid down by Lycurgus were embraced by the Spartans and were to last for over 800 years. The memory of Lycurgus's accomplishments, such as limitation of power, participatory Government, and social responsibility, endures into the modern day.

SOLON

The lawmaker and poet Solon (638 BC–558 BC) was important in promulgating early concepts of Athenian democracy. Modern scholars argue about his contribution because of the lack of writings by him and those who knew and observed him. Few of those writings survived the ages. Most of what was written about Solon by ancient authors occurred hundreds of years after his death. However, it is generally agreed that he was chosen both as a mediator and to set forth a new set of laws to replace the harsh edicts of Draco, which meted out death for even small crimes. "Draco" is the origin of the word "draconian." Solon restricted the death penalty to cases of manslaughter and murder. Another reform for which he is remembered is ending the practice of punishing mortgage delinquency by enslaving the debtor and even his children.

Of Solon's reforms, the most important contributions to Freedom were giving The People the power to elect officials and forming a court in which the common men at least had some representation. Some scholars believe the court consisted of all the citizens while others believe the court consisted of only a representative portion. He also eased the financial and social qualifications to stand for public office.

Solon abdicated his power and left Athens shortly after instituting his reforms. He lead a remarkable life. He was taught the history of Atlantis by the Egyptians. He wrote about it in later life. He interacted with the Lydian King Croesus, one of the wealthiest men of the time.

Unfortunately, many of Solon's reforms were undone by the tyrannical rule of Pisistratus whose ascension by force was publicly denounced by Solon on his return to Athens as an old man. But the nascent concepts of democracy that had been laid down by Solon would await those who would revive them in the future.

PROTAGORAS OF ABDERA

In Thrace, around 490 BC, a man was born whose thinking fostered a radical new direction in politics and morals. He was Protagoras of Abdera, and he was to plant the first seeds of Freedom and democracy. It is a commentary on our time that most of us who love Freedom have never heard of him. Perhaps even worse, his followers were called "Sophists," a word that in our time has a decidedly negative connotation. And yet we owe so much to this great thinker.

Prior to Protagoras there were two prevalent doctrines concerning human history—Primitivism and Cyclicalism. Primitivism held that all things were better at some wonderful period in the past rather than their present circumstance. Cyclicalism believed in cyclical or circular patterns in human history. What is relevant about both of these beliefs is that they offer no hope or mechanism for change in the present. In primitivism, society is in decline as a normal course of events and is expected to decline even further. In Cyclicalism, society has its ups and downs in a cyclic pattern that is disassociated from what is done in the present.

Belief in continuing progress was exceptional or nonexistent before the Sophists. But Protagoras, in a famous myth of the origins of society, saw human history in terms of the progressive development of arts and crafts for the supplying of human needs, with government in settled communities and organized living marking a vast step forward. This view directly attacked the dogma and popular beliefs of the time, and established the idea that mankind had more control over his own destiny than had previously been imagined.

Another dogma challenged by Protagoras was the belief that virtue was a function of class or birth. As in modern times, this assured elitist and aristocratic rule. But Protagoras and the Sophists challenged this view. "The belief that virtue can be taught was universal among the Sophists....The effect of this doctrine upon Athenian society was revolutionary, since it implied that anyone, after instruction, might become qualified for the exercise of power, and it left no special place for privilege by birth or the inheritance of a special family or class tradition. It is not surprising that Protagoras was probably the first man ever to explore the theoretical basis of democratic government." ii

This was no fluke or passing thought. Protagoras was a man of substance, well known in Athens, and close to Pericles, under whose leadership Athenian democracy reached its zenith, and there can be little doubt that Protagoras provided the theoretical basis for Periclean democracy; indeed, it is known that he was asked by Pericles to draft a Constitution for the new colony of Thurii in 443 BC.

Another major contribution of the Sophists was their teaching that moral precepts should be supported by reason. This was a significant attack on dogma that was not well received by the entrenched ruling intelligentsia of the day.

Possibly the greatest contribution Protagoras made to Freedom for mankind was his recognition of the importance of the individual. In a time when the individual had never been seen in any other light than his relationship to the collective whole, it was a radical departure to suggest this emphasis was misdirected. Protagoras believed it is the individual who is of primary importance as opposed to the collective, and that philosophical and political emphasis should focus on how the group relates to the individual rather than the reverse.

In more modern times, the famous basis for this departure has become known in philosophy as "Man the Measure." It is a concise and elegant statement, especially in consideration of the time in which it was written. It contends that "man is the measure of all things, of things that are that [or "how"] they are and of things that are not that [or "how"] they are not." Collectivists and those who believe that all rights arise out of Government have tried to distort and rationalize Protagoras "Man the Measure" by saying that it must be viewed as "man" representing the collective whole. Plato, in his *Theaetetus* takes the opposite view. He asserts, through the voice of Socrates, that Protagoras's original meaning was applied to the individual, although he may have subsequently extended it to groups. The individual comes first, and what is lost to the detractors is that Protagoras realized that the more important component of the relationship is the individual. The individual is the basic building block of all of the relationships that follow—to family, to group, to tribe, to local government, and to State. The process does not work in reverse! Protagoras's early understanding of this concept illuminates a key element in man's struggle for Freedom.

The ideas of Protagoras were a direct threat to those in power. As we observe in history, when given the opportunity, those in power will use that power to oppress those who would challenge it. Governments in ancient Greece were no exception. We know that at least one of Protagoras's books was publicly burned and he was ostracized from Athens in the latter part of his life. It is probable that because the thinking of Protagoras was gaining influence and acceptance among those not in power, he was saved from an even greater punishment; possibly even the ultimate punishment, such as that inflicted upon Socrates to quell his ideas supporting individual Freedom and in his highly reasoned attacks against the corruption and power brokering of those in positions of Government. However, Protagoras died at sea while on his way to exile in Sicily, so his ostracism was, in practical terms, a death sentence anyway.

As was the custom of his time, Protagoras's thinking extended to many subjects besides politics. Scholars may debate his contributions to other fields, but his seminal ideas about Freedom of the individual, democratic thought, the importance of reason, protecting The People from Government through a constitution and the dangers of authoritarian rule, have been a beacon to all mankind which followed him and should never be forgotten.

DEMOCRITUS

Among the other early Greek philosophers who made important contributions to the concept of Freedom was Democritus. Although he is most famous for his work, following Leucippus, on atomic theory,

Democritus also had insights on Freedom that should not be ignored.

Democritus was most certainly capable of an enormous degree of original thought and was prolific in his writing, being credited with over sixty works, extending from biology and the theory of pangenesis to the broad epistemological principles of atomism. He lived in the fifth century BC. and it is believed that he lived more than one hundred years. Considering the average life span of the day, this is an amazing fact in itself!.

Of Democritus's contributions to the concept of Freedom, several are noteworthy. The first is his skepticism about the usefulness of passing laws and using force through authoritarian rule as the basis of right and wrong. In other words, Democritus believed "it is one's own consciousness of right and wrong, not fear of the law or public opinion, that should prevent one from doing anything shameful." This brilliant insight stands in direct opposition to those who believe that we must use force and fear to control society, the instrument being a cornucopia of laws instituted to foster authoritarian rule. In addition, Democritus's ideas challenge those who believe that morality is the responsibility of the State instead of the individual.

A second noteworthy contribution is Democritus's lending of his support and prestige to Protagoras's fledgling ideas of democracy. Unfortunately, we have only fragments of his original works, and much of his thinking must be reconstructed from the reference of others to his works. The true extent of his contribution will never be known. However, there is little doubt as to his political leaning as exemplified by a surviving fragment of his writings:

"Poverty under democracy is as much to be preferred to so-called happiness under tyrants as freedom to slavery."[22]

---

22. http://www.humanistictexts.org/democritus.htm

Other important aspects of Democritus's thinking were his belief in a relationship between man and nature and his exclusion of teleological explanations. He rejected the idea of behavior being sanctioned by the supernatural and strongly believed that man is responsible for his own actions.

Other Greek philosophers contributed to the cause of Freedom, making it difficult to be certain of importance of the contributions of any one individual. But Democritus's contributions in other fields surely elevated him to a higher plane of influence, both with his contemporaries, and down through the ages. "The theory founded by Leucippus and developed by Democritus was the most coherent and economical physical system of its day, and the history of its influence can be traced from the fourth century BC, to modern times."[23]

THE SOPHISTS

As we have noted, Protagoras was the most influential of all of the Sophists. Who were these men, and what did they accomplish?

Prior to the fifth century BC, little attention had been given to the relationship of mankind to the State and politics. It was about the time of the Persian Wars (500 to 449 BC) that a group of enlightened men began to question the dogma of the past. There may have been a connection between the two events. The Persian Empire was a mighty and enormous authoritarian State based in modern Iran. Its kings had decided to conquer the world, and were well on their way. They wanted Greece next. How could small, fragmented Greece possibly defeat them and retain their independence? This is a question that Greek (especially Athenian) thinkers must have considered very deeply, and it is not surprising that many may have realized that their advantage, if they had one, lay in the creativity of their citizenry, a

---

23. ibid.

creativity born out of the Freedom to think for themselves.

Whether it was the urgency of repelling the Persian attack or not, the thinkers who developed this appreciation for the value of Freedom became known as the Sophists and are in large part responsible for one of the most productive and enlightened periods in all of history. In their investigation of politics and their challenge of the inadequacies of the old order, they insured that the subject of politics would be prominent among all philosophers who were to follow.

Unfortunately, much of what the Sophists believed and accomplished was distorted by one of their detractors, Plato. Due to the fact that the writings of Plato survived the ages, he has had an exaggerated importance in the way mankind has come to view the Sophists. As a result, the importance of their contribution has often been overlooked or maligned.

The Sophists were teachers. Along with Protagoras, we recognize Hippias of Elis, Prodicus of Ceos, and Thrasymachus as important in the initial Sophistic movement. Many scholars also include Socrates as a Sophist, or at least as adhering to many of their ideas and teachings. It is interesting to note that Plato (discussed next) greatly admired Socrates, but as an adherent of authoritarianism was also a staunch opponent of the Sophist movement.

Through the teaching their ideas and by their travelling from place to place in pursuit of their teaching, the Sophists initiated a movement that was to extend for centuries into the future. In point of fact, mankind is still struggling with many of the concepts laid down by these men. The only other period in human history that can compare with the Sophistic movement is the Enlightenment of the eighteenth century.

That movement returned, in large part, to many of the principles laid down by the Sophists. Just as the Sophistic movement had done more than two millennia earlier in Greece, the Enlightenment also stimulated one of mankind's most productive periods. It fostered improvement in the social condition of The People instead of promoting the dominance of a select few. This relationship of cause and effect must not be ignored by our generation. Twice, in their own time and in the Enlightenment, the ideas of the Sophists have promoted a productive expansion of Freedom. The first eventually withered as the lessons were forgotten. The result we call the Dark Ages and the threat of a repeat awaits only the abandonment of the philosophical principles that induce Freedom and its corollary: human achievement.

PLATO

The importance attached to the works of Plato may be due in large part to the fact that he was prolific in his writings and that so many of his works have survived the ages.

As a young man he had shown ambition in politics, but his allegiance was to those who lost power, and any future he may have had was finished. Some believe that Plato's scathing attacks against the cause of democracy were colored by this personal involvement. Whatever his motivation, Plato was an antagonist of democracy and Freedom, although most believe his contributions to other fields of thought are considerable.

THE UTOPIAN STATE

Most of us have heard of Utopia and the idealistic society that the word is supposed to represent. The word "Utopia" originated in a work by Sir Thomas More (1478–1535) as an allegorical description of a perfect society. We know that More did not believe that such a place could realistically exist because the word originates from an ancient Greek word literally meaning "no place." Plato also wrote about his vision of a perfect State. However, the present day connotation of

Utopia is not what was envisioned by Plato.

Plato laid down many of his ideas concerning the "perfect State" or "Kallipolis" in his now legendary work *The Republic*. In his formulation of Kallipolis, Plato utilized some of the ideas of the Spartan military State to create an entirely new, and to his mind "ideal," structure of Government. Plato believed that there should be three classes: a ruling class consisting of educated and enlightened philosophers; a governing class which included police-soldiers; and a laboring class which was to do the work of society.

The labor class was made up of farmers and artisans who, in order to keep them under control, were forbidden higher education. It is also significant that the labor class was to have no say in Government and was to be ruled through the authoritarian principles of force and fear, and through the enforcement of laws and decrees of the ruling class.

Plato concerned himself mostly with the ruling and governing classes, whose members, women as well as men, possess complete political authority, in return for which they live a garrison life.

In Plato's ideal State, the constitution was final and absolute, having no means of reform after its implementation. His idea of a constitution was to legitimize the power of the State, rather than, as in the American Constitution, to limit the power of the State.

In his economic theory of his ideal State, Plato taught that each person could perform only one economic role. Each class would be forever locked into the performance of a single role in society with no expectation or hope for change.

Let there be no doubt that the focus of Plato's *Republic* was total authoritarian rule.

He laid down some of the principles in *Laws*, which provided explicit and immutable rules for elections, legal proceedings, religious ceremonies, markets, schools and irrigation. Even the regimen of pregnant mothers and the games of infants are rigidly specified.

It is questionable whether Plato believed that his ideal State could ever be implemented; he may have been engaging in a mental exercise when he wrote the *Republic*. As he wrote, Plato also acted (either intentionally or accidentally) as an astute observer of the machinations of the body politic of his time. However, Plato's other writings such as the *Laws* leave little doubt as to his authoritarian thinking and that politics in general was a subject of much preoccupation. We observe from history that many of the themes of Plato's Kallipolis have been prevalent throughout the ages: centralization of authority, authoritarian rule, police state, subjugation of The People, and constitutions that are intended to justify and unleash rather than to limit the power of the State. These concepts have been far more prevalent than the Sophistic ideas of democracy and individual Freedom. It is in great part due to Plato's distorted legacy that the Sophists are only now being elevated by some scholars to the level of importance and recognition they deserve.

Like More's Utopia, Plato's Kallipolis suffers from the unavoidable weakness of all proposed ideal States—that it cannot be maintained without the application of force against Freedom, the Freedom if, nothing else, to try a different idea. It is difficult to determine the extent of Plato's influence on history. Although much of the Greek influence was lost for centuries, many of his ideas have been used to control the actions and fate of mankind throughout subsequent history. Was this the legacy of Plato? Did his teaching mold the thinking of many who followed him, or was he simply an astute observer of universal maxims regarding Government and its use of authoritarian rule to subjugate The People? We cannot be sure. We are left to deal with the fact that in the entirety of recorded history, humanity has been predominantly oppressed by the State, and that Plato's teaching endorsed such a state of affairs. From the viewpoint of Freedom, it is tragic that Plato's writings, rather than those of Protagoras, endured through the ages.

CHAPTER 8

NICCOLO MACHIAVELLI

ONE OF THE FIRST INDIVIDUALS TO write down or codify a set of maxims for the practice of statecraft was Niccolo Machiavelli (1469–1527), a bureaucrat from Florence, Italy. In 1513, while displaced from his job, Machiavelli wrote a short treatise, *The Prince*, which was not published until after his death in 1532. Few works have been popularly read for as many generations or had as great an effect on future despots.

Machiavelli's writings have been analyzed, and their intent has been a subject of much disagreement, almost since their introduction. *The Prince* was not his only work. In support of his maxims of statecraft, he also wrote *The Discourses*, and *Art of War*.

Other works included plays, poetry, and various stories. The writings of Machiavelli eventually became the foundation of modern political science. It is unfortunate for mankind that his legacy was one of deceit, ruthlessness, and inhumanity.

Virtually all of his commentators have understood the evil nature of his theories, and it is odd that a man so universally criticized would nonetheless have an enormous impact on history. True, his writings were extraordinary in style and clarity for the time in which he lived.

But his ideas were morally bankrupt, and so his name has come to mean, "attempting to achieve goals by cunning, scheming, and unscrupulous methods." He believed fervently that the end justifies the means and accepted the ancient belief in the universal wickedness of human nature. He had no concern whatsoever for The People, regarding them as mere pawns in a ruler's endeavors to maintain and extend the power of his Government and influence, and he utterly rejected the ideas of Freedom and Liberty.

But whether intentionally or not, Machiavelli wrote timeless instructions for oppressing humanity that have been widely studied and applied by some of the most evil despots in history, and—here is the main point—by many power-seeking politicians who would never accept being placed on such a list. Therein, I believe, lies the answer to the question of how Machiavelli has retained such popularity. No respectable leader admits to being a follower of Machiavelli, but they take his advice anyway.

Machiavelli was preoccupied with what he perceived to be the "greater truth" of history, and he set out to codify a set of maxims with which a ruler, or would-be ruler, could deal with almost any contingency. He proposed that even the most horrific of acts against humanity are justified to preserve order or to preserve the power of the State—any manipulation or deceit, even wholesale slaughter of one's opponents. Machiavelli proposes exploitation of the most base and cruel nature of mankind. He sometimes makes attempt at a moral justification using the age old "doctrine of necessity." He also justifies what he acknowledges to be monstrous and immoral acts as a means of "preserving order." Of course, this excuse was most often nothing more than a veiled means of maintaining power. As an example, Machiavelli approves the annihilation of the entire lineage of a leader's opponents to prevent future opposition from those who might be entitled to office by birth.

Machiavelli was a master in the art of deception, which he saw as nothing more than a useful tool in the exercise of Government power. He also viewed evil in much the same manner. Consider the following from *The Prince*:

Thus it is well to seem merciful, faithful, humane, sincere, religious, and also to be so; but you must have the mind so disposed that when it is needful to be otherwise you may be able to change to the opposite qualities. And it must be understood that a prince, and especially a new prince, cannot observe all those things which are considered good in men, being often obliged, in order to maintain the state, to act against faith, against charity, against humanity, and against religion. And, therefore, he must have a mind disposed to adapt itself according to the wind, and as the variations of fortune dictate, and, as I said before, not deviate from what is good, if possible, but be able to do evil if constrained.

Perhaps one could claim that Machiavelli was merely acting in the role of an observer of the time in which he lived or was engaging in a mental exercise much like that ascribed by some scholars to Plato in his creation of Kallipolis. However, this cannot be the case with Machiavelli and may not be true with Plato. He openly admits that what he proposes is often "against humanity" and "evil," but nonetheless is justified to maintain the power of the State. Machiavelli's writings regarding his statecraft are doctrinaire. They are a practical "how to" manual for those who would usurp power and oppress The People.

Machiavelli is the founder of much that is now accepted and admired by today's political intellectuals and ruling elite who often secretly, "justify" much of what he espoused by their support for the way modern Governments treat The People. They may attack their opponents with the epithet "Machiavellian" when they see it to their advantage, but that is nothing more than a backhanded acceptance of the belief in deception. The manipulating elitists along with the politicians they both lead and follow are the true Machiavellians.

How little Government has changed in its manipulation of The People. Even in our modern twenty-first century, "to preserve order" is the most commonly used maxim to justify oppression and usurpation of rights. It is used to create police States. It is used to justify secrecy that allows Government corruption to proceed unnoticed in the shadows. It is used to justify authoritarian rule. It is used to justify spying upon a country's own citizens. It is used to justify murder and torture of those who oppose the State. And "to preserve order" is being taught as "necessary" to our children in America's public schools!

Machiavelli was to influence a wide spectrum of political thought which was to follow him. Not all that he taught was bad or evil. A few of his maxims even found their way into the cause of Freedom. However, the legacy of evil has been far more prevalent. The cruel and despotic King Henry IV of Spain was carrying a copy of *The Prince* when he was murdered in 1610. The philosopher Hegel, who elevated statecraft into a cult, was very taken with Machiavelli in the German rediscovery of his works.

Lenin and Stalin operated with adherence to many of Machiavelli's maxims. Stalin, through his infamous purges, was an especially astute practitioner of Machiavellian "control" and "order." Mussolini wrote an introductory essay for an edition of *The Prince*, and Adolph Hitler reportedly kept a copy of *The Prince* by his bedside.

To many it seems an enigma that Machiavelli could have so great an influence on such a widely diverse collection of philosophies as Fascism, Socialism, Nazism and Communism. However, Machiavelli influenced many of the common themes that run through all of these philosophies: the belief that all rights are reposed in Government, and the liberal use of force, fear, and oppression to control society and to preserve order. The real purpose of Machiavelli's maxims is to increase the wealth and dominance, and to amplify the power of the political elite who rule through Government. Machiavelli taught that any means suitable for accomplishing this end is justifiable even if bereft of morality.

Secrecy, lying, trickery, murder, and even genocide in the pursuit of the "common good" are also Machiavellian legacies. There is almost no Government in the world today that does not use the justification of the common good to manipulate and deceive The People as a matter of day-to-day policy. However, closer scrutiny shows that these policies are generally used to cover embarrassment, to foster avarice, to hide corruption, or for the preservation of power, and have little to do with what is good for The People, common or otherwise.

Unfortunately, the excuses of *necessity, preserving order and the common good* are alive and well. They are the seductresses of power. Even men who are normally good and honest can find within these mantras a path to their own corruption. They defy human morality. A prime example is the now popular and often-quoted maxim popularized by the notorious Communist revolutionary, Che Guevara, that "to make an omelet you have to break some eggs." This is nothing more than attempted moral justification for admitted evil. And yet, look at the many good people who are seduced into acceptance of things that they would normally find abhorrent. Evil is evil; acts against humanity are not cases of the end justifying the means. However, the allure of these enticements will persist so long as men seek justification for their vile acts. Machiavelli's contribution included not only the justification, but also practical actions through which one could amplify and maintain the power of the State and oppress The People.

Machiavelli's influence on the philosophy of Statism extends not only from the brutal oppression and genocide of Nazism, Communism and other forms of totalitarianism, but also to the more cancerous and bureaucratically invasive philosophy of socialism. His legacy will continue to be a beacon for those who wish to derive power by worshiping at the altar of State hegemony. Machiavelli is certainly one of the greatest nemeses of Freedom and Liberty in all of history.

CHAPTER 9

THE ENLIGHTENMENT

IT IS DIFFICULT, IF NOT IMPOSSIBLE, for us to imagine the miserable condition and the despair of the common man during the Dark Ages. The latter part of the Middle Ages offered some improvement for a few, but there was little benefit for most of The People. Political dissent was brutally crushed. "Villeins ye are, and villeins ye shall remain," King Richard told participants in the Peasant's Revolt of 1525, before ordering the leaders hung. Although Freedom was oppressed for over a thousand years, it did not die. In the seventeenth and eighteenth centuries, a handful of courageous men rose up to challenge the concept that to preserve order and maintain security, the State must control every facet of the lives of The People. They did not lead an armed revolt; instead, they produced perhaps the most striking example in history of the premise that "The pen is mightier than the sword."

In books, pamphlets and speeches, they challenged the concepts of authoritarian rule and unjust laws. They asserted the radical concepts that all men should be treated equally and that human beings have inherent rights. They confronted the "old order" and asserted the rights of man, in spite of the direct threat to their personal lives and safety.

Each time we hear the justification of authoritarian rule as "necessary for security," or "to preserve order," we should think of the debt we owe these men who forged a path out of the darkness.

Of course, we should also remember the debt *they*, and therefore we, owe to the many whose names have been lost, but who did not yield their Freedom, and whose bodies were often broken and tortured until death became a blessing. The Peasants Revolt and numerous similar uprisings were failures insofar as the lives of those involved were concerned, but in the long run, they kept the torch of Freedom alive, and provided the inspiration for the pathfinders who led the world out of the darkness of the ages. Their era is rightfully called the Enlightenment.

JOHN LOCKE AND THE NEW POLITICS

In a radical departure from the past, the Englishman John Locke's (1632–1704) insightful reasoning challenged the old order in a fresh and unique way. Locke opened the minds of Europe and paved the way for other great thinkers whom he was to inspire. Locke's ideas stood the world on end, made possible the great revolutions, and were a foundation for the constitutional republic that America now enjoys.

Locke believed that it is mankind rather than the State from whom rights originate, and he set out to prove it intellectually. He showed that man was governed by the laws of nature before the existence of the State. The concept of "natural law" was not original to John Locke, but he strengthened the concept by appealing to reason, challenging the authority of the State. Locke's assertion that mankind could determine principles of morality by applying reason to the laws of nature was a direct challenge to the dogma and authoritarian rule of the past.

Locke reasoned that all men should be equal under the law and that Government should be a contract between equally free men. He believed that rights of men included "life, liberty and property," an assertion which Thomas Jefferson was later to use in his original draft of the Declaration of Independence, though "property" was changed to "pursuit of happiness" in the final document.

Locke believed that men were justified in rebelling against tyrannical rule, but he was not an anarchist noting in his *Second Treatise of Government* that, "The aim of revolution is the establishment of a new government, not a return to a state of nature."

Locke understood the need for some degree of Government, but he also realized that the governed are locked in a continuous power struggle with the Government. He believed that the best means of insuring the rights of The People was through a division of the powers of Government, that legislative powers should reside in the form of a parliamentary assembly elected by The People and that the function of the executive was to carry out the laws passed by that body.

Locke's assertion that ultimate rights arise from The People rather than from the State, and his reasoning in justifying these beliefs was arguably his greatest contribution to Freedom. These ideas originated a new way of thinking about Government and began a movement that was to elevate the rights of man to a level unknown since the decline of the Sophist movement in Greece over two millennia before. In addition, Locke's teachings on tolerance opened the thinking of his time and allowed more Freedom of expression for those who were to build on his ideas, including men of vision like Francois Marie Voltaire (1694–1778), Alexis de Tocqueville (1805–1859), Jean–Jacques Burlamaqui (1694–1748), the Baron Montesquieu (1689–1755), and Cesare Beccaria 1738–1794).

Almost as important as Locke's assertion that rights arise from The People was his integration of nature into Natural Rights and then into Natural Laws which Locke combined with the use of reason to investigate the manner in which man governs himself. Transferring the impetus from dogma to reason was a significant accomplishment, as Locke thereby established both intellectual justification and a mechanism for change and reform.

Because of the intellectual stature achieved within his own lifetime, John Locke was able to pry open the doors of public discourse that had been firmly shut for over a millennium by threat of no less than torture and death.

JUDICIAL REFORM AND THE ENLIGHTENMENT

Throughout all of history, few champions have more tirelessly advocated on behalf of the weak and powerless than Voltaire. His greatest contribution to Freedom was to articulate the principles of reform which he laid down for the legal and judicial systems.

The Enlightenment was a time in which fresh new thinking permeated society. Ideas about the origins of morality, presumption of guilt or innocence and the fairness of punishment were investigated and argued by the thinkers of the day.

In disagreement with Locke, Voltaire believed that morality was derived from instinct rather than reason. Another philosopher of the time, Jean le Rond d'Alembert (1717–1783), also a noted mathematician, believed man arrived at morality by experiencing injustices. However, questions over the ultimate origin of morality did not cloud the observation of most thinkers of the time that the political condition of mankind had become intolerable and had to be changed. Voltaire built on the ideas of other thinkers like Montesquieu and Beccaria and fought tirelessly to change Government's despicable use of the judicial and legal systems to oppress The People.

Although he disagreed with Locke about the origin of morality, Montesquieu, like Locke, believed in appealing to reason. He believed in trials by jury that should be open to the public. Montesquieu also believed there should be a relationship of fairness between the crime that was committed and the punishment for that crime. His most noted work, *De Esprit des Lois* (The Spirit of Laws) first published in 1748, was one of the earliest attempts to investigate and classify the differing functions of Government. He showed that the administrative powers of Government could be divided into the executive, legislative, and judicial. Montesquieu believed these powers should be separated in a manner to make them equal in influence. These ideas were to later have great influence on Thomas Jefferson, James Madison and the U.S. Constitution although Montesquieu did not favor American independence from Britain.

Building on the ideas of Locke and Montesquieu concerning Government's proper role in creation and prosecution of laws, Beccaria addressed the subject in, *Essay on Crimes and Punishment* (1764), in which he eloquently attacks the unjust suffering caused by the status quo system. Beccaria issues a cogent and rational appeal to correct the inhumanity, cruelty and torture that were common practices. He was against capital punishment and believed that punishment should be swift in order to reinforce its preventive function. Beccaria believed The People had a right of self-defense and that it was an improper use of law to disarm a population. Beccaria also made notable contributions in the fields of economics and philosophy. His ideas on "the greatest good for the greatest numbers" are part of the earliest foundation of what was later to become Utilitarianism.

Essay on Crimes and Punishment so impressed Voltaire that he wrote a commentary which was added to Beccaria's work. The commentary became Voltaire's first published work in America. It is often not the originator of an idea who effects the greater change, but rather the one who sells that idea to the rest of the world. So it was with Voltaire and Beccaria. As one of the most prolific writers of his time, the intensity with which Voltaire attacked the injustice of the day in promoting the ideas of Beccaria produced an immediate benefit to many of the oppressed.

Voltaire believed that the most important means of correcting the abuse of power by the State was to codify and publish the laws; that writing down the rules was essential to limiting the arbitrary power of the ruling elite. Voltaire also realized that standardization of procedures and codification of the laws was a means of limiting arbitrary abuse of power.

Voltaire believed that persons accused of crimes should be tried by a jury of peers and that they should have benefit of counsel. He further believed that men were innocent until they were proven guilty, and therefore that the charge of guilt was not sufficient to subject man to punishment until the charges could be proven and the individual declared guilty. This was a radical departure from the inhumane practices of the past wherein the test of torture until death was often imposed with divine intervention alone supposedly interceding to save the innocent. The number of successful divine interventions was most certainly not ignored by The People, and even the most powerful lived out their lives in fear of the church and State.

Voltaire's genius extended to many fields. He was strongly influenced by the theories of Sir Isaac Newton (1642–1727) and had a long collaborative relationship with the brilliant Marquise du Chatelet (1706–1749), one of the most notable female scientists of the day. He was fluent in numerous languages and achieved excellence in almost every literary form of writing.

Some think of Voltaire as being much like Socrates, the self-described "gadfly which God has attached to the State ..." Like Socrates, he was frequently in trouble with the authorities and was frequently imprisoned for his witty and often scathing attacks championing reform. He was even confined to the Bastille and later banished from France. But like Socrates, he even faced the consequences of

State punishment; Voltaire continued to expose and attack perceived injustice throughout his life.

The influence of men like Voltaire, Beccaria, and Montesquieu, as well as Locke, was such that even an authoritarian despot like Catherine the Great of Russia sought their friendship, and flirted, if no more than that, with constitutional reforms. The devastating revolutionary change in Russia was still a long ways off, but in France, the United States, South America and elsewhere, it was on the march. Some of those revolutions resulted in little new Freedom for The People, but others represented veritable laboratories for the ideas of the Enlightenment. Consider, for example the *Declaration of the Rights of Man* (1789) in France, not only influenced the revolution in that country, but also the U.S. Constitution. It is one of the best-selling books of all time; it has been adopted by political groups of every ideological stripe; and has been used from the time it was written to our own time both to justify revolution and to suppress it. It is hard to imagine any success in the establishment of the concept of Freedom without the reforms the *Declaration* set in motion, and yet the French Revolution produced little Freedom for The People of France.

ADAM SMITH AND ECONOMIC ENLIGHTENMENT

In our rapidly changing modern world, it is difficult to conceive that very little changed for over a millennium during the Dark Ages. "Order" and "security" were preserved through authoritarian force, and The People were locked into a static caste system that economically supported those who derived power from their association with the State.

By breaking this economic bondage, the Enlightenment unleashed the power of the individual and initiated the transformation into the modern world.

The Enlightenment was not just about reforms in governance, however. There was also a substantial "enlightenment" in many other fields of human endeavor as well, and the pace of societal change was impacted by virtually all of them. Sir Isaac Newton (1643–1727) directed his great intellect toward science and mathematics, but certainly he had a great collateral effect in helping Locke force open the issue of public discourse without fear of punishment or death. Open public discourse allowed men to challenge unjust laws and punishment.

Just as Newton forever changed the world of science, a Scottish philosopher, Adam Smith (1723–1790), forever changed the world of economics. In the early part of his life, Smith gained a reputation as a moral philosopher due to his ideas concerning the inter-relationship of sympathy and morality. Later, however, he turned his great mind toward economic theory, and in 1776 he published *The Wealth of Nations* directly challenging the economic ideas prevalent in his day. No single treatise has so greatly impacted the financial circumstance of the world as this insightful work for it unleashed the power of economic Freedom.

Prior to *The Wealth of Nations*, accepted economic theory was mercantilism, the belief that prosperity and wealth were a function of the amount of gold and silver maintained within a nation's borders, the possession of resources, buildings, and factories, and through land improvement. In other words economic worth was rooted in non-consumable "things of value" which a nation was able to maintain within its borders. Such things might be encouraged and hoarded, but mercantilism philosophy was also very different with respect to consumable goods. Mercantilists held specifically that Government should engage in protectionism by discouraging imports and encouraging exports, which was accomplished by using tariffs and subsidies, thereby discouraging trade among nations.

Adam Smith accurately rejected possession and retention of

non-consumable goods as the source of a nation's wealth. Smith recognized that it was production and control of consumable goods that is the driving force of economics. Surplus allows for the possibility of trade. Smith rejected Government protectionism and was a proponent of free trade. Smith also understood the driving force of demand. Sufficient demand allows for specialization of production. When that demand becomes great enough, the producer can satisfy his other needs by specializing in production of the needed item and using the profits to buy whatever else he wants. Smith believed this type of specialization would continue to the point that labor would be utilized to make small component parts of a larger item as a necessary outcome of efficiency. Think of how accurate Smith's prediction was, as evidenced by the specialization necessary today to construct almost everything we build.

Smith also believed general well-being was achieved by allowing the individual to pursue his own self-interest. He believed a capitalist would necessarily pursue the production of those goods most needed and demanded by society. As demand for an item increased, there would be a corresponding price increase because of the shortage of supply created by the lag time necessary to increase production. The capitalist would move into the vacuum of demand and supply the needed good. As more of the demand is satisfied, there is a corresponding price drop until there is a surplus of the product again. Some capitalists, as entrepreneurs, would then move their resources into other areas of demand where they could command greater profit. In this manner, the self- interest of the capitalist fulfills a basic need of society as if "led by an invisible hand to promote an end which was no part of his intention." Another cornerstone of Smith's thinking was that the industry and initiative of The People was a more important factor in creating wealth than land or natural resources. A creative and free People is one of the most powerful economic engines in the world.

Our forefathers of the American Revolution drew heavily from the thinking of Adam Smith in an attempt to provide for economic Freedom. Smith's observations and thinking became the basis for accepted economic theory and capitalism. Productivity as the foundation, the basic relationships of supply and demand, the role of the entrepreneur, advocacy of free trade, and restriction of the role of Government in economics are a legacy which help propel the world into a previously unimagined age of prosperity.

It is ironic that many of the modern detractors of Adam Smith return to discredited centuries-old economic theories. Many of our children are taught in contemporary public schools that the most important element in America's historic economic success was unlimited land and resources. As we have already noted in the first chapter, a comparison of modern day Russia, Mexico and Japan provides powerful confirmation of Smith's realization that unfettered initiative and innovation of its people is a country's greatest driving economic force. It also shows the intransigence of his detractors.

Even when confronted with overwhelming empirical evidence, his detractors cling to ideas that reinforce their belief in socialism, but which have little relationship to truth.

Whereas the Dark and Middle Ages had been a time of stasis, the Enlightenment was a fertile period of change. Newton and others began the scientific revolution that would soon enough lead to a technological revolution. The governmental reforms and revolutions that followed in the wake of the writings of Locke and his contemporaries relieved the fetters of bondage with which at least white men (not yet women or people of color, alas) had been shackled. More economic Freedom began to improve the circumstance of The People and began to fund extraordinary change. Unshackling the individual from oppression of the State collective fostered a flourishing in all fields of human endeavor. The Freedom kindled in the Enlightenment has fostered mankind's greatest achievements.

There were growing pains, unwanted side effects and unexpected consequences. The perfect society remained as distant as ever, and I'm certain it always will. But by any reasonable "misery index," the Freedom of The People had begun a steep improvement which has been sustained into the present generation. It has always been fragile, and founders in dire peril today. But thanks to the geniuses of the Enlightenment, we at least know what is possible.

CHAPTER 10

FREEDOM AND THE
FOUNDING OF AMERICA

IN ALL OF RECORDED HISTORY, THE list of truly seminal events that have ubiquitously advanced the condition of humanity is quite short. In various fields of endeavor, we could for instance cite the teachings of Aristotle and John Locke; the introduction of the scientific method; the marvelous achievements of Sir Isaac Newton; the biological insights of Charles Darwin; the introduction of economics by Adam Smith; the precepts laid down in the *Magna Carta*; the early twentieth century revolution in physics represented by Albert Einstein's relativity theories; and the development of quantum mechanics by Nils Bohr, Werner Heisenberg and others.

It is even more extraordinary that three monumental events occurred in relatively rapid succession to one another during the founding of America. First came the Declaration of Independence, a document unique to all history in that it not only put forth a justification for the revolutionary war, but also defined the role of Government and provided a rationale for *any* just revolution.

The Declaration was followed by the founding of a new nation by the creation of a Constitution designed to *limit*, rather than expound, the powers of Government. To this remarkable document was then appended the Bill of Rights, establishing in ten succinct statements the basis for Freedom constraining any scheme for the workings of State. No other three events come close in breadth and scope of improving the day-to-day lives of The People, or in accelerating and advancing the vast latitude of human achievement. By breaking the shackles of Government that benefitted only the elite few, and that oppressed everyone else, the doors were thrown open to achievement and advancement by all, and the result has been astonishing.

THE AMERICAN REVOLUTION

Rebellions, even revolutions, are not of themselves world-changing events. However, the rebellion "across the pond" became a seminal event not just because it succeeded, but because the underlying principles that were enunciated to create and support the separation also succeeded. The American Revolution became more than just a transfer of power, more even than a means of righting an injustice; it became a symbol of something far greater—a struggle for Freedom for the common man that transcended all such previous conflicts. It was an extraordinary triumph fostered by extraordinary men on behalf of all mankind. Yet, when the American colonies began their rebellion, the British ruling classes viewed it mostly as an annoyance. After all, Britain's Navy had long dominated the seas, and she was therefore a global superpower, arguably the most powerful nation in the world. Since conditions affecting life for the common man had been so bleak for several millennia, why hadn't there been other successful rebellions? Why weren't the British elite more worried, and why were they so slow to react to the growing dissent in America? Today is seems like monumental stupidity or indifference, but in the mindset of the time, the pervasive view that America's rebellion was nothing more than an annoying nuisance was not surprising. It arose from an arrogance based on a 2,000-year-old system of dominance *that had never failed*. War with another State or internal conflicts might succeed in wresting power, but a successful rebellion by The People ... by the common man? Never!

To be sure, the Swiss had taken advantage of the death of the Hapsburg emperor in 1291 to form a confederation which had proved durable, but to an eighteenth-century aristocrat, that was insignificant and dismissible. More to the point were the dozens of peasant revolts throughout the Middle Ages. The only ones that had even come close to success were those cases where some opportunistic aristocrat had taken advantage of the situation and become the revolutionary champion. The Cromwellian interlude in seventeenth-century Britain had ended in popular disgust and the restoration of the Stuart monarchy in a mere eleven years after the execution of Charles I, with republicanism thoroughly discredited, and Charles II once again ruling on the basis of alleged Divine Right.

The point is that prior to the American Revolution, all advanced countries of the world were governed by a ruling class, which had developed to derive personal power and wealth in a way vastly different from how the middle classes accumulate wealth in Tier 1 countries today. Today, wealth is created by people using the ideas of their minds and strength of their bodies to engage in productive work that has value to others. The earnings from these mental and physical efforts, when combined with prudent saving, create individual prosperity, even for those who earn only a marginal amount above subsistence.

That's how it is done today, but prior to 1776, virtually all of the rich and powerful people in the world held those advantages because they were born into an established elitist aristocracy based on the control of Government, and which had persisted in its dominance for so long that its members had to come to believe it was their *right* to rule, a right ordained by God. To set themselves apart, they gave themselves titles ordained by birthright or granted by the powers that be, notably the King, but other aristocrats as well. If the King knighted you, made you a Baron and granted you an estate with a castle or magnificent manor house, he had effectively bought your service for life, especially since he could take away all those privileges and your head as well, whenever he pleased.

The aristocracy that supported the King constantly clamored, flattered and schemed for additional power and a reconfirmation and extension of their existing rights and privileges. When the King was weak, the nobles tended to fill the vacuum and become relatively more powerful. Religious institutions, universities and cities could sometimes, when conditions were ripe, win rights from the rulers, but these were always precariously held and could be abrogated at any time.

The People were kept in servitude not only through force but also by maintaining them in a condition of ignorance whereby they would be unable to run their own affairs even if they did rebel. The only pathways to significantly improving one's life were through the bureaucracy, and the minimal educational system was totally controlled by the ruling class, which held sway over the power of admittance. By and large, The People were offered no opportunity of learning to read or write; they had no knowledge of organized warfare, economics or finance or even the skills necessary for minimal orderly governance. *The common men were barred from knowledge beyond the trade skills necessary to perform their functions of production to support the State.* A welter of societal barriers, from language usage to table manners were used to bar access, and to exclude the underclass. It was even forbidden for a commoner to dress like an aristocrat. This was a formidable system that successfully monopolized power to the elite for over 2,000 years. Eighteenth-century England had evolved perhaps the mildest form of this oppressive despotism anywhere in Europe. It had a Parliament with real, although limited power; and since the so-called Glorious Revolution of 1688, the understanding had grown that there were such things as "the rights of Englishmen." Still, the aristocracy controlled the nation, and it is not surprising that they were disdainful of the rebellious colonists in America. That the colonial uprising could be successful was simply unthinkable.

This elitist view was supplemented by the contemporary understanding of what constituted a colony. Simply put, the purpose of a colony was to enrich the mother country. Thus, the Spanish plundered Central and South America of its gold and silver, and the Portuguese, Dutch and British managed their East Indian and Caribbean possessions with a singular eye to how much profit could be made from the sugar, spices and other riches of those parts of the world. No one considered that those who went to live in such places had any rights worth speaking of. At best, service abroad was a pathway to advancement upon a person's return home, and the top tier seldom bothered to brave the dangers of an ocean passage themselves. From its founding in 1670 until the twentieth century, it is highly improbable that any director of the Hudson's Bay Company ever saw Hudson's Bay.

All of this was consistent with the economic theory called mercantilism—indeed very much its heart and soul, and it is one of the ironies of history that the intellectual justification for mercantilism came crashing down precisely in the year 1776, with the publication of *The Wealth of Nations* by Adam Smith.

The British colonies along the mid-Atlantic seaboard of America were different from other colonies in many ways. Here was a huge, fertile territory with a temperate climate, and a population density vastly lower than those found in Asia, Africa or tropical America— the other areas of the world where colonization was underway. There were minimal natural resources, at least not the kind that could be quickly exploited. There were no known gold or silver deposits, nor any rare, exotic (and thus expensive and profitable) fruits or spices. That the fertile land could produce agricultural bounties was obvious, but doing so—given the small population of natives that could be enslaved—demanded a large number of farmers, even if slaves could be imported from elsewhere.

From the early 1600s on, it turned out a great number of Englishmen and others were willing to uproot their European stakes and try their fortunes in the thirteen British colonies that came to be established between Georgia and New Hampshire. In addition, many early American colonists were transported as punishment for having committed some sort of crime, or as delinquent debtors. This penal colony system would later become more widespread in Australia. A third type of American settler was the religious refugee. Puritans, Quakers and even Catholics—who were discriminated against in various ways in Britain—came to America to escape the religious persecution ubiquitous throughout Europe.

Colonists came from not only the British Isles, but also from Germany, Sweden, the Netherlands and other parts of Europe, but as Britain gradually established control of the seaboard east of the Allegheny Mountains (the French continued to compete for territory farther inland), the settlers gradually came to think of themselves as subjects of the British Crown. Some had been granted titles to their new land and were educated members of the ruling class. They viewed themselves as an extension of British society engaged in carving a satellite civilization out of what was then essentially perceived as a wilderness.

This was important because it meant that the normal protocols of strict bureaucratic control that would have been forced on a newly conquered territory were not stringently imposed because the leading figures of the colonies were perceived as an extension *of* the ruling class. However, due to the fact that the aristocrats among the colonists lacked the ability to subjugate their fellow settlers to the extent prevalent in Europe, the American colonists, more than any other in history, were largely left to their own devices.

Thus, the early settlers in America were able to exploit Freedom to a degree previously unimagined, and they began to flourish in an environment that was relatively unregulated and untaxed by European standards. Many began to educate themselves and engage in entrepreneurship, creating jobs throughout the colonies. Many began to work the land and derive personal benefit, even land ownership that was unattainable in Europe. Out of necessity, they learned to manage their own affairs. It is of inestimable importance that a greater proportion of common men among the colonists had begun to improve their lot in life through their own initiative, and thus to reap innumerable benefits which can only be enjoyed in concert with a significant degree of Freedom, which had previously been reserved only for the elite ruling class.

Because Freedom leads to human achievement, colonial Americans accomplished much. It is probable that already by the time of the Revolution, Americans were living better than any other people in the world. It is recorded that when British ships loaded with Hessian mercenaries sailed into New York Harbor to confront Washington's rebel army, the Hessians, observing mile after mile of well-kept, prosperous farms on Long Island, Staten Island and the New Jersey mainland, were astonished at how rich these Americans were.[24]

Farther inland, the French had continued to pursue their territorial objectives. In the early 1750s, they constructed garrisoned forts on Lake Erie's south shore and other strategic points. The British responded with their own fort-proliferation program, including one where the Monongahela and Allegheny Rivers join to form the Ohio, the place that would eventually become the city of Pittsburgh. A group

---

24. McCullough, David, *1776*, Simon and Shuster, 2005.

of Virginia militia, representing the British Government and, under the command of a young man named George Washington, was sent to protect the building site, but by the time they arrived, the French had driven the British out and built their own fort, Fort Duquesne. Washington, aided by a contingent of Mingo Indians, ambushed a French force near what is now Uniontown, PA, and killed its commander. The incident triggered the French and Indian Wars, which in turn led to the Seven Years' War (1756–1763), the first truly worldwide war in history.

The war was fought in Europe, the Caribbean, off the coast of Africa, in India and the Philippines. The British and the French sent forces to America to protect their interests, initiating numerous conflicts throughout the disputed lands. Initially the British were slow to adapt to new realities of warfare in America and fared poorly against the French. However, the British troops gradually began to adapt, and superior naval forces were able to severely hamper French supply shipping. Population in the British colonies dwarfed those of the French, and the British eventually poured far more resources into their campaign, culminating in French surrender with the capture of Montreal in 1760, although the wider war was to continue for another three years.

Historians have noted that there was probably no time in the history of the colonies in which there was a greater feeling of devotion to the Crown than at the conclusion of this war. Together as British citizens living on both sides of the Atlantic, they had triumphed against French colonial efforts that had instigated many Indian tribes to create fear and havoc on the frontier. That feeling of patriotism was soon to be eviscerated.

Heavily in debt from the war, King George III induced Parliament to tax the American colonies with imposition of the Stamp Act (1765), the Townshend Acts (1767) and the Tea Act (1773), as a means of extracting much needed revenue. The colonists were both alarmed and offended. King George was considered an incompetent ruler by many in the world, and the new taxes were viewed by the colonists as unlawful. Instead of being respected as citizen partners by the Crown, as they were accustomed, they perceived they were being treated more like conquered territories, as Britain was imposing more bureaucracy, regulation, and taxation upon all of its foreign holdings in order to fund its expansive empire. The colonists' British sensibilities were offended, especially among the educated, as none of the colonies had representation in Parliament, and the cry "no taxation without representation" resounded across the land. Clearly, ideas about the proper role of Government had found their time and place, and the decade leading up to the events of 1776 was filled with a growing awareness in America that the colonists could no longer rely on mere geographical remoteness to protect their Freedoms. Initially demanding only the "rights of Englishmen," they gradually came to believe that nothing short of independence from Britain would do.

In 1765, delegate Patrick Henry introduced a series of resolutions in the Virginia House of Burgesses as a protest against the Stamp Act—among the earliest expressions of the sentiment that led to the Revolution. Henry was known as a radical in the revolutionary movement and later represented Virginia in the First Continental Congress; served four terms as Governor; was a signatory to the American Constitution; was one of the most ardent supporters of the Bill of Rights and was appointed Secretary of State by President George Washington. He had a long and distinguished career of service to the nation, but for all of that, he is probably most remembered today for his skill of oratory that produced the now iconic words from a speech at the Virginia Convention in support of his state joining the Revolutionary War, "I know not what course others may take," he said, "but as for me, *give me liberty or give me death!*"

In 1773, a Boston firebrand, Samuel Adams, led a remarkable demonstration of civil disobedience in response to the Townshend Acts and the Tea Act, when a group of men boarded ships in Boston Harbor and destroyed three shiploads of taxed tea owned by the monopolistic East India Company. At an earlier meeting organized by Adams on November 29, several thousand people had gathered and passed a resolution calling on the captains to return the tea to England without paying the import duty. Outraged that the Governor refused to let the three ships leave without paying the tax, the men went to the harbor and threw every box of tea from all three vessels overboard. Adams publicized the event as an act of defending the Colonists' rights, and word quickly spread, helping to solidify the sense of British injustice. The Boston Tea Party became an iconic moment in American history and has since been held by protestors worldwide as a symbol of Government over-regulation and unfair taxation. Even in present day America, a loosely organized grass roots movement, protesting high taxation, unconscionable debt, increased Government spending, and as a remedy calling for a return to constitutionalism, has chosen the honored name of the Tea Party as its symbol.

The Boston Tea Party was only one of many events that led to the American Revolution, but it became a major rallying point in both countries. The British responded with a decision to make an example out of Massachusetts by closing the port of Boston and in 1774 by passing five laws, which became known as the "Intolerable Acts" to punish the colony. The Colonists were outraged, and in the same year established the First Continental Congress as tensions grew.

The battles of Lexington and Concord, in Massachusetts, initiated armed conflict. On May 10, 1775, the Second Continental Congress convened; and although many of the delegates were still hoping for reconciliation with England, a significant faction now supported independence, including Thomas Jefferson, Benjamin Franklin and

John Adams[25]. Small-scale fighting had continued in the wake of Lexington and Concord, and uncoordinated skirmishes were taking place throughout the colonies. On June 14, 1775, Congress voted to create a continental army and appointed Washington as commander.

Even so, there was a pervasive hope that the grievances with The Crown could be resolved short of all-out war. The revolution might not have reached critical mass save for the publication of the pamphlet *Common Sense* by Thomas Payne in January of 1776, passionately and persuasively advocating both colonial independence and Republicanism. *Common Sense* was immediately immensely popular, circulating throughout the colonies and opening the quasi-taboo subject of separation from Great Britain to public debate. Paine's pamphlet was instrumental in lighting the fuse of the Revolution in that it excited growing public sentiment toward complete separation of the Colonies from the Crown.

In February of 1776, Congress learned that Parliament had passed the Prohibitory Act declaring American ships to be enemy vessels and instituting a blockade of American ports. Following on the heels of *Common Sense*, this legislation greatly increased sentiment among The People in favor of independence. In Congress, too, support for independence grew as it became clear that England was not disposed to negotiated reconciliation. The problem was that the delegates lacked the power to bind the colonial legislatures that had chosen them as representatives. Some delegations were specifically barred from voting for any resolution favoring separation. Congress began a proactive effort under the leadership of Massachusetts' John Adams to obtain authority from all of the Colonies to declare independence from Great Britain.

As the effort to secure valid endorsement proceeded, Congress appointed a committee of five men to draft a formal declaration: Jefferson,

_____
25. The future President was a cousin of Samuel Adams and a prominent Boston lawyer

Franklin, Adams, Robert Livingston of New York and Roger Sherman of Connecticut. Jefferson wrote the first draft, consulted with the others, incorporated some of their suggestions for changes, and presented the committee's final draft to Congress on June 28, 1776, only seventeen days after they had begun. Congress first voted for a Resolution of Independence. It then modified the committee draft declaration, eliminating a lengthy segment of powerful condemnation of the slave trade. That was the most upsetting of any changes to Jefferson. The final version of the Declaration of Independence was unanimously approved on July 2, 1776, and was engrossed and published two days later. It is arguably the most important document of Freedom ever written, and still has contagious appeal for all who love Liberty. The People were truly fortunate to have found such an eloquent and deliberative champion of Freedom and Liberty as Thomas Jefferson.

As noted above, a rebellion over egregious taxation and regulation was not in and of itself a remarkable event. What elevated the American Revolution to a seminal moment in history was the introduction of radical ideals of Freedom and Liberty used to justify the rebellion. What began as irreconcilable grievances soon became not just a struggle for power, but a *philosophical* revolution encompassing ideals of individual sovereignty underpinned by the concept of rights derived from nature, the true purpose of constitutions, and the proper role of Government. It became not just a revolt against unjust rule by the British, but an intellectual challenge to oppressive rule by *all* Governments. It recognized that in order for humanity to be Free from manipulation and oppression by the elite few, the *natural right* of individual men and women to sovereignty over their personal lives must *supersede that of the collective or of the monarch.* Imagine how radical was this notion of ranking the sovereignty of each individual over his personal affairs above that of the king! It fostered the concept that each individual is endowed with inalienable rights, and institutionalized that concept as a system of Government that emphasized not how men could be governed by the ruling class but how men could govern themselves, literally changing the trajectory of the world and heralding an unprecedented flourishing for all humanity.

Few things can galvanize the resolve of men as to struggle in a just cause against a perceived oppressor, especially when that oppressor is known to have superior strength and resources. So it was with the beginning of the American experience among the colonies. The hardships and resolve of the American army under General Washington are now of legend. Events like Valley Forge, where some men starved and others literally froze to death, yet the survivors did not abandon the cause of Liberty, will forever serve as an inspiration to men and women who love Freedom. In such a conflict, differences evaporated, and bonds were forged in the furnace of resolve that transcended the lines of statehood.

Among the colonists, the deportment and atrocities of the British army, and their Indian allies, cemented powerful feelings of alienation from their former countrymen. Although they still had strong ties to their local colonies, The People were also becoming more unified, more American, with each succeeding event. By the time the British were defeated with the surrender of Lord Cornwallis to George Washington's army at Yorktown, Virginia on October 19, 1781, there was great unity, borne of the hardships and by the enormity of what had been accomplished. The Tories, who supported the Crown, began to flee to Canada and the Caribbean after Yorktown, which further refined this sentiment. While it took some time to secure signing of the final documents, the Freedom of the colonies had been won, and in so doing the beginnings of a united nation had been formed.

Next, two events equally extraordinary to the American Revolution and the Declaration of Independence were on the threshold of taking place. Together, they were to foster the greatest leap forward across the gamut of human endeavor that the world had ever seen. For the first time, the power and initiative of The People was to be set Free! Even Thomas Jefferson did not fully realize the dynamic energy his ideas would help to unleash. He died believing it would take a hundred generations to fully develop the vast western territory of the United States. In the immediate flourishing of humanity that Freedom helped to foster, it only took a few decades.

THE AMERICAN CONSTITUTION AND THE BILL OF RIGHTS

In the aftermath of the Revolutionary War, the colonies recognized that their hard won independence could only be maintained through cooperation. Back in 1777, Congress had drafted the Articles of Confederation, which loosely bound them together and constituted the *de facto* American Government during and after the war. But the Articles were seen as inadequate by many of the leaders who saw the need for a stronger union. In 1787, a convention was called, ostensibly to propose amendments to the Articles of Confederation, mostly intended to improve trade. Once assembled, however, the body soon decided instead to propose an entirely new constitution that would create a new form of Government, and so it became known to history as the Constitutional Convention. It was to bear the mark of two exceptional men, only one of whom was present.

We are uncertain as to when Thomas Jefferson and James Madison first met, but we know that they were acquainted at least by May of 1776 when they were both serving in the Virginia House of Delegates. At that time Jefferson at age thirty-three would have been eight years Madison's senior. While Jefferson was drafting the Declaration of Independence as a delegate to the First Continental Congress, Madison was in Virginia helping craft Virginia's first constitution. In

1779 Jefferson became Governor of Virginia, and Madison served on his advisory council. Both possessed genius minds; both were classically educated; both spoke and read numerous languages; and both collected large libraries covering a wide range of topics; Jefferson sent Madison over 200 books while in France.

Jefferson's library was so voluminous that it became the basis of the Library of Congress after the original collection was burned in the War of 1812.

Most important, both Jefferson and Madison recognized and accepted the challenge thrust on them by their unique moment in history to improve the lot of mankind by redefining Government. It was an enterprise they accepted with vigor commensurate with the magnitude of what they were attempting to accomplish. They studied history, philosophy, economics and politics and were in constant communication both in person and in letters, stimulating each other's minds and challenging each other to attain the best of what each was capable.

The product of their studies and of their collaboration produced the three most important documents of Freedom and Liberty ever written, and if gauged by their importance to the advancement of humanity, the most important documents of any kind ever written: the Declaration of Independence, the U.S. Constitution, and the Bill of Rights. While others played important parts, Jefferson and Madison were the true architects of these documents, and through their writings we have a record of their remarkable deliberation. There is no doubt that both understood the historical importance and difficulty of what they were attempting. Much of our way of life can be attributed to these two incredible men.

Isaac Newton said of his own accomplishments, that if he had seen farther than others before him, it was because he stood on the shoulders of giants. That is precisely what Jefferson and Madison did. They learned from the ancient Greeks and Romans, Medieval and Renaissance thinkers and in particular the philosophers of the Enlightenment. They studied economics, including their Scottish contemporary, the father of economics, Adam Smith. In short, they absorbed as much information as possible and deliberated with great sense of purpose over that which was best for all of humanity, rather than that which served the interest of the powerful elite. For The People, it was one of the most fortuitous friendships and collaborations ever.

The Constitutional Convention convened in May of 1787; in all, fifty-five delegates would attend, although only thirty-nine actually signed the document. The delegates represented twelve of the thirteen states. Rhode Island did not send a delegation. The delegates agreed that a unifying Government was needed for purposes such as negotiating treaties and arbitrating relationships among the States. Free trade among the states was a must, but probably the greatest impetus for creating a Constitution was the need to establish a common defense: The British had refused to remove some of its troops in the North; the French were still active in the west; and the Spanish would not let Americans ship goods from the port of New Orleans in the South. With no independent stream of revenue under the Articles of Confederation, there was little means for unified defense, an oversight which was obvious—and a great temptation—to the other nations. Many among the ruling elite across the world believed that the Americans' experiment in governing themselves would fail in due time creating an opportunity for conquest.

Jefferson was not present at the Constitutional Convention as he was serving as Ambassador to France, but his ideas were championed by his good friend and confidant James Madison. John Adams was in London with similar ambassadorial duties. However the venerable Benjamin Franklin, by then eighty-one years old, was present, and undoubtedly a major influence.

The framework adopted by the convention was based on a document called the Virginia Plan, mostly drafted by Madison. The underlying principle was to have a form of limited Republican Government that reserved ultimate sovereignty for The People. The Virginia Plan proposed dividing responsibility between three branches: a strong bicameral legislature comprised of a House and Senate; an executive chosen by the legislature; and a judiciary whose judges would serve for life.

The Virginia Plan became the basic framework for the ensuing debate that would result in a final document. While some elements were changed, such as the President being chosen by a vote of specially designated electors rather than by the legislature, the overall themes were preserved. A system of checks and balances was implemented to limit governmental power. Moreover, the powers of the new national Government were specifically enumerated with all other powers reserved to The People and to the States. Persons accused of crimes were entitled to a trial by jury, and *ex post facto* laws and bills of attainder were prohibited. Treason was specifically defined, so Government leaders could not charge their political opponents with this crime as had often been done in England. The Constitution also provided for the admission of new states and included a procedure for its own amendment.

All in all, it was a utilitarian document, concisely defining the structure of the new Government. Yet supporting the structure were profound philosophical ideas about Freedom. There was much debate and compromise, and many of the delegates remained dissatisfied. It was finally agreed that only nine states would be needed for ratification. Even so, unless the delegates would support the new Constitution in their separate States, instead of continuing to dispute their differences, there would be little possibility of ratification. Just prior to the signing, a short speech was presented by Benjamin Franklin. Franklin was internationally recognized as one of the greatest minds of his day.

He was a self-taught polymath genius who had a long and venerated life as an inventor, philosopher, civic activist, satirist, political activist and statesman.

He was, and remains, one of the most revered of the founders, and influenced the thinking of all the important leaders. In the years before the war, he had been sent to England as the representative of the colonies to attempt to resolve the growing differences; and while there, he wrote numerous essays. The essays track his gradual disillusionment with the British elite, and in 1773, he wrote a scathing satirical essay, *Rules by Which a Great Empire may be Reduced to a Small One,* which had a profound influence on the debate back in the colonies, and which many consider today as a masterpiece of political satire. When the British closed the Port of Boston as punishment for the Boston Tea Party, Franklin gave up hope of reconciliation and at the age of sixty-nine returned to the colonies, becoming one of the most outspoken advocates of independence. In 1776 he became ambassador to France and successfully negotiated a crucial military alliance that many believe tipped the scales toward a successful outcome of the revolution. Later, in 1783, he was instrumental in negotiating the *Treaty of Paris* which ended the war.

At the Constitutional Convention, Franklin was still sharp of intellect but in feeble health due to his extreme age for the time. The Constitution was completed on September 17, 1787. Probably held in equal esteem to George Washington who chaired the convention, Franklin was one of the strongest supporters of unification, and he had asked to make a short speech prior to the signing of the final draft. Franklin was too weak to give it himself, so it was presented by his fellow Pennsylvania delegate, James Wilson. This speech is considered another of Benjamin Franklin's great masterpieces. It was a powerful appeal for unity, calling upon the delegates to put aside their individual differences and to support the final draft during the process of ratification. Though there were significant disagreements, the delegates largely heeded Franklin's plea, and they worked out their differences. New Hampshire was the ninth colony to ratify on June 21, 1788; the last state, unrepresented Rhode Island, did not ratify until May 29, 1790, two years after the new Government had begun operations. The second great document of Freedom engendered by the American Revolution was now complete.

Franklin, as much as any delegate, realized that if the Constitution had one great shortcoming; it was the failure to address the issue of slavery, and his actions stand as a great testimony to his integrity. Knowing that there did not exist in the nation the political will to end slavery, he would not deprive America of the document that solved so many other problems. But no sooner had the First Congress convened than the old and feeble Sage of Philadelphia petitioned to rid the nation of its principal blight. It would take another three quarters of a century and a catastrophic civil war to finally decide the issue, but Franklin, who had been strongly influenced by abolitionist Quakers, stands tall in his support of Freedom for all.

In several of the states, ratification of the Constitution was made contingent on the addition of a Bill of Rights. Madison, principal author of the Constitution, and its leading proponent,[26] proposed that such a bill be passed as soon as the new Congress convened; and he introduced the document himself in 1989, offering twelve separate articles as Amendments to the Constitution. In the end, only ten were adopted; they came into effect after being ratified by three fourths of the States on December 15, 1791. This completed the third great document of Freedom arising from the American Revolution.

The Bill of Rights protects The People and the States from the oppression of their own Government. They are brief in their wording,

---

26. Along with Alexander Hamilton and John Jay, Madison wrote *The Federalist Papers*, a series of essays supporting ratification that were hugely influential in building popular support for the new Constitution.

broad in their scope and momentous in the ongoing struggle for Freedom and Liberty.

The First Amendment guarantees Freedom of religion, speech, the press, assembly and petition, and reads:

"Congress shall make no law respecting an establishment of religion, or prohibiting the free exercise thereof; or abridging the freedom of speech, or of the press; or the right of the people peaceably to assemble, and to petition the government for a redress of grievances."

The Second Amendment establishes the right of The People to keep and bear arms. In modern times, it has become perhaps the most controversial of all the stated rights in the Bill of Rights as those who would like to expand the power of Government rightly see it as a huge deterrent to their goals. They have used all sorts of arguments in attempts to get around it, but to date, have failed to undo its status as one of the great protections of The People. The Amendment reads:

"A well-regulated militia, being necessary to the security of a free state, the right of the people to keep and bear arms, shall not be infringed."

The Third Amendment was one of great importance to The People of the time because it obviated one of the greatest British abuses during the war.

Indeed, it is one of the specific grievances against King George III listed in the Declaration of Independence. It reads:

"No soldier shall, in time of peace be quartered in any house, without the consent of the owner, nor in time of war, but in a manner to be prescribed by law."

The Fourth Amendment protects The People against several possible abuses of criminal law by the Government, and reads:

"The right of the people to be secure in their persons, houses, papers, and effects, against unreasonable searches and seizures, shall not be violated, and no warrants shall issue, but upon probable cause, supported by oath or affirmation, and particularly describing the place to be searched, and the persons or things to be seized."

The Fifth, Sixth, Seventh and Eighth Amendments follow up on the Fourth, and specify rights of The People in a number of important situations regarding law enforcement and judicial proceedings. The Fifth, containing its famous ban on self-incrimination, as well as several other important protections, reads:

"No person shall be held to answer for a capital, or otherwise infamous crime, unless on a presentment or indictment of a grand jury, except in cases arising in the land or naval forces, or in the militia, when in actual service in time of war or public danger; nor shall any person be subject for the same offense to be twice put in jeopardy of life or limb; nor shall be compelled in any criminal case to be a witness against himself, nor be deprived of life, liberty, or property, without due process of law; nor shall private property be taken for public use, without just compensation."

The Sixth Amendment gives the rights of the accused at trial, and reads:

"In all criminal prosecutions, the accused shall enjoy the right to a speedy and public trial, by an impartial jury of the state and district wherein the crime shall have been committed, which district shall have been previously ascertained by law, and to be informed of the nature and cause of the accusation; to be confronted with the witnesses against him; to have compulsory process for obtaining witnesses in his favor, and to have the assistance of counsel for his defense."

The Seventh Amendment extends the right of jury trial to civil cases. It reads:

"In suits at common law, where the value in controversy shall exceed twenty dollars, the right of trial by jury shall be preserved, and no fact tried by a jury, shall be otherwise reexamined in any court of the United States, than according to the rules of the common law."

The brief Eighth Amendment is self-explanatory:

"Excessive bail shall not be required, nor excessive fines imposed, nor cruel and unusual punishments inflicted."

The Ninth and Tenth Amendments are different from the others, and, sadly, have not been adhered to as strictly. The Ninth, in a single sentence, presents perhaps the most comprehensive statement of the doctrine of Enumerated Powers. It is a powerful affirmation that The People are sovereign, which has been far too little used by modern courts. Few things would do more for Freedom in our time than a reinvigoration and amplified application of this Amendment:

"The enumeration in the Constitution, of certain rights, shall not be construed to deny or disparage others retained by the people."

Likewise, the Tenth Amendment has been under-enforced by modern jurists. Often called the "states' rights" amendment, it is more than that. It is also a "people's rights" amendment:

*"The powers not delegated to the United States by the Constitution, nor prohibited by it to the states, are reserved to the states respectively, **or to The People.**"* (Author's emphasis.)

OUR LEGACY OF FREEDOM AND LIBERTY

With the completion of its founding documents, America charted a new course in governance that stood the old order on end, wresting power from ruling elites and placing it in the hands of common men. The succeeding two centuries have proven beyond a scintilla of doubt that when common men are Free to pursue their own destinies, they are capable of astonishing achievements. Freedom and Liberty are the pathways to economic well-being and achievement in every field of human endeavor.

CHAPTER 11

FLIRTING WITH THE EDGE OF DARKNESS

EVEN AS WESTERN CIVILIZATION BEGAN TO flourish as a consequence of the protection of The People from State rule, a new group of philosophers rose up to challenge the success of limited Government, capitalism and Freedom. While these men addressed a number of different concerns, the impetus of their ideas moved increasingly toward economics. In so doing, they largely rejected the laissez-faire ideas of Adam Smith.[27] Men like Rousseau, Hegel, Marx, Engels, Lenin, and the twentieth-century economist Keynes cast aside ideas fostered by the Enlightenment and developed a philosophy that rejected concepts of individual liberty, low-tax governmental minimalism and free markets, in favor of class identity, large bureaucracies and central economic planning.

The imposition of these policies inevitably demanded the use of force, and they were willing to sacrifice individual Freedom in the process. To put their ideas in the best possible light, we may say they were ostensibly concerned with reducing (or eliminating) the disparity between rich and poor. But by omitting Freedom from the equation,

---

27. Smith himself never used the term "laissez faire," which may be translated, "let it be."

they assured that the only path to achieving what would eventually be called "economic justice" was by impoverishing everyone alike. Thus were laid down the foundations of the collectivist philosophies of Totalitarian Rule; Socialism, Fascism, and Communism.

ROUSSEAU

The philosopher Jean-Jacques Rousseau (1712–1778) had what may have been an unintended effect on mankind. His *Social Contract* (1762) is deemed by many to be the foundation of "modern" totalitarianism. However, if we view Rousseau's ideas as a whole, it is difficult to believe he would condone the use of his work as a justification for oppression.

Rousseau was a tortured soul who led an unstable life, and it is possible that his personal struggles are reflected in the contradictory nature of his thoughts. He professed to believe that political rights arose from The People, and yet he endorsed strict authoritarianism and proposed rule by united Church and State. He believed Freedom and coercion were not mutually exclusive concepts, and held that the "common good" and "general will" were ultimate expressions of a self-governing process, which he viewed as collective rather than individual in nature.

In struggling with ideas beyond his grasp, Rousseau inadvertently endorsed principles of dogma and totalitarianism that his other writings indicate he vigorously and vociferously rejected. But the damage was done, and future authoritarians would appropriate Rousseau as one of their own as they sought roots for justifying their belief in oppression of The People. His thinking on these topics was so convoluted that no reasonable person could have given it much credence unless they desired to promote their own ulterior agenda. Those who believe in the use of Government to control our lives through force and fear found a ready-made "grandfather" in the muddled thinking of Jean-Jacques Rousseau.

HEGEL

Ideas of the German philosopher Georg Wilhelm Friedrich Hegel (1770–1831) were to have a great influence on both admirers and detractors. Most scholars agree that Hegel had a profound effect on twentieth-century totalitarianism, fascism, and communism.

Hegel set out to become the greatest philosopher by developing principles which would encompass all the ideas of previous philosophy. He developed a concept he referred to as the "Absolute," by which he meant all reality, seen as a material, rational system. History, or progression in time, could be explained through the process that came to be called "dialectic," that is, an initial thesis was challenged by an antithesis, resulting in a synthesis, which both subsumes the thesis and antithesis and transcends them.

The idea of the dialectic had been around since Greek times, and the notion of the Absolute itself is not dissimilar to Plato's idealism. And, like Plato, Hegel was an ardent believer in State authoritarianism. He downplayed individual Freedom in favor of obedience to the State, which, like Rousseau, he saw as a manifestation of the general will. A free and rational individual, he believed, would naturally choose to subordinate his own actions to the higher order of dialectic achievement. Therein lay the trap, one that would not manifest until some years following Hegel's death.

Hegel believed Christianity was the highest religion. Sympathetic to this sentiment, some Christian readers thus became Hegelians which are called "right-wing" Hegelians in the literature. However, he placed Christianity and all other religions below secular philosophy, so it was difficult for the right-wing Hegelians to identify the Christian

God with Hegel's Absolute, and they are of little historical importance. The left-wing Hegelians, however, based their support for him on his rejection of individual Freedom, natural rights, and natural Law, as championed by Locke and his followers. Hegel asserted that people enjoy concrete Freedom only when the various orders and groups of civilized life are maintained within and by the State.

Hegel shared with Rousseau the idea, inherent in their acceptance of the primacy of the State that an individual might be free even when being coerced, for although he might resent the force applied against him, this resentment would be an expression of his particular whims, not his rational insight. One early critic who saw clearly the root problem with Hegel's philosophy was the Danish existentialist philosopher Soren Kierkegaard (1813–1855), who noted that such systems "abrogate the distinction between good and evil, and destroy freedom." In his work, *Concluding Scientific Postscript*, he added that in Hegel, "Being an individual man is a thing that has been abolished, and every speculative philosopher confuses himself with humanity at large; whereby he becomes something infinitely great, and at the same time nothing at all."

For Karl Marx, "abolishing individual man" is precisely the goal; and measured by its impact upon mankind, Hegel's greatest achievement is the effect his ideas were to have on Marx. As such, his writings became the foundation and justification for some of the most destructive forms of Government ever to subjugate humanity. Like Rousseau, he has been badly served by his followers.

DAVID RICARDO

Another forerunner to Marx deserves mention here. The economist David Ricardo (1772–1823) has generally been regarded as one of the classical economists, along with Adam Smith and Thomas Malthus

(1766–1834). In *Political Economy and Taxation* (1817), Ricardo proposes a theory of "comparative advantage" in which he champions free trade and makes several astute observations about the specialization of labor, demonstrating that markets in economically inferior countries might still have a competitive advantage in producing certain goods, based on particular resources or labor skills. He also believed wages should be open to competition.

But in *Political Economy*, Ricardo also proposes his "labor theory of value," which holds that the value of different goods is determined by the relative quantities of labor necessary to produce each good. However, even Ricardo seems to have recognized that his idea was flawed for he continued to work on it, attempting to resolve some of the contradictions and the necessity of using unrealistic assumptions for most of his life.

Ricardo is also noted for a compilation of previous economists' theories of rent, drawing heavily from Adam Smith. Comparing the different points of view, he developed his own theory, which has become known in economics as Ricardian Rent. This theory was also seriously flawed as was immediately pointed out by his contemporary Malthus in his own work *Rent*.

Counter to Adam Smith's belief that capitalism could lead society progressively forward, Ricardo believed that economic equilibrium gravitated toward a standstill. His examples also draw a distinction between the different classes, viewing them as adversaries.

By emphasizing the importance of class struggle and formulating his labor theory of value, Ricardo's influence on Marx was substantial. Marx drew heavily from Ricardo in developing and supporting his own works.

MARX AND ENGELS

No single figure is of greater importance to the political systems of socialism and communism, and to the philosophy of collectivism in general, than Karl Marx (1818–1883). Marx borrowed aspects of writers such a Rousseau, Hegel and Ricardo in the process discarding virtually everything of value any of them ever wrote. In 1843, Marx was in self-exile in Paris because his radical behavior made it necessary for him leave his German homeland. In Paris Marx became close friends with Friedrich Engels (1820–1895).

They were to collaborate on their writings for the rest of their lives; Engels even edited and published the last two volumes of Marx's unfinished *Das Kapital* after Marx's death. In 1848 Marx and Engels published *The Communist Manifesto*, which was to have enormous influence on world politics from that day to this. Only about 8500 words long, it subverted all conventional political and economic philosophy, appealing in its directness and simplicity to many people, and appalling many others with its abrogation of individual human dignity and its promise of colorless conformity—a vision of drabness brought to life in the architecture of every communist-built city in Eastern Europe.

The first sentence of the first chapter of the manifesto reads: "The history of all hitherto existing society is the history of class struggles." What a stark contrast with Jefferson, who, following Locke, began the Declaration of Independence by speaking of *individuals*, endowed with *rights*, including *life, liberty* and *the pursuit of happi*ness.

Marx's economic theory drew on Ricardo's labor theory of value, but inserted capitalists instead of landlords as the villains of society. He believed workers were locked into misery and poverty by the economic laws of capitalism. Marx used Ricardo's predictions of stagnation to construct his belief that wealth will concentrate, and the workers will continue to become more impoverished until they rise up and depose the capitalists. That conflict, Hegelian to the core as Marx saw it, would lead to a synthesis, which he described in this way: "There would succeed a progressive, rational society with no wages, no money, no social classes, and, eventually, no state - a free association of producers under their [own] conscious and purposive control." It is doubtful that Ricardo would have agreed with, or approved of Marx's ideas because he was a strong proponent of free trade. However, the historical link is forever entwined.

Marx falsely believed his thinking to be "scientific," and it was proclaimed as such by Engels. But the convoluted thinking supposedly leading to his "Utopian" ideal world reveals more wishful thinking than the rigor of scientific inquiry. Even so, it was seen as credible to some in his own times when the early Industrial Revolution was producing unprecedented and confusing social upheaval. But now, over a century and a half later, both sides of his equation have been decisively demonstrated to be wrong. The proletariat turned out not to be locked into a life of misery. Instead, by leaps and bounds, it grew in affluence, education and culture—specifically because of the enormous productivity of capitalism when combined with political Freedom. And because the disciples of Marx's ideas *did* succeed in taking over the Governments in some parts of the world, we can also see that his communist synthesis was anything but a Utopia. Materially, emotionally and intellectually starved, The People of the communist world bolted for the exits the instant the terror was overcome, and the wall torn down.

Marx's ideas ignore that in a free society it is the potential and initiative of the individual which determine his status in the hierarchy, not the imposition of force or the caste system of the old order. In a free and capitalist system, the brightest and most gifted have an open pathway to positions of responsibility and influence and will gravitate toward the top. Moreover the wealth of the topmost does in fact trickle down—"cascade" might be a better word—throughout society. In the final days of the Soviet Union, Americans, even those far below the so-called poverty line lived in homes equipped with large screen color television sets, microwave ovens, and dozens of other signs of material wealth unimaginable in the "worker's paradise" behind the iron curtain.

Even in terms of public wealth, which one might suppose to be a strong point for a Marxist state, the comparison condemns communism. Plagued by shortages under all of the communist regimes, The People struggled to purchase even bare necessities while grocery stores in the West overflowed with a bountiful variety unavailable to even the wealthiest monarchs in previous times.

Infrastructure should be another strong point of a Marxist State, but again the comparison points to condemnation. The distance between the two largest cities in Russia, Moscow and St. Petersburg (then Leningrad) is about the same as the distance between New York and Chicago. Yet the principal highway between the two was nothing but a two-lane road. Imagine if there were nothing more than that connecting New York and Chicago!

Marxist economics begins with a false premise—Ricardo's labor theory of value. Defining value based on the amount of labor necessary to produce a good completely ignores the enormous variation in the factors affecting the choices of each individual as they consume. It also ignores supply, demand, and availability which are the cornerstones of accepted economic theory, and which any rational inquiry must include in determining value.

Nonetheless, Marx's ideas were to inflame the passions of revolutionaries such as Vladimir Lenin and Mao Zedong, and even today, he is considered as a grandfatherly influence by many who proselytize collectivist philosophies. Never mind that more misery, oppression, death and destruction are arguably attributable to the practitioners who implemented Marx's writings than any other individual in history. The tens of millions of broken bodies murdered by despots who professed a belief in Marxism, shout from their graves as a graphic reminder.

COMMUNISM

The communist doctrine conceived by Marx and Engels has been put into action by a number of leaders in various nations, most importantly by Vladimir Lenin (1870–1924) in Russia, and Mao Zedong (1893–1976) in China. Lenin originally believed that the communist revolution would sweep the entire world in a matter of a few decades at most. He later revised his thinking into a longer time frame as events unfolded and communism did not gain the rapid worldwide acceptance he had anticipated.

In 1909 Lenin published *Materialism and Empirio-criticism* in which he proposed a socialist revolution led by a "vanguard party" of professional revolutionaries. Lenin believed that the communist ideal could be achieved through ruthless prosecution of all dissent, and through totalitarian rule. After the revolution, Lenin became the undisputed ruler of Russia until his death in 1927. Due to Lenin's failed agriculture policies, it is estimated that between six and eight million people died of starvation in the 1918–1923 famine alone. Without the most massive effort of food aid distribution by America in all of history (before or since), the death toll would have been many tens of millions greater, and without which many scholars believe Lenin's revolution might have failed.

Totalitarianism under Lenin tolerated little dissent, but the authoritarian brutality of his successor, Joseph Stalin (1878-1953), is of legendary inhumanity.

Lenin's many writings were also to become the philosophical

basis of Marxism-Leninism, through a compilation by Stalin and in Stalin's own writing *Concerning Questions of Leninism*. Under Stalin's rule, Marxism-Leninism was proclaimed the official ideology of the State. After taking control of the Soviet Union, Stalin rapidly began to implement even greater economic collectivization by his now infamous "five-year" plans. Industrialization and modernization immediately plummeted, and the plans were especially disastrous in agriculture. It is estimated that tens of millions starved to death in the resulting famines. As if economic catastrophe and starvation were not enough of a burden on The People of Russia, in the late 1930s Stalin initiated the Great Purge to crush all dissent. Known by The People as "The Great Terror," credible estimates of victims by modern historians range from four to ten million. Including the numbers who died from famine, estimates of the total that succumbed to Stalin's socialism range as high as sixty million, although we will never know for certain because part Stalin's "purging" process was to erase the public record of many of those who were eliminated as though they never existed.

Communism is marked by total central planning and control. All individual rights are forcefully usurped for the supposed good of the collective whole while the power is in the hands of a small elite and closely held group. Rule and legitimacy are maintained through force, fear, and intimidation of The People. Thus, an elite class "temporarily" exercises power through their control of the power of the State.

Though similar to the total oppression of the monarchies and theocracies of the Dark Ages, in communism, Marx's uncompromising atheism is honored by depriving the church of any role. The ruling cadre is from a different class of society and central planning insures even more invasive control over the lives of The People. Total destruction of individual rights draws its "necessity" from supposed advancement of the collective good, but destruction of the initiative and innovative power of the individual fosters economic decline and stagnation in nearly all fields of endeavor.

The collectivist philosophies of communism and socialism predictably end in failure and misery for The People living under their dominance, precisely because they stress forced sacrifice to the collective, which is antithetical to Freedom of the individual.

They are not pathways to Utopia. They are group struggles for power and control of society. Rather than struggles to free mankind, they are a whitewashed means of *returning* to the enslavement of mankind. Rather than giving power and Freedom to The People, they represent merely a power shift from the old aristocratic class to a new group—the revolutionaries and Marxist intellectuals. Their arguments are but a new means of justifying State dominance over the individual by those who derive their wealth, power, privilege and status from their association with the State.

Mao Zedong was very candid as his group exerted their communist dominance over China at the end of World War II. Mao stated that all power ultimately "comes from the barrel of a gun." In other words power originates through force, fear, and intimidation, and in direct opposition to tolerance and Freedom. Mao's version of communism included such infamous policies as the Great Leap Forward (1958–1961) and Cultural Revolution (1966–1976). The Great Leap Forward involved forced collectivization of agriculture and results were similar to results of the famines and disasters in Russia. The Cultural Revolution mobilized the youth to ferret out all of those who might desire a return to capitalism. Many of the educated were caught up in the resultant turmoil that damaged not only the economy but also had a long-lasting negative effect on Chinese culture and society. It is estimated that between thirty and seventy million people died in Mao's socialist reforms.

JOHN MAYNARD KEYNES

Not all the people who championed Marxist thinking were ruthless dictators. Many were "merely" professors, economists and other intellectuals, artists, labor leaders and others whose common ground seems to be the sort of egotism Kierkegaard referred to in finding Hegel guilty of "confusing himself with humanity at large."

One of these was John Maynard Keynes (1883–1946). At the end of World War I, his book *The Economic Consequences of the Peace* (1919) bought Keynes to prominence. His attacks on Woodrow Wilson and British Prime Minister David Lloyd George stirred up a furor of controversy, and in its wake came recognition and fame. Thereafter, Keynes was to seek out controversy as a tool for promoting his socialist ideas about economics.

Two books in the 1920s, *Tract on Monetary Reform* and *Treatise on Money,* reflected Keynes' views on Monetarism, which holds that changes or manipulations of the money supply determine the direction of a nation's economy. Keynes believed stabilizing the price level would stabilize the economy; and as a matter of public policy, he was at the time a proponent of intervention by the Government central bank to lower interest rates when prices are rising and raise interest rates when prices fall. However, Keynes reversed much of this thinking a decade later in the policy he prescribed for aggressive Government economic intervention.

Keynes put forth his new ideas in a 1936 book on the cause of the depression, entitled *The General Theory of Employment, Interest, and Money*. Although there were dissenters from the beginning, the book was very influential, and his ideas remained mainstream for many years. Indeed, Keynes's reputation endured until, in 1971, President Richard Nixon sought to justify his own government's intervention in the economy (abandoning the gold standard and implementing a freeze on wages and prices) by endorsing Keynesianism. After the failure of "Nixonomics," Keynes' views appear to have declined in popularity, at least in name, although the link may be merely associative, and not causative. While politicians and bureaucrats no longer wish to be attached to Keynesianism, the policies of big Government agencies and institutions, such as the Federal Reserve, have remained Keynesian to the core.

In any event, *The General Theory of Employment, Interest, and Money* is clearly a monumental assault on Freedom and Liberty. Keynes's theories begin with an obviously flawed premise that consumption rather than production (aggregate demand is the sum of consumption) is the driving force of economics. He then uses this premise to justify the centralization of power and Government intervention in the free market. In the process, he outrageously asserts that full employment can only be maintained by Government spending, an idea that became accepted around the world and is still taught in American colleges today. A question arises. If Keynes's core theory is so obviously flawed, how has it gained such wide acceptance? The answer is simple. The Governments of the world embraced the ideas of Keynes primarily because they rationalize the growth of Government dominance of economics. Government promotion of Keynesianism resulted in academic appointments, research grants, publication opportunities and a plethora of other self-sustaining actions supported by Government funding, a dynamic seen not only in economics, but other disciplines as well. "Funding" is often the most important element in establishing tenure at colleges and universities.

Prior to Keynes, a balanced budget was standard policy with the U.S. Government, but Keynes justified Government intervention in the free market; Keynes promoted centralization of power and Government control of economics, and he advocated abandonment of the gold standard so Government could better "manipulate" the economy by controlling the amount of money in circulation and through the control of credit. Even more importantly, Keynes advocated creation of debt and deficit spending. All of these policies enormously increase the size, control, and the power of Government. It is obvious why Governments worldwide still wish to promote the ideas of John Maynard Keynes. Unfortunately, it is The People who ultimately pay the price for Keynes's policies of Governmental excess. Ultimately, the producers of society are harmed most.

In 1940, Keynes published *How To Pay For The War* and was immediately invited to become an advisor to the British Treasury. From that point his influence in World economics became firmly entrenched. After the war Keynes was instrumental in driving centralization on a global scale through helping create the International Monetary Fund (IMF) and the World Bank. The modern growth of Government and its intrusion into almost every facet of man's daily life began primarily with the acceptance of the socialist economic policies of John Maynard Keynes in World War II, and it set the World on an unsustainable path leading toward global economic disaster, which could ultimately make the Great Depression pale in comparison.

Keynes's theories hold that consumption rather than production is the basis of economics. He believed consumption drives production and is the fundamental driving force of economics. Keynes believed that demand was determined by expenditures.

Therefore, if Governments usurp more and spend more, creating debt through deficit spending, and/or manipulating the money supply, then Government can steer the economy toward prosperity for all. Keynes believed full employment could only be achieved by Government intervention to implement a policy of cheap money and public investment. It becomes obvious that Keynes aligns himself with Plato and Marx in positing that Government is the solution rather than the problem.

Promoters of Keynesian economics believe that Adam Smith never extended his theories into the arena of Keynes's thinking. This ignores the fact that Smith was a first order creative genius whose ideas were a radical departure from accepted theory rather than building on a common theme. How can anyone believe that he would not have given consideration to consumption as a driving force when Smith originated the concept of production of "consumable goods"? It is far more likely that he considered and rejected Keynes's thinking. Keynes's theory of the importance of investment in capital equipment and its financing is nothing more than reworked mercantile economic policy, only substituting the element of financing for simple possession. Keynes's ideas regarding stimulating production through stimulating consumption ignore three key economic elements.

First, there is no orderly mechanism for change, due either to technological improvement or change in consumer preference and desires. If Government induces large capital investment, it becomes locked into continuing that chain of production. If something better is invented the next year, production of the outmoded and technically obsolete item will continue because of the need to recapture the investment. The same holds true for the innovation of a better means of production. Government will protect its investment and hamper production of the more modern item or more modern means of production. Factories quickly become outdated and produce unwanted items with less and less efficiency.

In the final death throes of the unraveling Soviet economic machine, we found Government-protected production of unwanted items, with factories inefficiently using antiquated equipment and producing goods of low quality. Smith saw the entrepreneur as a risk taker who would fill this part of the economic equation. There would be no Government protected "sacred cows." If technology improves, the entrepreneur must either accept his losses and/or modernize for competition dictates that others will be willing to move into the vacuum of demand. Change is not obstructed or hampered as it is by Government, but instead change is enhanced. Modernization and technological improvement are sped up rather than frozen.

The second failure of Keynes's interventionist policies is that without production, there is no corresponding increase in the value of money. Someone somewhere must produce goods or a service which the value of money only represents. Deficit spending and the creation of debt create an illusion of gain and may produce some immediate benefit but inevitably, sooner or later, the producers of society must pay and square the deficit. Only the illusion of prosperity is produced. The debt then becomes a burden on future generations.

The third failure of Keynes's thinking is the precept that Government operates on the principle of creating good and prosperity for all The People (Government as the solution). As we have seen, this goes against the entire historical experience.

Government acts to create more Government, to increase its power, to centralize authority and to control and subjugate its people. And Government enriches those who derive wealth, power, privilege, and status from association with Government at the expense of those who actually produce.

Observation of history since adoption of Keynesian economics in World War II shows cycles of boom and bust with the recessions becoming more severe in each downturn. There has never been employment equal to that which was created by the policies of Freedom from Government preceding Keynes. Since the adoption of Keynesian "babble," history records a phenomenal growth in Government. And it shows an enormous and unprecedented growth of debt. If debt is created, doesn't someone have to pay it back? Is that not the very definition of debt? Who do you suppose that will be? The Keynes prescription of spending our way into prosperity through debt is a con game of the first order. It might pay for a war. It might even finance high times and the illusion of prosperity—momentarily. However, someone has to eventually pay for the present excesses. Will our grandchildren and even their grandchildren pay for the excesses of our generation through an increasingly lower standard of living? Will the burden on The People, which expresses itself in taxation, become so great that we are sowing the seeds of the decline of our great nation? Will we pay through the misery of worldwide economic collapse? The path we are currently on is unsustainable. Disaster is on the horizon. We cannot spend ourselves into prosperity. There is no free ride. It is ultimately the producers of society who **always** pay. Adam Smith would have laughed at some of Keynes's ideas. The eminent economist and philosopher Ludwig von Mises discounted many of Keynes's ideas as gibberish.

An entire school of thought now encompasses the name *Keynesian Economics*. While Keynes did make some contributions to economics, the vast majority of his thinking and legacy have been very detrimental to humanity. Analogous to the collapse of communist Russia, how much misery, both contemporary and to future generations, must The People endure before we return to the simple idea that there is a balance in economics? When Government creates debt, it is The People who must eventually pay it!

It is immoral to enslave future generations to pay for the excesses of this or any generation.

CHAPTER 12

LUDWIG VON MISES AND THE AUSTRIAN SCHOOL OF ECONOMICS

ONE OF THE TWENTIETH CENTURY'S GREATEST proponents of Freedom, and most vociferous critics of socialism, was the philosopher and classical liberal economist Ludwig von Mises (1881–1973). Born into a prominent Jewish family in Austria-Hungary, he received a doctorate from the prestigious University of Vienna in 1906. Forced to flee his homeland to Geneva to escape the growing Nazi threat, he taught there until immigrating to New York City in 1940. Living in the social and political cauldron of early twentieth-century Europe imbued von Mises with an insight into contemporary application of economic theory and philosophy.

Von Mises is the best known of the economists of the Austrian School of economics, which rose to prominence in the late nineteenth and early twentieth centuries. Austrian economics teaches that unpredictability in human behavior prevents accurate modeling of markets. Von Mises and other Austrians advocated sound money based on the gold/silver standard, laissez faire economics, and free markets; they taught against Government economic intervention and production of excessive fiat money, which is legal tender not backed by any reserves, but dependent solely on the population's faith in the Government that issues it. Though marginalized for decades by Keynes and other proponents of socialist economics, Austrian Economics has enjoyed a resurgence of interest in the years since the 1980s.

Like Voltaire, von Mises was prolific and capable of writing excellence in languages other than his primary language. He wrote over a dozen books in both economics and philosophy that are available in English. I personally believe that Von Mises's seminal work *Human Action: A Treatise on Economics,* published in 1949, is second in economics only to Adam Smith's *The Wealth of Nations* and ranks as one of the most important works on Freedom ever written. *Human Action* intertwines economics, philosophy and human behavior in a manner that explodes many of the contemporary myths regarding economics. It shows that *all* economic phenomena are the result of individual action in the form of choices. The ideas are elegant in construction from the simplicity of their beginning to the integrated complexity of their development. The rigorous scholarship with which Von Mises introduces his economic ideas makes them almost impossible to assail rationally, and many become self-evident in their concept.

Von Mises lived at a time in which socialism, communism, fascism and Nazism were sweeping the world, and to this catalog of collectivism must be added the "new liberal economics" of John Maynard Keynes, who lifted the term "liberal economics" from the followers of Adam Smith so successfully that we must now distinguish Smith's principles by using the term "*classical* liberal economics" in order to clarify our meaning. Von Mises perceived the fallacy of all collectivism and its threat to Freedom. The more brutal forms were relatively easy to deal with intellectually, but von Mises also attacked and discounted the ideas of Keynes and other "respectable" contemporary socialist economists, showing them to be unworkable and writing that,

"The essence of Keynesianism is its complete failure to conceive the role that saving and capital accumulation play in the improvement of economic conditions." Speaking out against an icon in the socialist revolution was not popular and was a significant factor in von Mises's ideas falling out of favor in the later part of his career.

In 1912, von Mises published *The Theory of Money and Credit* in which he explained that business cycles are caused by the expansion of bank credit. He also extended the marginal utility theory to money where utility is gained or lost due to respective increases or decreases in consumption. He showed that demand for money is due to its usefulness in purchasing goods and services rather than for its intrinsic value. In his early career, von Mises's ideas gained great acceptance to the extent that *The Theory of Money and Credit* was widely used as a college textbook. But as socialism grew in popularity, he was marginalized for his ideas supporting Freedom of the individual and laissez faire economics.

With publication of *Socialism* in German in 1922 (translated to English in 1936) von Mises declared open war on the perceived collectivist menace that he observed doing great harm to the well-being of humanity. He methodically attacked socialism's intellectual construct and almost everything encompassing the socialist idea. In the collectivist onslaught against Freedom in the twentieth century, *Socialism* stands out as an important bulwark of rational thought promoting the importance of individualism and warning of the impending disaster of socialism.

Today, von Mises is probably best known for his accurate prediction that socialism must fail due to what is now known in economics as the "economic calculation problem," which shows that socialism's central planning lacks the market information to rationally allocate resources. In a free market economy, this allocation is done by virtue of prices, which reflect the value individual human beings place on a given good or service.

Under socialism, prices are set either by a cost of production calculation or simply by Government order, thus ignoring the purchasing choices individuals make, which are influenced by factors such as personal preference, availability of resources and demand. Von Mises realized that the only way to gain knowledge of these factors is through the market itself—that is: You have to do it to know how it will work out.

Without this unobtainable knowledge, Government control of economics can never determine the proper allocation of resources and must fail. Unlike the market, Government cannot make adjustments on the fly and has no means of fulfilling the crucial role of the entrepreneur.

In 1944, von Mises extended his thinking on the economic calculation problem to accentuate the difference between bureaucratic management and profit and loss management in the free market through publication of *Bureaucracy*. He shows that bureaucracy can never make rational decisions or achieve efficiency, and how Government interference and impairment of the profit motive drives business toward bureaucratization. *Bureaucracy* is also important for its underpinning of individualism and its attack against collectivism in which von Mises insightfully predicted, "Socialism must result in complete chaos."[28] Von Mises dedicated his life to fighting for the cause of Freedom. He continued to speak out against Government intervention and in favor of Freedom of trade and economics, even though he was ostracized and even blackballed from many teaching positions which viewed him as outside of the main stream of current economic thought. With the perspective of time, he has proven to be a beacon of rational thought in what was the foggy and muddled mania

28.Ebenstein, Alan (2001), Friedrich Hayek: a biography (1st ed.), Palgrave, New York: University Of Chicago Press, pp. 116, ISBN 978-0312233440

encompassing the socialist revolution. Von Mises was correct in foreseeing the failure of socialism. Collectivist economics has proven to be a disaster in every country that succumbed to the siren promises.

It is worth reviewing the step-by-step destruction of nations that implemented socialism of one sort or another. The fascists and Nazis were defeated in World War II, specifically because their centrally planned, socialistic economies could not match the ability of market-oriented western economies. Although the Axis powers began the war with a decided edge in war-making abilities (newer and better weaponry, factories building war materials, etc.) they lost their edge the longer the war went on because of the enormous productive capacity of the United States and the other Allied nations. The collapse of communism in the 1990s fully demonstrated the truth of von Mises's ideas.

The Soviet bloc was able to afford a space program and a massive war machine, but because no economic resources were left to meet consumer demands, the system imploded. Today, only a handful of truly communist countries remain, such as China, Cuba, and North Korea. In others, Chile in the 1960s, for example, Nicaragua in the 1980s and several African nations throughout that period, communist leaders may seize power, but their takeovers prove to be short-lived At the time of this writing, Venezuela and Bolivia appear to be likely candidates for this category, which is not, in the big picture, of great consequence, devastating though it may be for the people of the countries involved.

Of the countries still under communist rule, all but North Korea and Cuba have reduced State control of their economies, but are still languishing ever farther behind countries promoting freer economics. Of those that have reduced state control, the most important is China, which has instituted "special economic zones" practicing market-oriented business, and is substantially free from central Government control and planning. The resultant two-decade-long growth and improvement for Chinese society from the pent up demand of such a large population has been phenomenal. However, without corresponding banking, monetary, corruption and social reforms, the parts of the economy still under State planning will eventually drag China into the abyss. This descent could possibly foster civil war as the ruling elite have a history of using draconian measures to preserve their power, and The People have finally had a first taste of Freedom.

In most of the rest of the world, including the Western nations that lived to see the fall of Fascist Italy, Nazi Germany, the Eastern European communist regimes and the Soviet Union, the phenomenon once pejoratively called "creeping socialism" has been the general trend throughout the past half century or more. This is Keynesianism, communism's wimpy little brother. Because it is a less extreme version of socialism, it has a correspondingly longer shelf life. But it, too, is unsustainable as we are currently observing around the world from California to Greece. As von Mises predicted, *socialism has been, and must be*, a chaotic and utter failure.

By notable academic achievement, Friedrich Hayek (1899–1992) has earned the distinction of being von Mises's most influential student and ranks as another important twentieth-century champion of Freedom. Born in Vienna, he became a British citizen in 1938 during the Nazi domination of his homeland. He taught at the London School of Economics, University of Chicago, and the University of Freiburg in Germany.

After graduating from the University of Vienna with doctorates in law and political science, Hayek was hired by von Mises who was working for the Austrian Government in an effort to deal with World War I debt. Hayek was profoundly affected by reading von Mises's book *Socialism,* and when they were both at New York University, he began participating in von Mises's private seminars. The innovative ideas of von Mises on business cycles and their relationship to money, the telegraphing of information associated within the economic calculation problem, and the interrelationship of economics and societal outcomes were to inspire Hayek to further develop these theories, becoming instrumental in his being awarded the Nobel Prize in Economics in 1974.

During World War II, Hayek wrote and published *The Road to Serfdom*. The title indicates inspiration by Alexis de Tocqueville's writings on the "road to servitude."[29] It is a monumental attack on collectivism, central planning, and unrestrained Government while promoting individualism and classical economic liberalism. Unlike most of von Mises's works, it received wide popular readership outside of the circles of academia and had a significant effect on economic policy in Hayek's lifetime, especially influencing British Prime Minister Margaret Thatcher and President Ronald Reagan.

Both Hayek and von Mises are widely associated with what is now known as the Austrian Theory of the Business Cycle, which deals with the cyclical pattern of growth and contraction. It denigrates central banking policies (meaning in the U.S. the policies of the Federal Reserve Board) as always being inefficient or harmful and as especially harmful when over-stimulating credit growth. The theory proposes that a sustained period of low interest rates and excessive credit creation results in a volatile and unstable imbalance between saving and investment.[30] It predicts that a policy of excessive money and credit creation will temporarily create a period of unsustainable "boom" which must then be followed by a "bust," in which the money sharply contracts.

The current business cycle of boom and bust, leading up to the economic crisis of 2007, tracks the progression of events predicted by this theory. It is reasonable to assume that the severity of the current

29. "The weeds of destruction". Economist. 2006-05-04.
30. Von Mises, Ludwig: *Bureaucracy*, P.57

crisis is proportional to the amount of Government intervention and unprecedentedly sustained low interest rates during Alan Greenspan's direction of the FED (Federal Reserve). But Greenspan's policies were only a warmup for the radical Keynesian expansion of his successor, Ben Bernanke, who has taken debasement of the dollar and creation of debt to an unprecedented extreme through creation of new fiat money. He even earned the sobriquet "helicopter Ben" after a comment about dropping new money from helicopters as a means of preventing deflation.

In the wake of President George W. Bush's Troubled Assets Relief Program (TARP), or bailout, program and the even more extreme "stimulus" and other spending programs of the succeeding Barack Obama administration, there has been a substantial revival of interest in the Austrian business cycle theory, as more and more Americans have become alarmed at the trend towards unrestrained exponential growth of Government. Led by economic thinkers generally labeled "libertarian" in their viewpoint, and including many leaders in the politically significant Tea Party movement, this trend offers at least some promise for a move away from collectivism and toward Freedom. Unfortunately, Keynesianism has dominated academia and the economic landscape for so long that the prescriptive "cure" of the Government bureaucrats has thus far been massive debt creation on a scale never before witnessed in any society considered Free. In addition, Government is using the newly-created fiat money to preserve and create more Government jobs, instead of stimulating the private sector and economic growth; and it is using the crisis as justification for giving even more power to the Federal Reserve and other regulatory bodies. While certain aspects of the Austrian business cycle theory may require further refinement, its core precepts are a significant contribution to modern economic theory. They predict that implementation of socialist Keynesian policies by the Obama administration portends almost certain economic disaster of global proportions. It is only the time frame that is unknown.

Another important student of von Mises was Dr. Murray Rothbard (1926–1995), who made notable contributions to the modern libertarian movement and to promoting and advancing Austrian School ideas. In scathing attacks, he condemned central planning, coercive Government, excessive taxation and the use of the monopoly force of Government. His book *America's Great Depression* (1963) showed that the depression of the 1930s was caused by central bank interference in the market through the inflationary policy of the Federal Reserve, and not, as Keynesians have always claimed, by stock market speculation. During his career he was an unwavering critic of Keynesian economics. Besides being a noted economist, Rothbard was a prolific author, promoting a libertarian theme of philosophy and political thought. He was also a political activist and social critic who, throughout his life, sought out different groups and associations in attempting to promote his belief in Freedom. Upon his death in 1995, the *New York Times* obituary noted that Rothbard was "an economist and social philosopher who fiercely defended individual freedom against government intervention."[31] Another prominent student attending the lectures of von Mises was the noted philosopher and novelist Ayn Rand (1905–1982). Born in Russia as Alissa Rosenbaum, she immigrated to the United States in 1926 and became an American citizen in 1931.

She is another of the twentieth century's greatest critics of all forms of collectivism and unrestrained Government and was a strong proponent of the role of the individual in society.

Rand was an ethical philosopher promoting what she coined as "Objectivism," which viewed man "as a heroic being, with his own happiness as the moral purpose of his life, with productive

31. David Stout, Obituary: Murray N. Rothbard, Economist And Free-Market Exponent, 68, The New York Times, January 11, 1995.

achievement as his noblest activity, and reason as his only absolute." For those seeking a more intellectual inquiry of her ideas, she wrote *Introduction to Objectivist Epistemology*. It was first published as a series of five articles in *The Objectivist* magazine between July 1966 and February 1967, and thereafter published together in book form. It presents a well–reasoned study of the core beliefs of Objectivism beginning with the premise that there are things which exist and are real, and concluding that action should stem from individual rational thought and objective investigation rather than dogma and doctrine.

Rand highly valued reason and intellect and believed extraordinary men could build extraordinary lives. She was a strong advocate of individualism and an opponent of democratic majority rule, stating that "Individual rights are not subject to a public vote; a majority has no right to vote away the rights of a minority; the political function of rights is precisely to protect minorities from oppression by majorities (and the smallest minority on earth is the individual)."[32] She was a strong advocate of, capitalism and realism, and opposed all forms of mysticism. But it was reason that she viewed as most important to her thinking. In an article in *The Objectivist* in 1971 she stated, "I am not *primarily* an advocate of capitalism, but of egoism; and I am not *primarily* an advocate of egoism, but of reason. If one recognizes the supremacy of reason and applies it consistently, all the rest follows."[33] viii Besides von Mises, Rand acknowledged Aristotle as having a great influence on her thinking. She also acknowledged the influence of St. Thomas Aquinas although she had been an atheist since her teenage years. She so disliked the philosopher Immanuel Kant that she referred to him as a "monster" and "the most evil man in history."[34]

Rand was also a major fiction writer whose novels show the strong influence of her philosophical beliefs, as well as her formative years

32. Rand, Ayn (September 1971). "Brief Summary". The Objectivist 10 (9):

33. "About the Author" in *Rand* 1992, pp. 1170–1171

34. Ayn Rand (1961), "Collectivized 'Rights,'" *The Virtue of Selfishness*.

growing up during Russia's transition to communism. *We the Living* (1936), focuses on the struggle between the individual and the State. *Anthem* (1938) investigates a future society totally dominated by collectivism and the resultant repressive and totalitarian outcome. Her first major literary success was her novel *The Fountainhead*, published in 1943 and released as a movie in 1949 starring Gary Cooper, with the screenplay by Rand herself. The book and the movie brought her financial success and led to greater interest in her previous works.

Arguably, Ayn Rand's most remarkable philosophical achievement was writing *Atlas Shrugged (1957)*, an epistemological novel in which the characters display and promote Rand's core beliefs in Objectivism and rational self-interest. Even though the book was criticized as too long and received poor reviews, it was immediately popular and is still widely read today. The book's depiction of gradually advancing social decay, collapsing infrastructure and overall societal decline prior to complete economic collapse, may fruitfully be compared to the decline which culminated in the disintegration of the Soviet Union. The book is proving to be remarkably insightful, especially since it was written during the period of worldwide ascendency of collectivist Governments.

Atlas Shrugged proved to be the perfect vehicle for Rand's ascendency as a popular philosopher and was her last fictional work. In the 1940s she had become a political activist, and her philosophical writings reflected her political, moral and ethical thinking. For the rest of her life, she promoted her ideas through writing and lecturing at some of the most prestigious universities in America.

She was hardly universally accepted, however; and was widely attacked because of her uncompromising stance against socialism, totalitarianism and any other form of collectivism, for her opposition to organized religion, and for her open marriage. Rand's greatest criticism has arguably come from her belief that most humans act in selfish interest, and this tendency is not evil but rather an observation of reality. She believed that people should be allowed to achieve to their fullest potential, and that to hamper this progress through teaching self-sacrifice and altruism ultimately does more harm to society than good.

Ayn Rand has gained the widest readership of all of those influenced by von Mises, having sold over twenty-five million copies of her books to a worldwide audience (not including those viewing movies based on her work), and her books are still widely read in the twenty-first century.

Her thinking is credited by many as important in the foundation of modern libertarianism although she rejected the libertarian movement.

Like Hayek and Rothbard, Rand has provided inspiration to a wide variety of prominent individuals from many fields of endeavor, including prominent leaders in Government and politics; among those who have acknowledged receiving inspiration from her are Ronald Reagan, Ron Paul and Clarence Thomas.

Ludwig von Mises consistently adhered to a regimen of rigorous scholarship in developing his theses. Unfortunately, rigorous scholarship and a meticulous academic presentation of themes and ideas does not necessarily equate to popular readership. He was not persuasive in debate and was often at odds, even with close associates. Von Mises was never able to achieve the change that he believed to be so important for humanity, but I personally believe his innovative ideas will continue to grow in importance and inspire others to ever-greater achievement in the unending fight for Freedom. He dared to confront the enemies of Freedom at a high point of their power and at great cost to his reputation and career. But in some of Freedom's bleakest moments since the Enlightenment, Ludwig von Mises did not waver or capitulate to the Marxist/Keynesian forces which he realized were dragging the world back toward a modern day Dark Age.

PART III. PROBLEMS IN CONTEMPORARY FREEDOM
★ ★ ★

CHAPTER 13

THE RULE OF LAW

LIKE MANY OTHER CONCEPTS CO-OPTED BY proponents of socialism in the past century, the phrase "rule of law" no longer has the same connotation it did when our country was founded. Fundamentally, America is not, and never has been, a country of laws. It is a country of rights, which are implicit to humanity, pre-exist any Government, and therefore preempt any laws. Viewed in this light, it is clear that the modern misuse of the rule of law concept is in fact a threat to Liberty.

But before examining the pitfalls of the modern distortion of the meaning of *rule of law*, I wish to point out its venerable history. The basic concept was that the rule of law was preferable to the rule of men, and was another way of stating that no man, not even a king, was above the law.

The rule of law was an important development in ancient Greece, where men like Solon and Lycurgus gave their people laws that, while in many ways harsh by modern standards, at least helped free men from the arbitrary and capricious rule of other men. If a king or dictator can yell "off with his head" arbitrarily, then no person is Free, and none have rights. Translations vary, but it was probably Aristotle who first stated that society would be better served following "the rule of laws, not men" in commenting on Plato's rejection of democracy.

Law in pre-classical Rome was mostly decided by "pontifices," who were high religious leaders of the patrician ruling class. In 449 BC, after having sent a delegation to Greece to study the Solonian Constitution of Athens and the laws of other Greek States, the Romans adopted the Law of the Twelve Tables. These statements of various rights and procedures, with strict religious underpinning, were the first attempt to codify Roman law.

They were literally carved into twelve separate tablets and posted in the forum for all to read. Combined with traditional customs, which could not be written down, these fledgling precepts of Roman law began a legal formalism that still influences law today, enshrining the concept that it was the form (not the intent) of actions that produced legal consequences. During the centuries of the Republic, the tradition of the Twelve Tables, although often compromised, was an important bulwark for The People. But with the advent of the Empire, they were relegated to little more than forceless heritage, while in practice the Emperor became the ultimate source of all law.

As Rome began to mature and control other states, it developed an alternate set of laws that applied to newly subjugated people (but not to Roman citizens). In the early fifth century, still another set of laws known as The Law of Nations were instituted to govern the relationship between Romans and foreigners.

Then, in the sixth century AD, the Emperor Justinian I began collating and publishing most of the collective Roman laws. Lost for centuries, this compilation of great historical importance is known today as the Justinian Code. Later rediscovered in the Middle Ages in Italy, it had immediate influence on church canon law and is generally considered an important foundation of civil law. Rule "by" law, as opposed to rule "of" law, was prevalent during the Dark Ages, and Freedom languished accordingly. The Middle Ages saw several attempts to limit the power of monarchs through written constitutions. This produced one of the most important early developments in Anglo-Saxon law: the signing of the Magna Carta by King John of England in 1215. The Magna Carta is important for its proclamation of rights, respect for legal procedures, and support of the right to appeal unlawful imprisonment. The Magna Carta implies that imprisonment should always be lawful and establishes the basis of what we now know as *habeas corpus*. Probably the most important aspect of the Magna Carta is its establishment of the precedent of limitation of the power of rulers. Starting with John himself, subsequent kings frequently attempted to ignore or repudiate the precedent, thereby stirring up opposition among The People. Sometimes it was the nobles, sometimes the fledgling Parliament, even on occasion the peasantry itself, as in the great Peasants' Revolt of 1381. But eventually, particularly in the wake of the Glorious Revolution of 1688, which fostered the English Bill of Rights, the concept of limited Governmental power became firmly established. This new development was given a firm intellectual foundation by philosophers and legal scholars. It was disseminated through western culture by documents such as the French Declaration of the Rights of Man and the American Declaration of Independence, the Constitution, and the Bill of Rights.

It was not until the flowering of new thought in the Enlightenment that the concept of "rule of law," as later espoused by the forefathers of the American Revolution, began to take form. Those who believe that rights arise out of Government support the formalist concept emanating from early Roman law, which emphasizes procedures and compliance without regard for whether the particular law is just. This view was challenged by philosophers of the Enlightenment. John Locke asserted that *substantive rights* to *"preserve and enlarge Freedom"* were *inherent in the "rule of law."* In his Second Treatise on Government, Locke states that:

> ... the end of Law is not to abolish or restrain, but to preserve
> and enlarge Freedom: For in all the states of created beings
> capable of Laws, where there is no Law, there is no Freedom.
> For Liberty is to be free from restraint and violence from oth-
> ers, which cannot be, where there is no Law: But Freedom
> is not, as we are told, A Liberty for every Man to do what he
> lists: (For who could be free, when every other Man's Humour
> might domineer over him?) But a Liberty to dispose, and or-
> der, as he lists, his Person, Actions, Possessions, and his whole
> Property, within the Allowance of those Laws under which he
> is; and therein not to be subject to the arbitrary Will of another,
> but freely follow his own.

Montesquieu's *The Spirit of the Laws*, published in 1748, is a monumental and multi-faceted gem in the struggle for Freedom. We have already noted its influence on Burlamaqui and penal reform. The *Spirit of the Laws* expands Locke's *concept* of "rule of law" *as itself inclusive of substantive rights* and offers practical application in both how the concept can be applied and how power can be restrained. His notion of the importance of the separation of powers greatly influenced James Madison and the other founders who wrote the American constitution. Montesquieu believed that, "Liberty involves living under laws that protect us from harm while leaving us free to do as much as possible, and that enable us to feel the greatest possible confidence that if we obey those laws, the power of the state will not be directed against us."[35] In determining the proper role of law in rela-tion to rights of the individual, the ideas of Locke and Montesquieu represent the clearest thinking. But it remained for Thomas Jefferson

---

35. Stanford Encyclopedia of Philosophy; Baron de Montesquieu, Charles-Louis de Secondat (first published 2003 with substantive revision Jan. of 2010); 4.2 Liberty

to put their ideas into the most succinct and famous statement ever on the relationship between rights, laws and Government as he began the Declaration of Independence. Humankind should never forget them:

> "We hold these truths to be self-evident, that all men are created equal, that they are endowed by their Creator with certain unalienable rights, that among these are life, liberty and the pursuit of happiness. That to secure these rights, governments are instituted among men, deriving their just powers from the consent of the governed."

The rights come first—pre-existing and not determined by any Government. The job of Government is to "secure" the rights. A modern writer might use the verb "safeguard" or "protect" instead of "secure." The People, "the governed," must in some sense give their consent to the laws the Government enacts, but neither Government nor governed can ever change the rights endowed by the Creator. The proper use of law by Government is to protect our individual rights.

Our American forefathers did not originate all of the ideas that produced the overall ideology fostering what became the greatest advance of Freedom and prosperity ever known for humankind. Instead, they gleaned most of these ideas from more than 2,000 years of struggle between Liberty and unrestrained Government. With the benefit of historical perspective, they were able to make judgments about the help or harm to society (by cause and effect) of the different applications of philosophical and political thought. Using both the good and bad, they distilled the ideas and practices of the ages into a new form of Government, encompassing rights of the individual. In order to prevent encroachment on those rights, they enumerated powers. Two cornerstones of their new creation were that Liberty is also inclusive of substantive rights derived from the rule of law, and that the application of law should be as minimal as is practical to provide for Liberty. Our forefathers were so opposed to rule by formalism of law that one of the safeguards they instituted was that juries are supposed to be charged with not only judging the guilt or innocence of the individual being tried; they are also to judge the validity of the law in question. We will look in more detail at this point later.

Those who misuse the concept of "rule of law" generally do so due to failure to recognize the crucial pre-existing nature of rights, and the proper relationship between rights and laws. If all rights arise out of Government, it is through the law that order is maintained. To correct almost any problem in society, Government must only pass another law and use its power to enforce it. Fear of punishment is supposed to modify behavior of The People. If any law meets resistance from a significant number of those in disagreement, the problem is solved by stricter laws, more force, and more taxation to pay for it. Since the first law is rarely or never successful, we find ourselves with volumes of practicably unenforceable laws attempting to solve a veritable host of social ills.

In addition to the inherent power of Government to enforce its will, this "Government First" thinking in either pure Marxian, or its more insidious Keynesian version relies on a belief in the ability of elite decision-makers to determine the appropriate kinds of laws necessary. These "social engineers," who know "what is right" for society, speak in terms of "percentage of compliance." They see law as a tool, to force The People into the patterns of behavior which they "know" are best for society. This approach does not work to shape the ethos of society because morality cannot be legislated, but it's often-unintended consequence is to increase the power and size of the State. While a more intrusive State increases the power and self-importance of the social engineers, unreasonable use of law breeds contempt for the true concept of a lawful society. The only valid laws are those which conform to the principles of Freedom and Liberty and respect the protection of the individual not only against the enforc-ers, such as secret police and other oppressors, but equally against the social engineers. At the expense of Liberty, many social engineers use Government as a tool to promote their belief in collectivism or to enforce their ideals of morality, economics and a host of other social consequences. Thus they pervert the nature of the term "rule of law" despite its more than honorable history.

The concept of "rule of law" as it is practiced today is a far cry from our Forefathers concept that the inclusion of fundamental rights is important for the support of Freedom. Viewed in this historical per-spective, laws have more often been used to subjugate The People. Some have tried to make the distinction between rule "by" law (as a tool of Government oppression) and rule "of" law (as a limitation of Government power). It is obviously one of the more important concepts of governance. The international bar association has even gone so far as to assert the principles as "the foundation of a civilized society"[36]. Where Freedom is concerned, "rule of law" has been a concept that has generated vast disagreement over meaning. What are the underpinnings of this concept and how have we gotten to the point of being a mantra for augmenting Government than a legal maxim supporting Freedom? I believe a better way of viewing the concept is that we are a nation founded on "rights" rather than "laws". More spe-cifically, America is founded on the principle that individual human beings have rights which include life, Liberty, property, to be born free of debt (without encumbrance) and to pursue our own course in life for the achievement of our individual happiness. Our Forefathers believed that the concept of "rule of law" encompasses substantive rights which assist us in that pursuit.

In America we have mostly abandoned a number of crucially important underpinnings of Freedom. Does the liberal application of

---

36. Council of the International Bar Association Resolution, September 2005

Government force through law promote the greater good for society when significant numbers of The People are in disagreement with those laws? *Or does it breed contempt and even less respect for more just laws?* Is the use of force a proper act, when used to enforce any particular ideal of morality where there is no victim? Our Forefathers realized that ethical ideals, morality, economic choices, lifestyles and many other important components of society should be left to the oversight of reason and persuasion, and not regimented by Government force. This is true even when that force is called the rule of law and whether the enforcement is performed by a regulatory agency or a police force. Law should exist for the purpose of preserving individual Liberty, securing rights, preventing and punishing activities in which persons attempt to violate the rights of others, and to arbitrating disputes. Laws should be singular in scope, easily understood by The People without need for interpretation, and they should be minimal in numbers in order to be practical in offering the greatest latitude of individual Freedom. The use of law to impose a moral viewpoint when there has been no victim is itself an act of subjugation and should be condemned by a free society.

You may hear the argument, "What if I believe that it is moral to kill—doesn't that mean that I would be free to do so under this type of society?" Of course not. Murder, rape, assault, robbery, and burglary are crimes. So are "white collar" crimes such as fraud. They create victims. One person is violating the rights of another. It is self-evident that such a violation of rights is a crime. Even the vast majority of those committing these types of crimes perceive that what they are doing is wrong and criminal, and it is a valid function of Government to punish such crimes.

What about laws that prosecute crimes where there is no victim? What about laws in which the matter is not self-evident, in which there is an honest disagreement as to whether the activity should be legal or criminal? Is it a valid function of Government and a reasonable use of society's resources to punish by fine or imprisonment those who do not wear seat belts while driving their cars? If so, on what basis? A generalized concern for safety? Perhaps, but macro safety statistics mean almost nothing to the individual. The U.S. fatality rate is 1.25 per hundred million vehicle miles. Yes, that adds up to some 34,000 fatal accidents a year, but it also means that you can expect to make your ten-mile commute almost ten million times without being involved in one, seat belt or no seat belt. What about insurance rates? These are often cited as an example of modern complexity necessitating some sacrifice on behalf of the common good. But the idea is specious because the market would adjust to the situation without the intercession of any law. Drivers who contractually agreed to use their belts, (for instance stipulating non-payment of damages in accidents where the belt is not worn) would get reduced rates, which would encourage usage, and the macro statistics would approximate what is achieved by making a law.

But with the law come a number of problems. Because it is impossible to enforce strictly, enforcement becomes arbitrary, inconveniencing even those who are in fact wearing their belts. In addition, the enforcers often engage in what economists call a moral hazard; because traffic enforcement laws create revenue streams for Government, they can be used as an unjust form of taxation. Then there's the issue of unreasonable search and seizure; these laws empower officials to stop someone under almost any pretext, even if their seat belt is in fact buckled. In a more general sense, these laws create a degradation of the spirit of Freedom itself as The People become more and more accustomed to the social engineers of the nanny State controlling their lives.

Supporters of this modern-day interpretation of the rule of law, which has strayed so far from the traditional and proper role of

Government, often claim they are doing so to protect the powerless "little guy." But who is more likely to suffer under such laws? The rich or the poor? The bank president driving his Mercedes, or the black man driving his aging Chevrolet? The Wall Street executive in his stretch limousine, or your teenager?

Who is more likely to be arbitrarily stopped? Undoubtedly, it is the poor and the powerless who are unjustly stopped and searched, breeding disrespect for both enforcers and for rightful laws.

And in the end, laws that overregulate simply don't work. Let us consider one that's been around for over 2,000 years. You be the judge of whether it has done more good or harm to society. How much of society's resources have been wasted trying to stamp out the ageless practice of prostitution? What have been some of the benefits and detriments to society? In prostitution there are no victims. The goal of prohibition is to enforce a moral ideal. Some argue that it is the prostitute who is victimized. However, this puts society in the position of making moral and economic choices for the individual, and it certainly runs counter to the feminist claim that it is a woman's right to do whatever she wants with her own body.

Laws enforcing victimless crimes like prostitution not only breed disrespect for valid use of force by Government; they do not work. We have been trying to use law to stamp out the horrors, real and imagined, of prostitution for at least as long as we have recorded history. But in the entire world, is there a city where prostitution does not flourish?

Prostitution laws are arbitrarily prosecuted and foster an inept allocation of resources. Increasingly important in today's world of more virulent sexually transmitted diseases, they spread disease by forcing prostitution into an underground setting. They breed corruption through bribes and payoffs. They financially support organized crime. They take wealth from the productive class at the expense of jobs and a higher standard of living. They make honest citizens into criminals. They breed contempt for valid laws. And especially important: They do not work to prevent prostitution.

The true purpose of law is not to be an agent of conformity. Lawmaking is not a moral act, and does not create, protect, or reflect morality. America was founded on the principle that the historical concept of "rule of law" is inclusive of substantive rights, and that *the valid use of law is to protect the Liberty of the individual against acts by others and to arbitrate disputes.* Our forefathers believed that the purpose of the law is not to arbitrarily restrict the actions of The People, but instead is to create an atmosphere fostering the greatest Freedom to accomplish. The use of law in violation of these principles drains the resources of The People, creates more Government, increases authoritarian rule and is in direct conflict with the principles of Liberty. To use Government to enforce any ideal where rights are not violated is itself an immoral act.

One final point is important in this discussion. If respect for the rule of law is to be restored, the law must adhere strictly to its legitimate purpose, the securing of the rights of The People; it must also be written in such a way that it can be easily understood by The People. The simpler and clearer a law is written, the less likely it is to be usurped by interpretation. As an egregious example, today's tax code in America would fill a small room if printed, and is unintelligible to even linguistic experts. Therefore, in practical reality, the law's meaning is whatever it is interpreted to be by the agents and lawyers of those exercising the power of its enforcement. In this manner, the law becomes a tool of oppression rather than a guarantor of Liberty.

Today's laws are verbal behemoths thousands of pages long. Not only are they unintelligible to ordinary citizens; they are unintelligible to, and unread by, even the legislators who voted to pass them. Their intricate clauses and codicils conceal details that always work to the benefit of the cunning Government itself, and never to the benefit of The People. Laws not written upon a single topic, easily understood by The People and brief in construction will always become tools of oppression for the State.

CHAPTER 14

THE SUPREME COURT

IN THEIR ATTEMPT TO KEEP MANKIND Free from the inherent tendency of Government to gravitate toward despotism and oppression, our Forefathers envisioned a system of representation that had previously been unknown in history. They created a Government that was severely limited by a Constitution and Bill of Rights. And, they devised an ingenious set of checks and balances to prevent any one branch or group from seizing too much power. They split the legislative body into two houses of Congress, each with its own powers. They made the executive branch dependent upon the legislature for funding. And they set up a separate judicial branch, not only to render justice in the general sense, but also to make sure the other two branches do not violate the Constitution.

What they created was truly remarkable in its scope and foresight. However, in the process, they made a grave omission regarding the balance of power in that they failed to provide a workable check on abuse of power by the judiciary. They should not be blamed for this omission. They were greatly concerned to make sure that the judiciary didn't fall under the thumb of the other branches, as had often been the case in England and other Governments with which they were familiar. Sitting in Constitution Hall, it was difficult to imagine that the branch of Government they set up to specifically insure the constitutional limitation of power over the executive and legislative branches, would itself usurp power that it was never intended to wield. A few did raise the point, but the truth is that any system of checks and balances has to stop somewhere, and the general feeling was that the one they had created had gone about as far as was reasonable.

More than a decade later, during his presidency, Thomas Jefferson recognized the problem and did his best to warn future generations. Jefferson realized that the framers of the Constitution had left no adequate mechanism for correcting the abuse of power by the Supreme Court. The Supreme Court is charged with seeing that there is strict adherence to the Constitution. The members are appointed for life, for the purpose of elevating them above the realm of political influence.

What the founders did not envision was a Supreme Court that would enter politics *of its own accord* and in violation of its specific constitutional duty. Today we call it legislating from the bench, and its negative impact on Freedom has been serious. The problem arises from the fact that there is no check in the Constitution for a Supreme Court derelict in its duty. To be sure, justices can be impeached; but this is tantamount to no remedy at all since impeachment requires a super majority vote in Congress and almost inevitably bogs down in the morass of politics. The founders imagined impeachment as a way to get rid of a corrupt or derelict judge, not one whose decisions represent a philosophy that sanctions the gathering of institutional power for the Court, and justifies, rather than limits Government power. Thus, any impeachment case would immediately become a political dispute, rather than a matter of jurisprudence. Nor do we want judges impeached because of their political views, which could easily lead to a bloodletting every time Congress changed hands.

The practice of legislating from the bench has always been justified by its adherents on the grounds of supposed benefits to The People, but no matter how laudable its proponents' intended goals, the operative outcome of their usurpation can only produce a momentum toward the loss of Freedom and Liberty. Yet today, many do not see the Court in that light.

In contemporary America, a decade into the twenty-first century, many view the Supreme Court only in light of its current voting make-up; the court's five to four majority has been more inclined to a stricter interpretation of the Constitution than the current far left Obama Presidency, initially backed by a Democrat-dominated Congress.

In 2010, Congress mandated a new health care entitlement. Polls consistently showed The People did not want the law passed, as it represented a clear attack on their Freedom. There were notable demonstrations against individual Congressmen and Senators in an attempt to influence them to vote against the bill. But it passed anyway. This legislation represented arguably the Government's greatest move toward socialism to date, as a government-run health care system has always been a key plank in the socialist platform of all countries. The law not only represented a takeover of approximately one-sixth of the U. S. economy, but set a remarkable new legal precedent. For the first time, the Government claimed the power to *mandate* purchases, that is, to force The People to buy something, specifically health insurance. Where did Government get the right to do that? In a remarkable bit of convoluted reasoning that only bureaucrats and lawyers can appreciate. Even with a wink and a nod, the Government claimed that a decision *not* to purchase health insurance qualified as commercial activity, thus bringing the non-activity under the jurisdiction of the commerce clause of the Constitution! Note that this was not like requiring a person to purchase a license to engage in some activity, which a person could always decline to engage in.

This was a requirement to buy something they might not even want or need.

A number of plaintiffs, including almost half of the Attorney Generals of the various states, have joined in a lawsuit to halt this power grab. They are depending on the Supreme Court with its current fragile center-right makeup, to find the law unconstitutional, which it clearly is. But who can say which way the decision will actually go? By the time the case winds its ways through the lower courts, the political makeup of the Supreme Court may have changed. And if the Court upholds the Government's position, an enormous expansion of Federal power can easily fit under the tent thus created. As an example, if the Government wanted to stimulate the auto industry, it could mandate that certain segments of society, for instance those owning cars more than ten years old, or those making a certain income, must buy new cars under penalty of law. The commerce clause reasoning would be the same as in regard to health care insurance—that not purchasing requires the Government to subsidize more of the poor due to less economic activity. And of course, the principle would be supported by the hallowed precedent of the previous health care decision.

The point is this: The Supreme Court should not be considered as merely one more player in the political decision-making process. That they are now so perceived is a serious threat to the Constitution and the Liberty of The People. Perhaps at the moment the Court's makeup is ever so slightly tilted against the left-wing assault on the Constitution. But the Justices should not even be operating within the left-right continuum in the first place; they should be protectors of the Constitution, pure and simple. The next threat to the liberties of the People could, after all, come as easily from the right as from the left; and that would no more justify unconstitutional laws than the present left-leaning trend of the legislative and executive branches.

At the moment of this writing, one death could change the makeup of the Court; and send it once again on a course of promulgating its own ideological, political prejudices rather than basing its rulings on what is constitutional. In addition, the Court over the centuries has created countless historical precedents in its usurpation of power to the federal Government, many of them by abusing the commerce clause. This enormous archive of decisions acts as an inertial force against a return to constitutionalism. Some judges, after all, while not inclined to innovate and legislate from the bench, are nonetheless predisposed to give deference to existing rulings and precedents. These may themselves be unconstitutional. Unfortunate decisions go back to the early years of the nineteenth century, and for many decades now, the Court has ruled in support of Government expansion far more often than not.

But possibly most important is that the focus has become *political*, and politics is outside the Court's constitutional function. The perception of the Supreme Court as a partisan institution, by either or both sides of any debate, tears at the fabric of the balance of powers conceived by our Forefathers. Resolving the dilemma is confounded by the reality that The People have no practical remedy against a Court that is acting in the political arena. We go through periods where The People are placated or upset as the pendulum swings back and forth, but with time, the overall direction has been toward gradual usurpation of unintended powers to the Federal Government. The Court has been drifting toward decisions that make it more a squabbling part of the "elitist ruling class" than a defender against the overreach of Government power.

Let us review a smattering of what "interpreting" the Constitution has brought us from our past. John Marshall (Chief Justice from 1801–1835) in *Marbury v Madison,* an otherwise insignificant case involving a minor bureaucratic argument, stooped into the politics of his day and in the process claimed the right of the Court to overturn any act of Congress it did not agree with. Chief Justice Roger Taney

(1836–1864) brought us the despicable *Dred Scott* decision, which prohibited Black people from American citizenship even if freed by their owners and recognized as citizens by the laws of the states in which they lived. This was impossible, Taney wrote, obviously presuming expertise in genetics, because Black people were "inferior beings." His decision made the Civil War almost a certainty for there was no longer any other way for society to resolve the matter.

Heinous on its face, the *Dred Scott* decision is important for our purposes because it represents a most egregious example of the Court being used (and allowing itself to be used) as a *political* instrument. Unlike *Marbury v Madison*, however, the political question involved was not minor; it was the consuming issue of the time. We even know how the political conspiracy was carried out as historians have unearthed correspondence between then President-elect James Buchanan and Supreme Court Justices John Catron and Robert Grier. These correspondences demonstrated that a five to four decision based on narrow grounds was turned into a six to three vote decision on grounds that far exceeded the scope of the case and (unlike what Buchanan and the justices had imagined) inflamed the nation.1 Moreover, the decision, however much Taney attempted to couch it in constitutional language, represented a gigantic *de jure* power grab by the Court, even as it secretly conformed to the will of the Executive Branch, i.e. Buchanan.

The political and moral prejudices of the justices have changed over the decades ever since; but through a series of decisions, the Supreme Court has consistently usurped more and more power, regardless of the cause to which they applied it.

Recent history finds the courts ordering the busing of school children against the wishes of their parents (both black and white), dictating in detail the management of jails and mental health facilities and determining to the minutest degree the drawing of legislative boundaries and mandating taxation never approved by any legislature.

This unprecedented usurpation of power has been portrayed as "activism," but let there be no doubt; it is an integral part of a major battle in the struggle between those who believe all rights arise from the State and those who believe that all rights arise from, to use Jefferson's felicitous phrase, "nature or nature's God." Those who believe in centralization of Government power consider it just and moral to use almost any means to circumvent the limitations on that power by the Constitution. The general flaw in their view is, however, that the end justifies the means. If Freedom is to survive, we must save ourselves from those who are intent on imposing what they perceive to be positive change, and arrogating unto themselves the power to make such decisions without regard to other public institutions, or The People themselves.

It is a sad commentary on the time in which we live, that to foster Liberty, we must save ourselves from our own Supreme Court, the very men and women who are charged with upholding the Constitution and the Bill of Rights. Herein lies another testament to Lord Acton's adage that, "Power corrupts; and absolute power corrupts absolutely." We must save ourselves from those who claim to know what is better for us than we know ourselves and whose concept of what is good or moral is superior to that of all others.

What has been the position of the opposition to those who would usurp our Liberty? What of those who believe that all rights derive directly from nature to The People? I have already mentioned Jefferson, who was so infuriated at Chief Justice Marshall's decision in *Marbury v Madison* that he initiated an impeachment proceeding against another justice with the implication that Marshall would be next. The impeachment failed by one vote, but the implications for Marshall were clear. So clear in fact, that John Marshall never used the power of Judicial Review again in his long tenure on the court. Jefferson attacked the court with all of his rational insight and oratory, aimed at what he correctly perceived to be a most grievous usurpation of power. He called it "rule by oligarchy."

As Jefferson was angry over *Marbury v Madison*, so Abraham Lincoln was furious at *Dred Scott* and used his great eloquence to attack the court both in his 1858 debates with Stephen Douglas and later after his election. In the debates, Lincoln decried abuse of power by the Supreme Court as a "trampling of rights," of "chains of bondage," and "servitude." After his election Lincoln continued with his attacks on the Supreme Court. Consider the following quote from his first inaugural address: "...if the policy of the government, upon vital questions affecting the whole people, is to be irrevocably fixed by decisions of the Supreme Court, the instant they are made, in ordinary litigation between parties in personal action, the people will have ceased to be their own rulers, having to that extent practically resigned their government into the hands of that tribunal."

It may well be that Lincoln would have attempted to limit the Court's power, or possibly even correct the omission of accountability in the Constitution, had he lived. However, after the Civil War, Reconstruction-era Congresses were not challenged by a more timid Supreme Court. The issue of Supreme Court abuse of power and accountability faded as abuse ceased and hotly contested issues diminished. The power struggle became moot for the moment and was forgotten. But the allure of unrestrained power is difficult to resist, and as the issue was never resolved, it had only to await those who would abuse it at some future date.

We will find the full flowering of this abuse in the twentieth century, but before we leave the nineteenth century, we must pause to consider one other Supreme Court decision, in which once again the Justices' prejudices and preconceived notions overrode their dedication to the Constitution. Nowadays, if someone mentions the case *Plessy v*

Ferguson, or perhaps even its notorious catch phrase, "separate but equal," most people imagine it was a case about school segregation. But in fact the 1898 case before the Court headed by Chief Justice Melville Fuller dealt with a black man who had the nerve to sit in the whites-only coach of a train in Louisiana.

In his excellent book *Who Killed the Constitution?* of which more will be presented later, constitutional scholar William Eaton summarizes the case thus: "All the Court had the Constitutional authority to do was to say that such matters had been left to the States. But the Court did not stop there. Rather, it produced a gratuitous discussion about 'equality' which violated constitutional boundaries by rewriting the Fourteenth Amendment in order to satisfy its appetite for social 'justice,' as then perceived by the majority.[37] The result was creation of that gross hypocrisy, the 'separate but equal' doctrine.[38]

In 1898, social justice consisted of keeping Black people in their place. A half century later, it would mean the opposite. And in both eras, the Supreme Court would violate its Constitutional responsibility by deciding that it, and not the Constitution itself, was the arbiter of what the phrase meant.

If Taney and Fuller were guilty of usurpation of power and trampling on the rights of The People, history must now surely view them as pikers in comparison to the twentieth century Supreme Court, particularly under Chief Justices Earl Warren (1953–1969) and Warren Burger (1969–986). For it was in the latter part of the twentieth century that those who considered their ideological agenda more important than the Constitution or the Bill of Rights came into full stride.

Though I am sure they believed their intentions to be most laudable and honorable, the unintentional consequences of Chief Justices Warren and Burger and the Courts over which they presided, must

---

37. Baker, Jean H. – *James Buchanan*, 2004, Times Books; Pp 82-86
38. Eaton, William – *Who Killed the Constitution*, 1988, Regnery Gateway; P 35

be seen as infamous to those who believe in Freedom and Liberty. St. Bernard of Clairvaux is often credited with originating the famous dictum that, "The road to hell is paved with good intentions." Regardless of who said it first, it is unquestionably applicable to the world of Government—perhaps even more so than in theology. In civil society, the end most assuredly does not justify the means; for once any Liberty is lost to Government, it is rarely regained without paying a most grievous price. As we have seen, the perception of what intentions are good varies from time to time. The Constitution is the compass that should keep the country on course, and The People free, as popular causes come and go. Legislatures will create and repeal laws according to the spirit of the times in which they were elected.

As long as the laws they make do not violate the Constitution, this is as it should be. The Supreme Court is the protector of the Constitution and charged with the duty to make sure that boundary is not crossed. When they succumb to the spirit of the moment, they fall victim to a maxim I hereby propose, that *popular causes make bad law.*

The early years of the twentieth century was a period of somewhat restrained, but nonetheless ongoing expansion of its own power by the Supreme Court. For example, in a 1905 case, *Lochner v New York,* the Court ruled five to four that a New York State law regulating the hours that could be worked by bakery employees was unconstitutional, a case that changed both the original meaning of the Fourteenth Amendment and the traditional understanding of the phrase *due process* in ways which have been a troublesome precedent ever since. In this very political decision, the Court stated it was acting in order to keep the country from being "at the mercy of legislative majorities." Unfortunately, in the process, it placed them at the mercy of the barest of judicial majorities.

When President Franklin Roosevelt's New Deal program was

begun in 1933, the Court responded initially by striking down several of its early programs. Relying on the principles of *Lochner*, the Justices threw out Roosevelt's National Recovery Act, as well as the Agriculture Adjustment Act, and appeared poised to dismantle the whole New Deal. But remember, the *Lochner* decision, rather than relying on a *constitutional* basis, had relied on a *political* basis. Just as the turn-of-the-century Court had bent with the political winds in *Plessey,* so it had in *Lochner*. But now the political winds had changed, and the enormously popular Roosevelt was able to use some of his political capital to intimidate the Court by threatening to "pack" it by increasing the number of Justices. Fearful for its turf, the Court backed off, and the rest of the New Deal was enacted without serious judicial meddling.

The point here is not that the New Deal was good or bad, or that the New York law overturned in *Lochner* was good or bad. The point is that the Supreme Court, after more than a century of straying from its Constitutional principles first abridged in *Marbury v Madison*, had become so entangled in the web of its own politicization that it had become just another player in the day-to-day, topsy-turvy of interest group and ideological bickering.

That sort of bickering is fine within a legislative and elective process. Indeed, it is what those processes are all about—resolving the political differences that divide free people in a free society. But the Court is not a legislative body. It is not elected. It is, or should be, the living, breathing manifestation of the Constitution itself, above the political process and responsive only to the plain and unambiguous meaning of that document. Its answer to any and all attempts by the political process to circumvent the Constitution must be, "If you want to do that, you must find sufficient support among The People to amend the Constitution so as to allow it. Until then, the Constitution as written forbids it."

I wish I could say that the New Deal era was the high point of judicial politicization, but in fact it was to get much worse before, in the past two decades or so, getting a little bit better. A thorough history of these events is beyond the scope of this book, and the principles upon which the difficulty rests were in place by the New Deal days. I have chosen, therefore, to discuss only briefly the problems presented by the Court's actions during the terms of Chief Justices Warren (who served from 1953–1969) and Burger (1969–1986), as well as the modest improvements under Chief Justices William Rehnquist (1986–2005) and John Roberts (2005–).

In so doing, I will pass quickly over many of the most famous cases of the era, such as *Brown v Board of Education* and *Roe v Wade*. Vast literature exists on these high publicity cases, so I will confine myself to noting that in *Brown*, the necessity of undoing the absurd separate-but-equal doctrine of *Plessey v Ferguson*, did not lead to a withdrawal of Federal intrusion into local schools. Instead, an even greater intrusion was orchestrated, which quickly metastasized into a counterproductive micromanagement of the public schools by judges. This led to unworkable social experiments such as forced busing which not only failed to integrate public school systems, but in many instances actually led to their being more segregated than ever, by causing "white flight" from the impacted areas. The practice of school busing to achieve racial balance in schools was virtually ended by the Rehnquist Court's 2007 decision in *Meredith v. Jefferson County Board of Education*.

In *Roe v Wade* (1973), a difficult and emotional controversy that should have been resolved by The People through their representatives in the state legislatures was instead resolved by fiat. The Justices decided they were competent not only to make judgments on generalized moral questions such as "when does life begin," but also to evaluate conflicting and constantly changing scientific data about matters such as fetal viability. The only question the Court should have asked is, "What does the Constitution say about this subject?" to which the only rational answer would have been, "nothing." At that point, the Court was obligated by its sacred trust to say that the Federal Government had been delegated no authority in the area, and therefore it was reserved to the states respectively, or to The People.

Certain clauses of the Constitution have proven to be particularly susceptible to expansion by the courts in their great sweeping trend of continual aggrandization of the power of Government, and in particular, the power of the court system itself. Among these are the spending power of Congress, the Commerce Clause, which gives Congress the right to regulate interstate commerce, and the Equal Protection clause, which is contained in the Fourteenth Amendment and says that the individual states cannot "deny to any person within its jurisdiction the equal protection of the laws."

The Commerce Clause was placed in the Constitution because the founders believed in domestic free trade and wanted to end the states' practice of erecting trade barriers, such as tariffs between one and another. To end these restraints, they took such powers away from the states and specifically gave them to Congress, making the regulation of interstate commerce one of the "enumerated powers." Early cases involving this provision dwelt on matters such as (in *Gibbons v Ogden*, 1824) whether the State of New York could grant a monopoly to a steamboat company which would prevent another company from operating a steamboat from Elizabethtown, New Jersey to Manhattan. It would be desirable that modern cases were about such modest, relevant matters. But instead, the twentieth century courts have construed the Commerce Clause so broadly that virtually any transaction, even a purely local one, is held to be involved in interstate commerce and thus under the jurisdiction of the Federal Government. For example, in *Heart of Atlanta Motel v. United States* (1964), the Court ruled that a local business is engaged in interstate commerce if any of its customers came from out of state, and in *Daniel v. Paul* (1969), it held that the Federal government could regulate a recreational facility because its snack bar sold some items that were manufactured in another state.

At the present time, an even greater expansion of the definition of interstate commerce is being sought by the Obama Administration, for this is the grounds on which it seeks to require, on penalty of a fine, that citizens purchase health insurance. In the process, they argue that the person's *failure* to make such a purchase constitutes an act of interstate commerce, and thus may be regulated (e.g. prohibited) by the Federal government.

With regard to the Equal Protection Clause of the Fourteenth Amendment, we have already seen how its application in *Plessey v Ferguson* and *Lochner v New York* was twisted to increase the power of the Court, and the Federal Government as a whole. In the 1960s, the Court had a very different ideological makeup, but it still managed to interpret the Equal Protection Clause so as to extend Federal power, and produced a doctrine regarding the apportionment of legislative districts that continues to amaze many observers. The Warren court, in a series of decisions beginning with *Baker v Carr* in 1962, enunciated what has come to be known as the "one-man-one-vote" doctrine. It requires that all election districts, from local school boards to the U.S. House of Representatives must be drawn in a manner that all citizens are entitled to "equal" legislative representation no matter where they reside. How close do the populations of districts have to be in order to be considered "equal"? It apparently depends on what side of the bed the justices got up on the day they make the decision. In one case 16.4 percent was good enough; twelve percent was required in another, while in a third, a 4.1 percent differential was *not* good enough. The Warren Court, in rejecting a six point differential, called in one case for "precise mathematical equality," without, however, specifying on what precise day (or hour?) that condition was to apply. One can almost imagine an army of local elections board officials scattering on Election Day to cover every maternity ward, funeral parlor and real estate closing in order to adjust the lines of the districts for state representative.

As to the spending power of Congress, the elastic view of enumerated powers may be illustrated by the cumulative effect of cases involving the right of the Federal Government to withhold program money from state Governments in order to force the states to comply with policies that may even be unrelated to the purpose of the programs themselves. This often involves Federal highway grants. In *South Dakota v Dole* (1987), for example, one of the last decisions of the Burger court, it was determined that Congress had the power to coerce a state to change its legal drinking age by denying highway money if they failed to capitulate to the demand. In this case, and others involving the distribution of highway money, including some which they simply refused to consider, the Supreme Court has circumvented the Constitution in precisely one way that worried Jefferson, and which he termed "the power of the purse." Once the precedent of coercion and circumvention were set, there is literally no realm which cannot be subverted, the views of The People notwithstanding. The scope of intrusion into our lives seems to have no boundaries, as this precedent is being used on all levels of society by lesser interventionist Federal judges. Each has become his own petty tyrant who can use the threat of financial coercion as a method to fiat whatever social change he deems worthy. And low and behold, these judges have discovered that they can "stack" these decisions one upon the other, like rotting carcasses they have partially devoured, to seize even more power, and circumvent even more of the Constitution.[39] In perhaps the most

---

39. Stacked legal decisions supporting each other are termed "legal precedent" and are used as support for subsequent cases with similar issues.

FREEDOM AND HUMAN ACHIEVEMENT

egregious decision of this type, a district court actually ordered the Missouri State Legislature to tax its citizens to pay the expenses of the Kansas City school district, which the court was literally managing in the vain hope of engineering a vast desegregation scheme, which ultimately collapsed.

In the 1970s the Nixon Administration decided that, in order to deal with what they called the "energy crisis," it would establish a mandatory fifty-five-miles-per-hour speed limit on all highways. Speed limits had always been set by the states, but as they had before and would again, the Federal government simply coerced the states with threatened denial of highway funds. The law itself was silly and contributed nothing in particular to energy conservation, nor to highway safety, another supposed benefit. In a few years, it was repealed. But the legal point was retained, along with the drinking age rule and other items in the growing bag of precedents which constitute a Federal protection racket that induces a steady passage of power from the Sates to the central Government.

Moreover, the process threatens not only the relationship between the national and state Governments, but also forms a direct threat to those powers supposedly retained by The People. Take, for instance, the Federal mandate that we must each wear a seat belt in the operation of our own motor vehicles. Once again the States are coerced by the threatened loss of funds, and this decision is used to reinforce the precedent set by the coerced fifty-five-mile-per-hour speed limit. Does anyone truly believe (as an analogy) that the framers of the Constitution intended that the document would be used by the Federal Government to mandate that all men must wear steel leggings and footwear when using an ax to prevent leg and foot injury, because we must be coerced into protecting ourselves? We could all laugh if it were not so serious. I can easily imagine what Jefferson or Lincoln would have said at such an abuse of power. But this act is only a symptom of how far the abuse of our personal Liberties is beginning to reach. And as another discarded carcass on the stack of our Liberties, the seat belt mandate had been used to set precedent for even greater usurpation of power. No matter that the original fifty-five-mile-per-hour speed limit mandate has long ago passed into history, the precedent lives and has grown into a serious threat to our Freedom and Liberty. The effect has been to give Federal judges power that was never intended for them to wield as mini-tyrants.

Seat belt laws are an excellent example of rule by fiat. A fiat is an arbitrary order or decree from the Latin "let it be done." Not only is it an arbitrary order; it becomes a law which is arbitrarily enforceable, so it can be used to the disadvantage of the weak or the politically out-of-favor. The Constitution guarantees us Freedom from unreasonable search and seizure. In this regard, it has always been held that a person could not be stopped in his automobile without probable cause. But it is not difficult to imagine how something as seemingly innocuous as a seat belt law could be used to circumvent our Constitutional protection from search and seizure.

Legal drinking age laws, highway speed limits, seat belt laws— none of these may seem like grievous curtailments of the balance of power the founders worked so hard to establish between the Federal government and the states. But the cumulative effect of such intrusions is significant, and their use as precedents in a court system that has become tilted in favor of an unconscionably loose construction view of the Constitution is grievous indeed.

Today, a decade into the twenty-first century, we find ourselves at an important crossroads with regard to the future of Freedom in America. The Obama Administration has again and again demonstrated its intent to move the nation toward a much more regulated and regimented Government, while at the same time pursuing wealth redistribution and other class warfare goals. Together, these impulses point to a vision of the future for which the word "socialist" is not inappropriate. In the 2010 mid-term elections, a significant negative reaction exerted itself; and it seems likely that the coming years will be characterized by a power struggle between the philosophy created and inspired by the Constitution, and the collectivist principles of the left. Those who value Freedom should bear in mind that the lengthy trend away from the Constitution that has occurred in the American judiciary represents both a necessary cause and a potentially horrific component of a socialist victory.

Dr. William Eaton, in his aforementioned, excellent 1988 book on the history of the decline of constitutionalism in the Supreme Court, *Who Killed the Constitution?* wrote:

> "The true purpose of the courts can be vividly perceived by recalling, as in reverse image, the function courts are made to perform when any fully socialist system comes to prevail. In such a system the courts do not serve as a protection against a tyrannical minority, [or majority], not to guarantee the rights of persons. Rather, they function to advance the ends of the state, as a means to disguise the uses of illegitimate power, as willing instruments of tyranny and oppression. Law vanishes, and the courts become thoroughly political institutions."[40]

Under socialism, *law vanishes*. As America has drifted leftward over the decades, the ultimate law of the land, the Constitution, has been vanishing apace. The prime culprit in this regard is abuse of power by the Supreme Court, first evident way back in 1803, when John Marshall allowed a petty political squabble to escalate into the principle of judicial review. This precedent has been utilized by courts again and again to expand the power of the Federal government, and not coincidentally, the Court itself.

---

40. Eaton, William – Who Killed the Constitution, 1988, Regnery Gateway p. 226

The result has been a plethora of *Freedom-restricting* laws, which have replaced the Freedom-granting law upon which the nation was founded, and Freedom-granting laws are precipitately vanishing. Founders like Jefferson and Madison worried that something like this would happen, perhaps in their wisdom perceiving what Eaton would write with the benefit of 200 years of history, that "... Government exists in a continual state of attempting to increase its power. If Government can assign rights to the "collective" rather than the individual it becomes the arbiter and eventually even the master over those rights... In the case of the Constitution, there can be no honest doubt but that its master intent was to *control* and *restrain* power. One of the most heinous offenses of Judicial revisionism is that the allegedly ambiguous phrases upon which the Court has relied to invent new constitutional philosophies have not been read in the context of this clear and obvious purpose." [41]

That is a very profound criticism of constitutional law as it has been practiced in the court system. The first question any judge should ask when he is asked to interpret a given passage is simply this: Does this reading tend to control and restrain the power of the Government? That was, after all, the purpose of the Constitution as a whole, and it is only logical to assume it applies to the parts as well. But the courts have repeatedly looked for some way to interpret this or that passage in such a way that it can allow the expansion of Government power.

We now find the courts readily engaging in what clearly should be the realm of politics. The courts have invaded the education process. The courts are mandating taxation. The courts are realigning legislative districts, and thus, even entering the elective process. All of the powers the courts are usurping to the federal Government are supposedly for the purpose of righting wrongs or remedying social ills. What these interventionist judges have probably never stopped to consider

---

41. Ibid. – p. 215

is the longer term implications of the mechanism they are creating. What happens when, inevitably, activist authoritarian judges ascend to the Supreme Court? In their zeal for social change, our present activist judges are setting into place the foundation (legal precedents) for authoritarian rule under which The People as individual human beings will have no rights.

Eaton is correct in his assessment of the source of the problem in the process of judicial review. "Judicial veto," he writes, "brushes aside all of the complex considerations of the political process and suspends the theory of democratic responsibility." But it is important to note in this regard that judicial review is even more likely to violate the Constitution when it sweeps the process under the rug than when it brushes it aside. Historically, for every time the Supreme Court has erred by using its power of judicial review to strike down a law, there have been many times more in which it has erred by giving its sanction to laws which a true devotee of the Constitution would never have done. I have cited a handful of such cases above; the number could have been expanded many fold.

Eaton is also on solid ground when he observes that, "Unfortunately, the trend is not one of restraint. In a constitutional republic, the Supreme Court must realize that its function is not a means to an end. More importantly, it must realize that its function is not that of a political legislative body. The rightful function of the Supreme Court is to limit the power of Government and to protect The People's barrier between themselves and their own Government—the Constitution." [42]

Congress must also recognize and accept the responsibility for its constitutional function. In a free society the success or failure of any agenda must not rest upon decisions or decrees of the courts, or the legislature would have no right to exist. It is just as immoral for Congress to condone or acquiesce to the abuses of the Supreme Court

42. Ibid. – p. 241

in order to promote the social agenda, as it is immoral for the Supreme Court to do so.

The Supreme Court beginning the twenty-first century has been composed of a tenuous majority of judges who support less activism and greater adherence to the Constitution. While such a Court may allow the country to avoid some unfortunate and unconstitutional mistakes, it cannot be considered a real answer to the problem. When decisions on most major issues are consistently decided by a five-to-four majority, event-oriented change—a plane crash, car wreck or heart attack—could produce a radical swing back toward liberal activism. With one party domination of both the Senate and the Presidency, radical change in the makeup of the Court was literally only a heartbeat away in the first term of the Obama administration, and such a situation will no doubt recur again from time to time.

But two greater threats may not be so readily apparent to the current actors. First is that the precedents set and reinforced by the Warren and Burger Courts could be used to a truly evil purpose should a radical majority come into power on either the Left or Right fostering *totalitarian* ideals that could sweep away rights of the individual, and with them Freedom and Liberty for The People. Both Right and Left need to stop and think what would happen if ultra extremists from the other side were to ascend to power in the Supreme Court.

An even more likely threat is Dr. Eaton's prediction that as the Supreme Court becomes more and more perceived as just another political body, the true purpose of the Constitution becomes lost entirely. This process is well underway, as the Court has descended into the mud wrestling of politics. Today, the power of the President to appoint Supreme Court justices has become a significant factor in presidential elections, and the campaigns of both Republicans and Democrats appeal to the fear of their constituencies by citing the havoc which the appointees of the opposition could cause.

As a result, the perception of the court as a fair and non-political body erodes further.

We must let the Constitution work. We must allow change to take place through constitutionally prescribed means—even if change may not be as swift as some might desire. Or we may face the prospect that our Constitution will no longer preserve "Freedom from" and protect us from Government but instead will be interpreted by the Supreme Court as a legal justification for asserting Government domination and power over The People. The barrier protecting us from our own Government is being turned into a "living document" justifying usurpation of our Freedom.

We must now correct the omission by our Forefathers as recognized by Jefferson and Lincoln. If Freedom in America is to prevail, we have no choice but to limit the power of the Supreme Court. We must hold those accountable who would rob us of our Freedom in order to enforce their personally perceived values of morality and of social change.

Any system of checks and balances must end with some final arbiter. Otherwise, the system is an infinite regression in which no action can ever be taken. Jefferson and Madison worried that ending the system at the Supreme Court opened up the possibility of an oligarchy, presided over by a small body of nine men and women, appointed for life and presumably therefore removed from The People. But none of the founders were Athenian-style Democrats, who would have proposed putting the decision in the hands of a national plebiscite. Jefferson suggested, rather, a special council chosen by the separate states, but it is difficult to see how such a body would differ from the Senate, itself chosen by the states.

I will have some other suggestions to offer in the "prescriptive" chapter of this book, but in the end, what matters most is the devotion of The People to the Constitution. That in turn depends on the strength and character of the educational, cultural and information institutions of the nation. Where these institutions are faithful to the vision of the founders, almost any organizational system will do; where they reflect views at odds with that vision, none is likely to succeed.

CHAPTER 15

THE POWER OF SLOP

FOR THOUSANDS OF YEARS, MAN HAS used food as a means of manipulating animals. No doubt it all started when some particularly clever Paleolithic hunter came up with the idea of baiting an ambush. Success in hunting with primitive weapons consists mostly of getting close enough to the animal for the weapon to be effective. Most prey animals have very acute senses of hearing, sight, and smell and are difficult to approach. Early hunters learned that ambushing animals along trails they follow to watering, feeding, and bedding areas was more productive than randomly trying to walk up on them. Creating feeding areas to draw animals to specific locations turned out to be even more productive, as terrain and timing could be used to better advantage, and the probability of encountering game was considerably improved.

As early man became more sophisticated, someone tried another innovation and learned he could use food as a means to domesticate some species, thereby acquiring the luxury of being able to choose the time and numbers that were harvested. As the animals became ever more dependent on the provided food and less able to fend for themselves in the wild, secondary products such as milk, eggs, and wool became available. The next step was to use selective breeding to make the animals more docile and improve specifically desired characteristics, such as size, or giving more milk. Through essentially the same process, grain and other vegetable species were domesticated, too, with soil enriched by manure and garbage supplying the "food." Thus was agriculture born, and the days of the dominant hunter-gatherer society numbered.

The technique of manipulating animal behavior through the use of food is still being used on most farms and ranches in the world today. I remember as a young man asking my uncle, who was a rancher in central Texas, why he didn't own horses. He told me he hadn't owned a horse in twenty years because he didn't need one, and riding was difficult on his back. He then took me out into the pasture near one of his stock pens and shook a line of corn from a feed sack in the back of his truck. He made a calling sound and vigorously shook the sack making a lot of racket. He continued right through the gate and into the pen. From the moment he started shaking the sack, I could hear his cattle bawling in the distance, and in just a moment they appeared, literally running toward us. Many were already on the feed line by the time he was back to the truck. Within a few minutes, all his cattle were in the pen, and he simply walked over and closed the gate. His goats in the next pasture responded in the same way. On horseback, it would have taken a considerable amount of time and effort to round up his livestock, yet with one four-dollar sack of dried food, they were safely enclosed in ten minutes.

In most mammals the fear of loss is a greater motivator than the anticipation of gain. Where there is a limited concentration of food, animals will often engage in frenzied competition to preserve their share. They frequently become so focused on guarding their portion of the food that they lose perspective and become easier to manipulate.

These primitive responses in mammals can be analogously observed in some species of fish which may enter a "feeding frenzy" when presented with an overabundance of prey and may literally bite anything near them, including each other. The term feeding frenzy is most often associated with piranhas and sharks but occurs in many species of fish, and has even been observed in alligators. Competition for food is a very powerful and primal response that can be enhanced by additional factors such as quantity and how the food is presented.

Even though my uncle's animals were range fed and foraged off the land, he taught me the importance, for his purposes, of continuously feeding small amounts to keep them habituated to the food he provided. The sophistication of his plan was truly remarkable. Occasionally, he fed the livestock at the pens so they would get used to being there, but he also randomly fed small amounts throughout the pasture so they would not abandon their general habitat. If he fed them large amounts at the same spot every day, the livestock would stay in very close proximity to that spot, waiting for the next handout, no doubt worried that others might get there ahead of them. He trained his animals to come to him when he called them with specific sounds, including shaking the feed sack and a special yell he used. Feeding an insufficient amount made them more competitive, and the stimulus of his calls produced a strong and immediate response. It certainly worked. They would literally run to wherever he wanted them.

I remember jokingly telling him he was like the "pied piper" of cattle, which made him laugh. I think it pleased him to think how, through country wisdom, he had reduced his difficult workload by eliminating the roundup task that was bad for his back, saving money in the process by being able to get along without a horse. It was all accomplished by manipulating his animals to want to be where he desired them instead of trying to force them to go there.

The ideas, of course, are not unique to my uncle. Dairy farmers, who must get the cows from the pasture to the barn two or three times a day for milking, use a similar method, and can actually train individual cows to go to a particular stall every time.

Near the end of the nineteenth century, the Russian physiologist Ivan Pavlov (1849–1946) was investigating the gastric system of dogs. While studying the salivary glands, he noticed that the dogs would involuntarily salivate when food was presented to them, but *before* it reached their mouths. This simple observation began a field of study that has unlocked many aspects of animal behavior. Though Pavlov won the Nobel Prize for his work on the gastric system, he is most remembered today for his work on what he called *conditioned response*. He would condition his dogs to different stimuli by presenting the stimulus just prior to feeding the dogs. The most iconic stimuli is ringing a bell. The animals would come to associate the stimulus, the sound of the bell, with the availability of the food. In time, merely ringing the bell would produce the involuntary salivating, even if there were no food.

All species of higher mammals exhibit similar, primal and involuntary characteristics—"hard-wired" we might call them today. In certain circumstances, they have no choice as to whether the saliva will flow. When presented with the proper stimulus, it just happens. Pavlov's experiments represent the laboratory-testing phase of the science of controlling animal behavior. Farmers and ranchers like my uncle have provided the field-testing as well as the practical application.

Armed with the practical and theoretical knowledge of a century or more of behavioral research, along with millennia of practical agricultural experiments, could we domesticate a wild species, even today? Let's design a program to exert manipulation and control over some generic animal's behavior by using some of these more ubiquitous traits. Since we have no actual product in mind, nothing like meat, eggs, milk or wool, we will simply attempt to impose our will on them to the greatest possible extent so they will work for us, amuse us, or otherwise respond to our control. Let's reason out how to use some of the characteristics attached to food, and to fear of loss, to make it happen.

We would probably begin by selecting the most vulnerable, weak-willed and least mentally-acute individuals among our wild species—those living on the margins and who frequently lose out in the constant competition for food that goes on in the wild. Being most fearful of losing out, we reason that they may be more willing to accept our offer. Being less successful in their world, they also have less to lose from negative side effects that might come attached to the handout.

As my uncle noted, we can habituate our animals by a program of substantially uninterrupted or repetitive feeding. He only fed small amounts because he wanted his livestock to forage rather than become dependent. But our goal is to exert maximum power and control, and so we will offer sufficient food necessary to provide a level of subsistence. If we offer a level of subsistence for sufficient time, the animals will gradually lose their knowledge and ability to compete, and they will become increasingly dependent on the food we are providing. As they become more dependent and have fewer options, our control and ability to manipulate them will be enhanced. The number under our control will increase as those we are manipulating into dependency will recruit others of similar type and circumstance.

We will be fortunate if we get bad weather—drought, for example. Under times of stress, it will be easier to entice more animals into the scheme, and difficult circumstances will accelerate the progress of those already partially habituated as necessity makes them more dependent. If we continue this program through generations, progeny will come to accept our program as the norm because it is all they have ever known. Instead of learning from their parents and other influences around them, important skills of self-reliance, such as foraging for ruminant animals, the newborn will learn to accept only our food. When the norm becomes our feeding program, and they have lost both the will and the skill necessary for independent survival, our control will be solidified. The program can be perpetuated by maintaining them with barely enough to survive. This will naturally increase fear of loss as the consequences become more accentuated because the threat is amplified if resources are already in short supply. Gradually, we can use increasing fear of loss to control and manipulate as we induce them to become more dependent on the resource we are providing.

Unfortunately, I think we just described Government welfare and entitlement programs mushrooming in size during the last half of the twentieth century.

Since Pavlov's early studies, an enormous amount of investigation on such responses and similar psychological traits in human beings has been undertaken, often funded by those who would use this knowledge to attempt to manipulate The People. Using such methods, how far can our manipulation extend? If we can evoke the competitive fear of loss response, we can literally lead farm animals to slaughter. Picture hogs at the slop trough squealing and fighting. As they lose perspective while they are trying to "get theirs" before others take it, we simply close the gate.

How does this relate to the Government welfare and entitlement programs? As The People are convinced that they are entitled to receive, many will lose perspective as fear of loss is evoked, and they rush to the metaphorical trough to "get theirs." The loss of perspective, as they fight to preserve their handout or entitlement, can even become so overwhelming as to subvert their natural sense of obligation to future humanity, and for many, even their desire for the well-being of their children. The domestication of The People becomes endemic, and Government slop has done its job.

Note, too, that the manipulators can utilize a wide range of techniques available that agriculturalists cannot utilize. People, after all, can read. To the extent Government can control *what* they read (and by extension, see on television, hear on the radio, etc.) it can employ *intellectual* persuasion.

This allows a degree of manipulation even among those remaining outside the system, the "wild" humans, if you will. They can be induced into participation as well, their role being to provide the resources to buy the slop. By showing pictures of abject poverty (or even starving children) and evoking a caring response, productive members of society can be induced to support Government programs to help those which they perceive to be less fortunate, with the unintended result of supplanting the centuries-old system of community based charities with bureaucratic "programs." Replacing community based charity with institutionalized Government largesse has dramatically increased the size and power of the State and has become an unseen threat to the future of The People. Both those being herded into the pens and those providing the resources are being manipulated.

Among humans no less than other animals, the fear of loss is a greater motivation to action than the anticipation of gain. This knowledge is used as one of the most basic precepts of sales advertising. When a company wants to hold a special sale on a product or service, it will inevitably advertise prominently that the sale is limited in time, thereby sparking the fear of loss, and thus stimulating action that will result in purchase of the product. If the ad states that the sale ends on Sunday, the message is clear: Act now, or the opportunity will be lost forever.

Another example is that value is often associated with size. When presented with two similar objects, the larger is generally perceived as having more value. Thus advertisers often use relatively small people to advertise products on television in order to make the product appear larger. Also, packaging is often considerably larger than necessary to contain the actual contents inside.

These commonplace examples show how many different and varied forces are utilizing knowledge about the basic nature of man to promote all kinds of agendas, sales being only one of the most common. Some are very subtle; for example, there are no clocks or windows in gambling casinos as the managers want customers to lose a sense of time, so they will continue gambling longer and without interruption. The manipulators use fear, sex, colors, music, and often they use graphic images that have become pervasive in a world constantly subjected to stimulation overload.

We must not underestimate the power of subjugation through use of the primal impulses we humans share with our fellow animals. It is a menacing reality for Liberty and Freedom that normally good and caring people are being duped and manipulated into unconscionable acts against their progeny and future humanity. Keep this perspective as you read the next chapter on debt.

CHAPTER 16

DEBT

EVERY CHILD HAS AN INALIENABLE RIGHT to be born Free of Debt. Indebtedness is morally reserved solely to those by whom it is created. It is immoral for any generation to obligate future generations to pay for its own excesses.

The concept of natural and inalienable rights was of upmost importance to many of the great thinkers of the Enlightenment and American Revolution. The Founders of America built on the concept of natural rights originating with the Stoics, particularly Seneca (AD 1–65) and expounded upon by Martin Luther (1483–1506) and John Locke (1632–1704), together with the ideas of Scottish philosopher Francis Hutcheson (1694–1746), who stressed inalienability; they merged these concepts espousing a doctrine of inalienable rights arising from nature and being, in the words of Thomas Jefferson, "self-evident." This combination resulted in terminology which allowed the founders to satisfy the entire spectrum of religious thought on the subject of rights.

Elsewhere in the Declaration of Independence, Jefferson (1743–1826) used the phrase "the Laws of Nature and of Nature's God" in reference to rights. Individual human rights were thus a law of nature, self-evident, and compatible with any religion, or non-religious school of thought which recognized the existence of the natural world, regardless of how it was created.

In his original draft of the Declaration, Jefferson said that all men "are endowed by their Creator with certain unalienable rights, that among these rights are life, liberty and property," but in the final version, two changes were made. "Unalienable" became "inalienable," which is probably an inconsequential grammatical correction. "Property," a direct quotation from Locke, was changed to "the pursuit of happiness." There has been much discussion and anguished parsing, of this phrase change, but in the final analysis, it is probably merely a broadening of the terminology to include non-physical sources of happiness. Though there is some debate, it was probably Benjamin Franklin (1706–1790), a member of the Committee appointed to draft the Declaration and a veritable connoisseur of the pursuit of happiness, who convinced Jefferson to make the change.

Our Forefathers had witnessed how the force of Government had been used by the privileged, titled, and landed classes to oppress The People through enforcement of indebtedness. Serfs being "bound to the land" through debt was a poignant topic for the Founding Fathers, having witnessed this injustice at the hand of the privileged class in the monarchies of Europe. Debt was also used as a means of indentured servitude.

Concern about the historical use of debt as a form of oppression and enslavement was a grave concern for Jefferson and James Madison (1751–1836) as they corresponded about the construction of the United States Constitution. They realized that Government creation of debt could be used as a form of enslavement of future humanity, and could lead to the eventual destruction of Freedom. To inhibit this possibility, they attempted to devise a way to prevent future generations from being bound by Government through the debt by incorporating a restrictive provision of the Constitution. Unfortunately, they never found proper wording to impose the restraint. The following excerpt of a letter from Thomas Jefferson to James Madison dated September 6, 1789, was part of their discussion and indicates how crucial they believed this issue to be:

> The question, whether one generation of men has a right to bind another...is a question of such consequences as not only to merit decision, but place also among the fundamental principles of every government.... [It is] self-evident that the earth belongs in usufruct to the living; that the dead have neither powers nor rights over it. [Usufruct is a legal term meaning the right to utilize and enjoy the profits and advantages of something belonging to another, so long as the property is not damaged or altered in any way]...no man can, by natural right oblige the lands he occupied, or the persons who succeed him in that occupation, to the payment of debts contracted by him. For if he could, he might during his own life, eat up the usufruct of the lands for several generations to come; and then the lands would belong to the dead; and not to the living ...The conclusion then, is that neither the representatives of a nation, nor the whole nation itself assembled, can validly engage debts beyond what they may pay in their own time.

Jefferson is one of the most eloquent of our Forefathers as evidenced by this beautifully constructed excerpt. We do not own the land; we are only stewards of it; and we have a moral obligation to pass it on to future generations without damaging it. Burdening the land with debt is a primary violation of this principle. Jefferson clearly states his belief that the principle may be considered a natural right when he states, "no man can, by natural right oblige the lands he occupied…to the payment of debts contracted by him". He also leaves no doubt as to the importance of the matter when he asserts that debt cannot be conveyed as being "self-evident."

In looking for a means to restrict Government from carrying debt into the future, Jefferson investigated "burdening of the land" as a potential justification. As it applies to individuals, this concept was adopted by our Forefathers and has been carried forward into our current law. In America, debt of the individual is not carried forward past death. It was the goal of Jefferson and Madison to extend this principal to include generations and Governments, and the "burdening of the land" concept was a potential basis for doing so. To reiterate, Jefferson reasoned: "The conclusion then, is that neither the representatives of a nation [the politicians], nor the whole nation itself assembled [The People] can validly engage debts beyond what they may pay in their own lifetime" [their generation]. They struggled with how to impose this constraint within the Constitutional framework, believing it "is a question of such consequences as not only to merit decision, but place also among the fundamental principles of every government." Their objective was complicated by the fact that Governments as entities survive individuals, and because of the strong historical precedent of Government borrowing and debt.

Unfortunately, this most important precept was never included in the American Constitution. Resolving the moral justification sought by Jefferson and Madison can be accomplished by viewing the matter from a slightly different perspective. Before moving the importance of the question forward to the debt of future generations, which is complicated by historical precedents, it should first be moved back to the birth of the individual. To be *born* free of debt, or any other encumbrance, is a *natural and inalienable right that is unequivocally self-evident*. If the newborn cannot be encumbered, any debt being incurred is the sole obligation of the living who create it, including "the representatives of a nation" and "the whole nation itself assembled."

No valid intellectual argument can claim that a child born into this world should be burdened by folly or excess which he had no part in creating or accepting.

Even the collectivist arguments of "social responsibility," "inter-connectedness," or "social contract" become hollow when carried back to birth. The newborn have a right to be born into this world with a clean slate both in mind *and* circumstance.

In a perversion of once noble thinking, the term "save the children" has become a mantra and rallying call justifying many forms of governmental expansion and usurpation of rights. It is shamelessly used by social engineers and collectivists to bludgeon down almost any dissenting argument. It harkens back to a hallowed tradition in America—willingness to sacrifice for our children's future. Sadly, today's predominant culture of self and instant gratification recognizes no obligation to pay the price of what we consume, which is problematic enough with regard to the accumulation of personal debt, but even worse when it manifests itself as perceived entitlement to receive Government largess. "Creating debt so our children will have a better future" is not only oxymoronic; it is one of the most inimical of all lies because it appeals to greed in the present, and because the debt it creates is literally *enslaving*, rather than *saving*, the children. Our Government, sadly with the support of many citizens, has embarked on a spending spree that is certain to encumber our descendants for generations to come, by shackling their productivity, even before they are born, to pay for the gluttonous excesses of the current generation. I can scarcely imagine a more immoral action.

Corporate debt and business debt both carry forward into the future because the entities survive the individuals. Collectivists want us to believe this same principle applies to Governments, which also generally outlive individuals. But this is nothing more than legal slight-of-hand. Corporate debt binds only the corporation itself. The liability of the stockholders is limited to the extent of their investment, and is in any event not collectible from the heirs of the investors.

The collectivist's corporation analogy is an attempt to erode one of the most fundamental foundations of our Liberty. America is a nation based on *rights of the individual*, and no entity (including Government) can legitimately infringe upon those inalienable rights. It is inherent in Freedom that each individual must have the widest possible latitude of choices to pursue life as he sees fit, so long as he does not infringe upon the rights of others. This concept is a component of the substantive rights of the rule of law as conceived by our Forefathers. Being born free of indebtedness is one of our inalienable, self-evident rights. Enslavement of the unborn is immoral, and that includes financial enslavement (through debt) by Government.

In order to rectify this omission from our Constitution, we must use a means that cannot be subverted by politicians over time. We need a Constitutional-balanced budget amendment that requires a supermajority for change or circumvention, and that prevents deficit spending, except for very brief periods of extreme emergency such as a Constitutionally declared war; and even in the event of exigencies, the budget must be brought back into balance, and any debt repaid, within a prescribed, short time period.

Should the budget not be brought back into balance and all debt repaid in the constricting time period as their terms of office expire, the President and the members of both houses of Congress could be barred from reelection. Those newly elected should face the same restriction if they fail to resolve the imbalance. Every State in our union has some form of balanced budget requirement except Vermont (as does the Constitutional Law of some nations, such as Germany). The recent decade has proven that our future well-being is becoming ever more threatened by the pervasive growth of Federal debt. Thus the restrictions binding both the Federal Government and the politicians need to be far more binding and onerous.

In America, our Forefathers insured that our laws have never permitted individual debt to be carried forward past death, which had not been the case in many nations they were familiar with, and the threat posed to Liberty by that situation represented greatly concerned thinkers like Jefferson and Madison. They recognized that a child born saddled with the debts of his father could face a virtually hopeless prospect, and they understood too that it was equally wrong for the nation to hand down a massive public debt to future generations.

What if your father could have obligated you to pay for his indebtedness, not just to the extent of his estate, but from money earned by the sweat of *your* brow? Wouldn't you agree that credit would be most easy to come by if children were obligated for the debts of their parents? It would mean the creditor has almost no risk in the long run.

For as long as there are descendants, the lender could carry the indebtedness into the future. Government force would be used to insure that the debt was paid. Any bad business decision could plunge all future progeny into financial slavery. An irresponsible man could borrow enormous sums and simply live in luxury. Another could borrow against even the most unsound business practices, with little regard for the risk. His kids and grandkids would just have to pay. But we do not need to assume that the debt problem must be precipitated by any such malfeasance. Many have been plunged into debt through no fault of their own, say by a costly illness of a spouse or other loved one. Such a debt too would be passed on to members of the next generation who would face assessments, wage garnishment, and other settlement schemes. And if such measures didn't work, it is not improbable that the authorities would be entitled to take even more drastic measures, such as seizing their possessions, incarceration, perhaps even forcing the descendants to work in labor camps to settle the debt. While

Americans have been largely spared such fates due to the foresight of the Founders in restraining Government, such things happen not infrequently in the world. During the Middle Ages, once self-sustaining families often became reduced in circumstances to serfdom; in modern times, innocent families were forced to work the collectivist farms of the now defunct communist countries. The prisoner-serf treatment of its citizens continues in North Korea to this day.

With this discussion of the consequences of private debt being extended to the descendants of the original debtor, let us now consider the path we are taking with respect to the national debt. In that respect, the fears of Jefferson and Madison have come to pass in our own time. Because we have not respected the right of every person to be born free of debt, we are in the process of creating financial ruin for those who come after us. Every American alive today has a solemn duty to posterity to correct this situation, or be guilty of enslaving future humanity to pay for the excesses and mistakes of our generations. That any newborn child should have to face any lower standard of living because of immoral acts by the aging and dead is despicable beyond words. It is unworthy of our role in the world as Americans.

Our politicians want to squander the vitality of future generations to buy votes and maintain their power, and far too many citizens are willing to sell their vote for Government "slop." It might be a welfare handout, an agricultural subsidy, a Federal job with a generous pension, an exemption from regulation that benefits the bottom line of a corporation, a Government-paid health care program or some other example of excessive Federal spending, abetted by the manipulation of interest rates and the pumping of more paper money into the system. Such policies are unsustainable and are already reducing standards of living for our children and grandchildren. We have overspent on such a grand scale that we are very near the point where even passing the burden to the next generation will not suffice. This is the point at which total economic collapse becomes inevitable. We must recapture the true spirit of sacrifice for our children and future humanity, and accept responsibility for the actions of our generations. It is self-evident that children have an inalienable right to be born free of indebtedness, and I believe that we are morally obligated to future humanity to both pay the debt we have created and to amend the Constitution to insure that the politicians can never steal from the newborn again.

How bad has the crisis become in present day America? It is probably much worse than most of The People are led to believe because our Government hides the truth by using accounting methods that would be illegal in the business world. They cook the books by reporting and focusing on a narrow definition of the national debt which represents only the sum of our outstanding marketable and non-marketable securities. By this calculation, the current national debt is something in excess of $15.25 trillion dollars, an enormous figure that is increasing at a faster rate than at any time in the history of our country, and in terms of real indebtedness, rivals any profligate empire in history. We have created more national debt in the current and past administrations than was previously created in the entire history of America.

The unprecedented expansion of our national debt is rightfully a cause of serious concern to our Freedom and the well-being of our nation. Unfortunately, it is only the tip of the iceberg if we are to make an honest accounting of the burden of debt that has been accumulated. There is a second set of books where the vast majority of our indebtedness is hidden from sight. This off-the-books debt is known as "unfunded liability" and includes Social Security, Medicare, and Medicare Part D (Prescription Drugs). By the time this book is published, our true debt—the official national debt plus the unfunded liabilities will be not just the staggering sum of $15.25 trillion, but a number that exceeds it by a full order of magnitude. Here's how the components break down: Social Security liability: $15.5 trillion:

Medicare Part D: $20.5 trillion: and Medicare itself a whopping $81.5 trillion.[43] So our unfunded liabilities are in excess of $117 trillion dollars. Combined with our official national debt, what America now owes over *$132 Trillion Dollars.*

Science has long been interested in human perception of numbers. After a certain quantity (for most humans a few more than ten) it becomes difficult to perceive a number of objects without actually counting. The ability to visualize or conceptualize larger numbers also varies, but most of the world's population has difficulty visualizing the number 10,000. Only a few exceptional humans (mathematical savants) are capable of visualizing one million. It is only in the last decade that the number "trillion" has emerged in our everyday economic lexicon. Scientists deal with large numbers by increasing the powers of ten (with an exponent representing the number of zeros) which, if written out would become so cumbersome as to be impractical. However, humans cannot relate to numbers of that size. This makes it much easier for the politicians to gain acceptance of their policies because the numbers are not grounded in any understanding of meaning. When the number reaches a billion, it just becomes a number as the human mind has difficulty finding any reference, and a trillion has even less context. Yet it is crucial that we find some understanding of the scope of the problem we and our politicians have created. As a means of attempting to grasp the size of our debt, let's view it analogously by referencing things with which we are familiar.

In comparison to time, ten thousand seconds is less than three hours; one million seconds is approximately 11.5 days; one billion seconds is approximately thirty-two years, while one trillion seconds equates to about 32,000 years (thirty-two thousand years!). In perspective, 32,000 years ago, civilization did not exist, and humans lived in caves. Humans have only left written records for around 5,000 years.

---

43. http://www.usdebtclock.org/

Possibly more helpful, let's make the analogy to money as we can all visualize our largest denomination in circulation, the $100 bill with Ben Franklin's picture on it. A packet of Franklins with a value of $10,000, is about half an inch thick and will easily fit in your inside coat pocket. A million dollars' worth of Franklins would easily fit in your airline carry-on bag, and a billion dollars' worth will fit into a small kitchen. But if you had a trillion dollars' worth of Franklins, you could pile them up in stacks eight feet high over a whole football field and still have a veritable fortune left over. Our national debt combined with our unfunded liabilities, that $132 trillion, would cover 132 football fields stacked eight feet high and overflowing with hundred-dollar bills. Or, to look at it another way, imagine a football field-size base stacked up to a height of almost 1,000 feet with hundred-dollar bills. Only four skyscrapers in New York would be taller,[44] Here is one last way of understanding the magnitude of the problem. In 2008, the total value of all U.S. bills, including federal reserve notes and currency no longer being issued, was only $853.2 billion.[45] In the two years since, it has grown to over one trillion, which is a dire problem in and of itself due to the debasement of the value of each dollar. If our politicians continue spending at the present rate, each and every year, our national debt will increase by more than the value of all of the paper currency we have in circulation!

The shift in the last ten years to referencing our debt in trillions instead of billions should have been cause of gravest concern for The People. Unfortunately, since even a billion was too large to conceive, the term trillion became just another number. Most Americans have never stopped to think about how vast the actual difference is.

With some sense of size, let's now investigate how much we owe by breaking it down into more manageable numbers. The U.S. national

---

44. http://www.emporis.com/en/bu/sk/st/tp/wo/
45. http://www.visualeconomics.com/the-value-of-united-states-currency-in-circulation/

debt owed by each citizen alive today is now in excess of $49,000.00 But this is a misleading number because the burden only falls on *those who are producers* and *who pay taxes*. Each taxpayer owes excess of $135,000.00 But if the idea of owing $49,000.00 sounds frightening, remember that the biggest part of the debt is the off-the-books unfunded liability. The U.S. unfunded liability of each citizen is in excess of $375,000.00. The unfunded liability per taxpayer is in excess of $1,000,000.00 (one million dollars). When we add the totals of both the national debt liability and the unfunded liability, *each producing taxpayer* is now faced with an unconscionable debt burden of more than *$1,375,000.00 (One Million, Three Hundred Seventy Five Thousand Dollars)! Each!*

In 2008 the number of American families with a net worth of one million dollars (not including the equity in their primary residence) was only 6.7 million households and was in steep decline. Those with a comparable net worth greater than five million dollars (who might have some possibility of paying what they owe) numbered only $840,000[46], and was also in steep decline. Our current President and politicians are spending at the greatest rate since the founding of our country, and the prospects for any favorable outcome to the current economic crisis, which the Government continues to exacerbate, are also in steep decline. The disciples of the economist John Maynard Keynes, who may reasonably be called the "Father of Economic Socialism," are rapidly leading us to financial ruin, and any hope of correcting the problem without undue hardship is rapidly receding.

Whether you wish to argue that a child born in the United States of America comes into this world enslaved with a debt of only $425,000.000[47], or if you want to assume that child will grow into adulthood, be productive and pay taxes, thereby facing a current (and

---

46. http://www.luxist.com/2009/03/11/number-of-u-s-millionaires-falls-steeply/
47. National debt per citizen of $49,000, plus unfunded liability per citizen of $375,000

growing) debt of $1,375,000.00, what our generation has done to the unborn is …

I pause. I try to think of a word strong enough to describe the immensity of the evil of saddling The People with such an impossible burden. Unconscionable? Immoral? Criminal? Irrational? Profligate? I can come up with no word to adequately describe the perfidy of what we have allowed our politicians to do to us and our progeny. It is bereft of conscience, contrary to any and every moral code ever advanced, a crime against humanity, and worse. The politicians who have created this dereliction will someday be justly compared to the slave traders of old, whose unspeakable atrocities against the weak of Africa have heretofore been justly regarded as the nadir of inhumanity. And the scope of the present abomination is growing as our debt is increasing at an unprecedented rate. Congress has just passed a new health care entitlement that will dwarf Social Security, Prescription Drugs and Medicare combined. What our politicians are doing is not only immoral; it is economically unsustainable and has brought the specter of worldwide financial collapse to our doorstep.

Every child has an inalienable right to be born free of debt. Those of us who do not make the personal commitment to join and sustain the fight until we can secure this right and correct the heinous negligence of our fiduciary responsibility to the future will be joined in culpability with the collectivists and politicians who have fostered this atrocity while placating us with the ability to live beyond our means in the present. This is a seminal moment in the history of America. We must rise to the purpose that is now demanded of this generation just as so many have joined in the fight for Freedom before us.

Repairing the damage will not be without a price, but this is a burden from which we must not shrink. Americans have always risen to threats against our Freedom, and I have unbounded optimism that once they come to perceive the scope of the debt our elitist politicians have created, they will do so once more. Nothing less than Freedom, Liberty, and the well-being of humanity are at stake. In order to prevail, those who truly believe in Freedom must reclaim our birthright. We must unite!

CHAPTER 17

JOBS AND PRODUCTIVITY

ONE OF THE MOST IMPORTANT FIELDS of study in relation to Freedom and Liberty is economics. Disciplines such as economics and sociology are often termed "social sciences," but this is misleading because such fields of study are not sciences. By definition, science is a means of gathering knowledge that can be tested; about things that are repetitive or can be measured, and that can be duplicated by repeatable methods. It encompasses laws which are inviolable. While economics may achieve some predictive power, it is far too variable and inaccurate to meet the most basic definition of science. This is not to denigrate the field of study for much has been added to our knowledge by great minds like Adam Smith. The misnomer leads people to believe those making decisions are more certain about the theories they espouse, and the predictions they make, than they can ever possibly be. There is a great danger in thinking of them as scientists. A real scientist, such as a chemist, can tell you that if you mix hydrogen and oxygen, you will get water *every single time,* but no economist can really know that an increase in Government spending will stimulate the economy. Moreover, the unintended consequences of the "stimulus" are unknowable. Finally, even if the stimulus is applied and the economy does in fact subsequently improve, there is no proof of causality because a myriad of other factors may have influenced the outcome, and there is no way to repeat the experiment. What all this means is that because economics deals with broad concepts rather than absolutes, it can easily be used by Government leaders to dupe and misdirect The People into accepting false premises that promote political agendas. Where Freedom is concerned, one of Government's most dangerous abuses is in promoting the concept that it "creates" jobs. Fostering this myth is used as a means to justify growth both in the size of Government and the degree of control it is able to exercise over The People.

At election time, the American public is inundated with political commercials selling the idea that certain jobs will be lost to the community if The People do not vote to retain the local politician. These may be direct Federal Government jobs, military or civilian, or local Government jobs financed through some Federal program; they may even be private sector jobs, which the politician claims to have impacted in some way. One message always fostered near election time is that Government creates jobs. If we vote for less Government, our community will lose those jobs.

But the message is false. In order to understand why, let us begin by considering the supply chain and how its relationship to Government impacts the productivity necessary for a healthy economy. Does the productivity of a nation depend on which goods are being produced in order to give value to its currency? Guns or butter? Police cars or delivery trucks? Paper for Government reports, or cardboard boxes in which to ship shoes? Does it matter if the production is done in Government-owned factories, privately-owned factories stimulated by Government subsidies or private factories stimulated by consumption in the private sector? Nothing less than the overall health and vitality of all nations' economies are impacted by the answer to these very basic concepts.

The term *productivity* is the measure of output in relation to input, and the total productivity of a nation must decrease as the size of its Government increases. The vast majority of money used by Government sucks vitality from the chains of true productivity necessary for creating jobs and a healthy economy. This is not to say that some functions of Government are not necessary and important, and even seem to create productivity. But the operative word in that sentence is *seem*, and thus we may speak of this phenomenon as *semblant* productivity. It is not, in the end, real, because Government itself supplies no input to the supply chain; all the resources it has must come from the confiscation of resources from the private sector, resources that otherwise would have been available for innovation and for creating and expanding supply chains that are the real source of jobs crucial to the nation's economic health.

Moreover, this confiscation involves a loss of productivity. Indeed, the act of confiscating is itself a cost because to give one example, all the Government employees involved in managing the confiscation and subsequent allocation of the resources in question have to be paid, given office space, desks, computers, retirement benefits, and the like.

When consumable goods are supplied on any significant scale, activities are set into motion that may be termed a chain of productivity, which is repeatable and willcontinue so long as the good is manufactured. It creates jobs along the supply chain of each component up to and including construction and sale of the final product. When a product does not do so, we may say that its post-sale economic value is *quiescent*.

The goals of Government are not the same as the goals of the private sector in economics. However, when functioning within its means, Government can provide some important benefit to economic productivity. This mainly arises as a *nutritive* function rather than being directly productive. As an example, infrastructure necessary to move perishable foodstuffs can be crucial to agriculture. A responsible law enforcement capability, sufficient to see that the goods can be transported securely and without interruption, is another valid function of Government, and serves as a nutrient to productivity. Another nutritive function is technical advancement that occurs as a byproduct of pursuit of other valid functions of Government such as defense or war. But as we will see by example, construction of the tools of war is semblant rather than real productivity. However necessary they are, we construct our tools of war at the expense of jobs and economic growth. Furthermore, waste, corruption and inefficiency of bureaucracy in Government are inevitably a component of even its valid functions in every field of its endeavor, and are totally counterproductive.

Entitlements and the national debt in America now account for about 71 percent of Federal spending while expenditures for defense make up about 14 percent, and discretionary spending including law enforcement, transportation and education make up the other 15 percent. The greater the size of Government, the greater percentage of its spending that will be quiescent to productivity. That is spending that is not nutritive and which will not create new activity or expansion along the supply chains. As an example, Government will claim that it is creating jobs due to the subsequent spending of those it gives money to such as welfare recipients and Government employees, but again this is only semblant productivity. If the money were left in the private sector to begin with, it would be far more efficient in creating new activity and expansion along the supply chains: The inefficiencies of Government, corruption, and bureaucracy would be eliminated; the workers would find employment in the private sector and turn their talents to productivity rather than bureaucracy.

To all these productivity factors, we must add a monetary

component. The base value of a nation's money should be determined by the goods and services it produces in relationship to the number of units of currency in circulation. In reality, it is more complex and includes such things as Government debt, and in America, the dollar being used as the world's reserve currency. Government's only sources of revenue are taxation and inflation which is a subversive form of revenue generation analogous to taxation. When Government prints more money than is matched by a corresponding increase in productivity, the value of each unit is reduced. However, there is a lag time before the economy adjusts to the new influx, and the Government benefits before the perceived value is reduced. Since every unit of currency is worth less, the purchasing power of everyone holding that currency is diminished. Except in extreme cases, the devaluation happens so gradually that The People rarely even realize they are being "taxed."

Both taxation and inflation destroy productivity in the private sector. This does not mean that a certain amount of Government revenue is not necessary or valid. It is simply pointing out that less is better. It is obvious that a nation must purchase certain items. However, Government must obtain all goods with the realization that it is costing jobs and decreasing the value of its currency with each expenditure because the role of Government is not productive. The creating jobs mantra of Government is a lie.

Do the types of goods purchased by Government stimulate true productivity?

Let's consider the question by investigating Government's defense-related expenditure of $21 billion to acquire twenty-one Northrop Grumman B2 Spirit stealth bombers.[48] People were employed from many different sectors of the economy, from mining the

---

48. Example only: Procurement cost alone was $929 per aircraft. Including engineering and development costs each plane cost more than $2.1 billion (estimated in 1997 dollars).

ore to the electronics industry. At the peak of construction, more than 13,000 people were employed at the dedicated plant in California. At election time, you consequently have a great number of people whose jobs are directly related to continuing the manufacture of the product. But the goal of the expenditures is not productivity. The goal of the expenditures is defense. Once produced, the bombers become an enormous additional drain upon the resources of the State. They actually become an economic liability rather than an asset because the bombers must be maintained, serviced, and operated, which is a very expensive proposition. In 1997 each hour of flight time required 119 hours of maintenance.[49] and these jobs produce no goods or services, as their *goal is defense*. More important, the money now tied up in the bombers becomes quiescent. The bombers, individually or as a group, do not produce consumable goods or services. Nor do they create jobs. They are thus a drain on the resources of the nation, but it is the quiescent predisposition of the investment that is most detrimental to true productivity.

Let's leave our $21 billion in the private sector and build shoe factories with it. Of course we realize that even $1 billion put into the manufacturing of shoes would likely upset the worldwide supply and demand, but it will serve as an example. Don't you think that it is also worthy of consideration that we might upset the worldwide supply of a commodity as basic as shoes with the price of one plane?

Let's assume we build our first shoe factory for $1 billion and investigate a few of the continuing supply chains of employment. Who will have jobs? Those who grow the cattle, ship the cattle, slaughter the cattle, ship the hides, make the chemicals to tan the leather, ship the leather, make the parts (the soles, the heels, the thread, the laces) construct the shoes, etc.—all the way to the point where these shoes are sold to us in the store. And all along each, chain employment is

49. http://en.wikipedia.org/wiki/Northrop_Grumman_B-2_Spirit

created for bookkeepers, accountants, clerks, secretaries, warehouse-men and truckers. Each supply chain has its own offshoots; for instance the factories making the thread have their own supply chain. Today there is a movement to lump all of the associated supply chains together into what is termed a "value chain." The difference between our shoe factory and our plane is that *the goal* of our shoe factory *is productivity*. Shoes are a consumable good, and the supply chain will continue to be vibrant for as long as the owners make good business decisions, and the public buys their shoes. The first billion dollars we invested will continue to produce for as long as we continue to build shoes.

Since the goal of our shoe factories is productivity, we now can build twenty more shoe factories (to spend our equivalent $21 billion) and create twenty times more jobs, and those jobs will continue far into the future! The money we invested toward productivity will vigorously move through the economy with great velocity. The goal of the stealth bombers we built was defense. Past the actual construction of each plane, the money becomes quiescent and produces nothing. It even becomes a drain on our resources. Each additional plane we build takes that much more money out of the cycle of productivity, and produces nothing. Building of the planes may temporarily create jobs, but it is not true productivity; it is in fact semblant productivity.

I am a strong advocate of defense. It is a valid necessity of any nation to defend itself, and defense is a valid expense of Government. However, *we must realize that we construct the means of our defense at the expense of true productivity.* All nations must balance their needs for defense against the economic health of The People. The People will be willing to give up a part of their gains in order to support the defense of the Nation. But growing defense or any other function of Government to the point of causing economic detriment ultimately does more harm to the security of The People and the Nation. We used defense as our example, but the principle holds true for every valid function of Government. Our Forefathers well understood this relationship and were adamant about trying to keep Government as small as possible so as to foster the greatest economic and overall well-being of The People. Whenever defense spending is touted for its alleged positive economic benefits, and justified on those grounds, the point is utterly invalid; this often happens when Congressmen try to get defense installations set up or not closed down in their districts in order to create or save jobs. As we have seen, every job that Government claims to create, in reality reduces the overall availability of jobs.

The gluttony of Government, combined with its continual attempts at more growth and taxation, has fostered the destruction of many an empire and nation. "Defeat" has most often been a product of poor economic health and *the failure of great States has been caused by growth of Government in times of economic expansion that cannot be economically sustained in times of economic contraction.* Government leaders almost universally have raised taxes in order to maintain their positions of power, and this has brought on the failure of small business and thus general economic failure and chaos. It is a cycle that repeats itself again and again throughout history. Growth of Government and over-taxation initially causes a concentration of wealth, a destruction of the middle class, and an increase in the disparity between rich and poor. This leads to the failure of small business, which is the true engine of more jobs and economic well-being. When the problem becomes more severe, it leads to economic collapse and often an even greater loss of Freedom, as Government uses additional force to "preserve order" arising from the chaos created by its own economic and social policies. The Government tends to grow even more dramatically, at least as a percentage of the whole economy because the productive private sector is weakened. Those who are a part of the Government, or associated with it derive wealth, power, privilege, and status from the process, whether they are great landowners, as in feudal economies or third world nations today, or labor union bosses in modern social democracies. Those who suffer most are the producers of society.

A striking example of the growth of Government causing the failure of a powerful state is the implosion of the Soviet Union at the end of the twentieth century. If Government spending could create jobs and increase productivity, as proponents of Keynesian economics believe, then the Soviet Union should have been one of the richest and most productive nations in the world. The Russian ruble should have become one of the world's strongest, most sought after currencies. It did not, and it is a remarkable phenomenon that those former Communist countries that have adopted principle of Freedom and reduced the size of their Governments the most have had the most economic success in the time since the collapse of the Soviet Union. On the contrary, nations such as Cuba and North Korea, which have clung most tenaciously to central planning and repression, have remained at the very bottom of the prosperity curve.

Their economies are in a perpetual state of depression, and their currencies barely worth the low quality paper they are printed on. I ask you, will you sell your house and accept Cuban pesos as payment? Neither will the rest of the world.

Return with me now to our own country. What would happen if we were to greatly reduce the size of Government and put this money back into the private sector? Certain people would logically be displaced for a short time. But what would happen in the overall picture, in the long run? I believe it would initiate an economic boom of proportions unseen since we embarked on the mad experiment of big Government: *fuller employment* for greater periods of time, business cycles with fewer dips of less severity, much shorter time frames for corrections of efficiency in manufacturing and jobs for all those willing to work.

Instead of building billion dollar airplanes, those workers might produce butter or shoes, computer components or video games. They might also provide services instead of physical products; these are part of a productive economy too. In whatever way, they would compete for jobs in the private sector, but the available jobs would out- pace the trained workers. Full employment would become reality instead of a campaign mantra!

In the 1980s, the Government of Japan created an economic bubble of massive proportions by credit manipulation, which made credit cheap and misallocated resources within the economy. One result was exceptionally high land values and low interest rates. Around 1991, when property values peaked, the land under Tokyo's Imperial Palace was worth more, on the books, than all the land in Florida. Prime slivers of downtown Tokyo were valued at ludicrous amounts: About ten square feet of the Ginza shopping district cost $200,000.[50] Beginning in 1991, the bubble burst, initiating a steep economic decline. The Government began bailing out the banks and large unprofitable private businesses terming them "too big to fail." However, in practice it consolidated the banks into even larger entities until there were only four national banks left in Japan. Massive public debt was created as money was injected to salvage Government jobs and unprofitable, debt-riddled companies. This produced what economists today call the "lost decade," which is a misnomer as it has now gone on for more than *two* decades. The Japanese stock market reached a new low in 2009, off more than 70 percent from its peak, and the upturn proclaimed by economists simply has not occurred. The economic malaise created by Government manipulation of credit and subsequent deficit spending, has lasted more than twenty years so far. Japan

---

50. http://archive.mailtribune.com/archive/2005/0711/biz/stories/02biz.htm

has immorally followed inept Keynesian economic policies that must burden future generations through debt creation to maintain the power of the politicians and Government. Enormous resources have become quiescent through Government spending, instead of reentering the cycles of productivity. All this malaise could have been averted, and Japan could have restored its economic health just by reducing both the size of Government and taxation. Government rhetoric aside, it is improbable that Japan has even yet reached the bottom of its economic decline.

Another recent example is the American Government's response to the economic crisis of 2008. The crisis was created by Government manipulation of credit, which, like the similar stimulation in Japan, caused an economic bubble that primarily manifested itself in real estate, housing, and banking. The Government then initiated a "stimulus package" of historically grandiose proportions that the politicians claimed was to create jobs and to restore the economy to health. In reality, the stimulus package was spent mostly defending the power base of Government employees to preserve their jobs, and on infrastructure, which we learned earlier may in some cases be nutritive, but which is only semblant productivity and actually makes the money spent quiescent. This has made credit more difficult to obtain, especially for small businesses. Instead of creating jobs, Government reacted in a manner to preserve and extend its power, rewarding those who derive wealth, privilege, and status from association with it. Crony capitalism became rampant. The true effect of the stimulus package as it was applied has been to kill jobs, and to immorally saddle our children and grandchildren with the responsibility to pay for the massive debt created.

If the Government had been honest about wanting to create jobs, it might have implemented an income tax holiday equivalent to the size of the stimulus and reduced taxes for one year. Congress passed its stimulus package on February 11, 2009 in the amount of $787 billion dollars. Like most Government programs, the price soon grew to $862 billion.[51] Yet, total personal income tax revenue for 2009 was only $915 billion dollars! Income taxes could have been reduced by an incredible 94 percent and there would have been no change in the deficit created. Which do you think would provide a greater stimulus to jobs and the economy: reducing the taxes of every producer (taxpayer) in America by 94 percent for a whole year, or Government's targeted response of semblant productivity *designed to insure that Government employees did not lose their jobs*? If there were an across the board tax holiday, the politicians would lose control, and with it the ability to siphon tax money to their cronies. On the other hand, not taking that money from the producers would insure that the majority of it went to stimulate jobs in the private sector. Furthermore, reducing the corporate tax rate from 35 percent to 15 percent would have an immediate stimulus effect on job creation and business investment, as the U.S. rates would then become competitive with most of the rest of the world. The choice is between true stimulus of jobs and productivity in the private sector or making money quiescent through the public sector, which is a detriment to jobs and productivity. The politicians will always choose the latter to preserve their power and control, and will sell the lie that Government is creating jobs when in fact the opposite is the truth.

With today's bloated Government and the number of jobs that are directly dependent upon spending our tax money, it is reasonable to ask if the voting power of those who live on the Government dole and jobs has become so great that there is no hope for change. I know of no way to truly calculate that, but I believe that the present generation will ultimately be condemned for the loss of Liberty if we do not bring about change. If our grandchildren are to live in Freedom, we *must*

---

51. *The Economist*, July 3rd-9th, 2010, A Prophet in His Own House, P.31

bring about change. It is never too late for hope or to join the struggle for Freedom.

The reestablishment of Freedom and Liberty will not be easy to achieve. There will be some short-term economic displacement. Things worth having are seldom easy and without cost. But we have a solemn duty to so many who have sacrificed to pass the torch of Freedom to the present day. That duty is to pass it on undiminished to those who come after us. In a later chapter, we will investigate what we may do in order to fulfill our ethical responsibility to future humanity.

CHAPTER 18

TAXATION

SOME OF THE EARLIEST WRITINGS OF humanity reflect the burden of oppression arising from excessive taxation. The earliest historical records chronicle taxation as being one of the primary means by which the elitist ruling class has dominated humanity. This legacy of excessive and inequitable taxation is particularly dispiriting in that The People are forced to pay for the rope with which they are hanged.

From the perspective of Freedom and Liberty in the modern world, taxation is a necessary evil, which if not explicitly limited with constricting restraints, becomes a significant threat to the flourishing of humanity. Taxation comes in many forms and under many guises, and is the means by which Government extracts all of its revenue from The People. The legal definition of a tax "is not a voluntary payment or donation, but an *enforced contribution,* exacted pursuant to legislative authority" and is *"any contribution imposed by government* [...] whether under the name of toll, tribute, tallage, gabel, impost, duty, custom, excise, subsidy, aid, supply, or other name." Note that even in the legal definition from *Black's Law Dictionary*, the "myth" of contribution is fostered. Both the terms "enforced contribution" and "contribution imposed" are oxymoronic terms as they should violate the very definition of the word "contribution," which should indicate an act of volunteerism. But meaning of the word was co-opted in the early twentieth century, and a secondary definition of the word "contribution" now includes "an imposed tax." The word has now come to mean both an *act of volunteerism* and an *act of forcible confiscation,* as a means of fostering the myth that taxation is somehow voluntary.

Collectivists view taxation as a crucial tool to achieving dominance and social manipulation. Taxation is used to create fear of, and compliance with, the wishes of the State, and is one of the primary applications of Government force. It is used to punish those who would detract from the omnipotence of the State, and to reward those who promote its policies. It is used to shape social behavior. It is used to divide society and to pit diverse interests against one another. And taxation has never been fair or equitable in all of recorded history.

In modern context in America, taxation is being used to enslave the productive part of society by bribing power from the nonproductive part of society through the election process; by fostering class distinction; and by creating self-interest dependency. It is stealing from Peter to buy Paul's vote.

As it has become more difficult for Government to extract revenue from the producers of society while maintaining consensus, two great myths have been fostered by the liberal ruling class. The first proposes that a primary function of Government is to oversee the "fair" distribution of wealth across society. This is grounded in the misguided belief that production of commodities is somehow a "social process," and that shares of the proceeds are allotted. It is asserted that the capitalist system unfairly allots a disproportionate share to those near the top (for instance to entrepreneurs and landowners). Out of this muddled thinking arises justification for forcible confiscation from those receiving "too much" and redistribution to those who "have less." The second socialist myth asserts that Government intervention in the market and control of economics is the best and most fair means to economic health and prosperity.

Taxation, manipulation of credit and currency, and redistribution of wealth are promoted as the means to achieving a society that is more successful, fairer, and more equitable. These myths are enduring in that they still find great appeal, even though in practice they are observably destructive to the flourishing of humanity. The tortuous failures of almost all of the socialist States during the twentieth century stand as recent reminders. Those with no understanding of economics can often be hoodwinked by the argument for "fairness," as its message and appeal have been developed by the ruling political elite for centuries. As a modern example, the Obama administration dragged out the time-tested mantra of "tax the rich" in the 2010 mid-term election by proposing a tax increase on those earning over $200,000 claiming, "It is only fair that the wealthy should shoulder a greater portion of the burden." While its appeal to fairness may be popular, the economic reality is diametrically opposed to what is stated. *All* of The People will be negatively affected in that the triggering threshold of $200,000 could not be more centered on small businesses, and the success of small business is at the core of job creation and economic health. Disproportionate confiscation from those most responsible for new channels of economic expansion and job creation has a direct negative effect on jobs and the overall economy. But "tax the rich" will always be asserted near election time because of its appeal to certain segments of society, most notably the less educated and poor. It is a paradox today that those most harmed by job and wealth destruction due to excessive taxation are some of its most ardent supporters. It is a vicious cycle; those believing they are benefited by Government largesse never stop to consider that the size of Government, and the correlative taxation necessary to maintain it, are reducing the number of available jobs in the private sector. Such policies keep them mired in poverty and dependency.

Another false claim of proponents of high taxation is that it is possible to tax consumption in a manner that will only affect consumers (but not producers) which is easily proven to be unworkable. This could only work conceptually if the levies also increased demand, but in fact the opposite is what occurs. Demand decreases because of the higher prices. It is another testament to modern day propaganda that such a myth can gain any purchase at all because it approaches borderline absurdity. If the tax burden can be shifted to the shoulders of the consumers, why wouldn't the producers simply raise their prices and immediately reap higher profits? It is because price-setting has a direct correlation to demand that causes the producer to engage in a balancing act to maximize profits. If he believed higher prices would give him greater profits, he would have already taken advantage of the increase.

Producers are constrained by both consumer demand and competition, which encourage prices toward their lowest level as the producer must be price competitive to sell his products. Since Government expropriates all of its revenue through taxation, it has no such constraints toward any form of moderation. The State is also not constrained by price competition in that it can tax and regulate competitors and even mandate (fix) prices. If Government is allowed to wield these powers in a manner that is not uniformly applied to all citizens, it can manipulate taxation to "reward" favored segments of society while "punishing" detractors. And Government can create monopoly powers by fiat, a practice that has spawned many of the world's largest companies. In modern terms, these practices are known as "crony capitalism."

Laws and policies that prevent one individual from accumulating more than another violate the basic tenets of economics and are destructive to jobs and economic well-being. One of the driving forces in capitalism is unrelenting competition among those supplying the wants and desires of consumers. It is consumers who decide winners and losers. Those who are most efficient in fulfilling the customer's mandates are rewarded with The People's affirmation of purchasing their products. The profits created provide for jobs and expansion. Disproportionate confiscation through taxation from those who are more successful in the competition of society produces a depressing effect on jobs and growth. There is a point at which confiscation reaches a tipping point that so hampers entrepreneurship that it produces "confiscatory stagnation" where the economy languishes in a malaise of chronic joblessness and inability to grow. A prime example is Japan's economic malaise of the past twenty years. If the economy is tipped even further, it can produce economic catastrophe such as national default, or even the more extreme possibilities of collapse or depression.

Contrary to what is intuitive; policies that would seem detrimental to the private sector are often promoted by big business and the large, established corporations, as a means of maintaining dominance. Small, growth-oriented companies are less capable of overcoming the handicap of "progressive" taxation due to their need for capital for expansion. *The large entrenched companies are far more fearful of new competition than the threat of taxation.* Progressive taxation becomes a formidable barrier to upcoming competitors as large companies do not face the same critical capital and credit requirements, and large companies can also wield their resources to buy off politicians and to create "tax loopholes" and other dispensations unachievable by smaller companies. There is a point at which excessive taxation can substantially choke off growth in small and intermediate businesses, producing confiscatory stagnation. One of the first indications that the tipping point may have been surpassed is a decrease in the availability of jobs. The vast majority of jobs are created by small businesses during the growth spurt made possible by their success. This expansion of new products or new ideas can be quite dynamic and requires new employees to fill the rapidly expanding jobs being created. Large companies have already successfully traversed the rapid growth stage, and for them jobs often revolve more around "replacement" rather than from new jobs being created. Higher taxes dramatically affect the growth-oriented companies while having more limited effect on the larger companies. In times of economic stress, jobs are often the first thing businesses in their dynamic growth stage must cut. This is the main reason jobs are one of the first indicators of confiscatory stagnation.

Confiscatory stagnation can also be readily observed through business migration. When taxes become over-burdensome and regulations so great as to make it difficult for companies to compete, they migrate to areas with lower taxes and a more friendly business climate. This is true of both large and small businesses. While jobs are an early indicator and may serve as the canary in the coal mine, business migration is an indicator of an even greater problem. Companies rarely want to move from the areas that brought them initial success. However, when excessive taxation causes an impediment to growth, they often feel they have little choice other than to move in order to stay competitive—or in some cases, to even survive.

This situation is readily observed by the migration of jobs from States with high confiscatory policies into those States with low taxes. The State of California is currently in dire financial circumstance because of profligate spending, strangling business regulations, and excessive taxation. Any recovery is going to be hampered because existing businesses are leaving California in droves, and new businesses are wary of moving to a State with an unfriendly business climate. Loss of businesses reduces the number of available jobs and produces a corresponding loss of tax base. For example, in 2005 California-based

Intel decided to build a multi-billion dollar chip-making facility in Arizona due to its favorable corporate income tax system.ii That companies are fleeing California's unfriendly business climate, is an unfolding disaster that its politicians seem unwilling or incapable of addressing. It is only unfolding in slow motion in the hi-tech industry because California's concentration of available talent is still attractive to highly technical enterprises. However, as more hi-tech companies such as Intel migrate and create pools of technical expertise outside California, there is a growing probability that what is now a trickle of migration will become a flood. Unlike the immediate indicator of jobs, the trends that shape economic migration are slower to develop but are more difficult to alter once they gain momentum. States that have reversed course and lowered their taxation have seen a gradual return of jobs once the market comes to believe the policy will be sustained. Companies move back to take advantage of the friendlier business climate. Some factors affecting business location are fixed, such as a need to be near resources or the availability of a deep-water port. Some businesses need to be near pools of highly trained experts. But many businesses face no such constraints and taxes and regulation become a primary factor in determining where they will reside. Another enticement for businesses to move is that States with the lowest taxes also tend to have the best economies.

Taxation and regulation in America are also primary motivators for businesses to expatriate, moving jobs to other countries. With America's top corporate tax rate of 35 percent, only Japan (at 39.6 percent) currently has a higher rate. They recently stated their intentions to lower the rate. The high cost of doing business in America is further exacerbated by State and local taxes, and many innovators and entrepreneurs opt to move their companies to other countries as they find it more difficult to compete in the world market The phenomenal growth, expansion, and robust employment created in America between the Revolution and the early twentieth century primarily occurred by becoming one of least taxed and least regulated societies in the world. This flourishing of The People through implementation of Freedom should be viewed in context with the loss of competitiveness and chronic unemployment of today's over-regulated and overtaxed society. Governments rolls in capitalism should be nutritive and should maintain a level playing field.

The historical perspective shows that the ultimate collapse of most Governments has been preceded by an increase in taxation, an increase in the number of Government employees, an increase in business strangling regulations, and an increase in the number of those dependent upon the State as a provider. The State is weakened economically because Government uses of money suck vitality from the private sector and are nonproductive; and when taxes become excessive, they foster economic decline. In periods of economic retraction, the Government bureaucracy has almost universally raised taxes and/ or created excessive debt in order to maintain the wealth, power, privilege and status of those associated with Government. This increase in taxation and/or debt, at a time of decreasing productivity, weakens the economy of the State even further and leaves it open to attack or internal chaos as the misery and despair of The People increases. In short, huge increases in the size of Government and the corresponding increase in the burden of taxation forced upon The People to pay for the burgeoning growth have been instrumental in bringing about the decline and destruction of almost every great State which has ever existed on the face of the Earth.

Excessive taxation sharpens the distinction between rich and poor by the destruction of the middle class, destroys wealth creation, reduces availability of jobs and severely penalizes the producers of society. Freedom, as the driving force of human achievement, is directly impacted by the tax policy of every nation.

The Forefathers of the American Revolution had no illusions about the threat of excessive taxation. As a coalescing force, it was probably more important than any other single issue in fostering the Revolution. Yet the Boston Tea Party was sparked by what today would be considered an absurdly nominal tax on tea that was imposed on the colonists by Great Britain.

Excessive taxation kept the serfs of Medieval Europe in poverty. Excessive, unjust, and unequal taxation prevented the establishment of a middle class and financed the monopolization of power by the ruling political elite. What is lost to Americans today is that *we are taxed far more than the poor serfs of medieval Europe in percentage of real income.* And, taxation is rapidly bringing about many of the same circumstances over which our Forefathers rebelled. Those associated with running our Government are being maintained as a privileged ruling elite. The United States Congress exempts itself from the laws it imposes upon us modern day "serfs."

Congress also approves its own pay raises and has its own medical and pension plans. Median and upper level bureaucrats are now paid at an inequitably higher level that is almost double that of comparable jobs in the private sector. Disproportionate compensation is not limited to upper management, but is extending its tentacles throughout the system. Some high school educated service providers can even command six figure incomes at a time when many in the private sector who have college educations can only command salaries at half of that rate.

A significant number of our "professional politicians" cry for more taxes and more regulation as their solutions to all problems. The money raised is used to buy votes from the nonproductive segment of society, to line the pockets of special interests, and to put more people on the Government payroll. These "public servants" will naturally have a vested interest when they cast their votes at election time. If the financial future of enough voters can be linked to more taxation and the creation of more Government, what will happen to Freedom? As a preview to the potential future that some of our collectivist politicians are bent on fostering, simply view the current strikes and riots by the public service unions in France and Greece. In 2010, strikes by French public service unions, that were protesting increasing the retirement age from sixty to sixty-two, shut down oil refineries and transportation. In Greece, where *almost 50 percent of all jobs are Government related*, there have been massive demonstrations and strikes by public service unions. Government employees have used strikes to create gridlock and orchestrated chaos over attempts at austerity, even though Greece is now on the verge of national default from its embrace of socialist economics. Greece can never repay the massive debt it has created without inflating it away, and that option is blocked because its currency is no longer sovereign since adoption of the Euro. This is creating a crisis that may ultimately tear the European Union apart. Yet those fostering socialist economic policies refuse to face the reality that Greece is bankrupt.

Will we create so many Government jobs and so many dependents in America that the same turmoil presently occurring in Greece and France will eventually happen here? Recent demonstrations in America by public employee unions over attempted reductions in deficit spending in the states of Wisconsin, Indiana and Ohio are ominous indicators of future unrest, as the federal Government continues its profligate spending.

THE TAX LAW

"No law should be written in a manner the common man cannot understand it." – Thomas Paine [52]

There is no excuse or justification for the behemoth labyrinth that comprises tax law in America today, but the purveyors of big Government are striving to make it even bigger and even more complex.

Thomas Paine saw through one of the ways in which Government maintains its dominance over The People. Laws left open to interpretation are subject to Government manipulation. This discussion will be carried much further in the chapter on Crime, but it is also necessary to bring it up here because there are few places where Government abuses this principle more than in the area of taxation. In March of 2006 the U.S. tax code comprised "only" 16,845 pages,[53] but is increasing at an almost unfathomable rate, and after only four years (in 2010) has exploded to encompass 71,684 pages.[54] To put this in perspective, page numbers vary due to factors such as page size, font size and spacing, but in order to have an equitable comparison, let's use an equivalently printed Bible containing almost 1,300 pages. The U.S. tax code is now more than fifty-five times as long as our comparably printed Bible. This omnibus monstrosity is beyond any comprehension. Even the Government lawyers admit that they do not understand it, and that it is open to interpretation. In this atmosphere of obfuscation, it becomes quite easy to punish one's enemies and reward one's friends because *the tax laws can be claimed to mean almost anything;* and Government bureaucrats are left to decree and implement whatever tax policy they claim arises from the law. The bureaucrats point out that each individual has the right to legal remedy if they feel they are treated unfairly. The lawsuit will be titled:

---

52. The Rights of Man

53. *Black's Law Dictionary*, p. 1307 (5th ed. 1979).

54. http://www.taxfoundation.org/research/show/22658.html

The United States of America versus "Poor American Taxpayer." Few Americans are able to take on the taxation bureaucracy with its unlimited assets and Government-paid lawyers. Since the rich can defend themselves with high priced lawyers, and since *advancement in the power structure of the IRS depends upon successful collections*; and since the poorer individual is far less likely to contest the decrees or interpretations of the agency, the wealthy are rarely audited and the burden is centered on middle class Americans who are less capable of fighting back.

What has evolved in America is an agency run wild. The tax collecting arm of the United States Government, the Internal Revenue Service, is beyond legal checks and balances that are supposed to insure our Freedom. In order to create fear (which they believe improves "compliance"), the IRS sometimes pursues a strategy of high profile audits of celebrities, those who challenge their authority, and also of those who publicly oppose them. Many believe that the singer Willie Nelson was targeted with just such a high profile media audit in the early 1990s, resulting in far harsher treatment than would normally be expected, because of his disdain for marijuana laws. Willy had not tried to cheat on his taxes; the federal tax agents had ruled the deductions his previous tax advisers believed to be legal were now invalid, and the penalties and interest from the many years had grown to more than he could handle. When the IRS auctioned off Willy's Dripping Springs ranch, considered his family homestead, farmers from across the country showed up at the courthouse and convinced the crowd not to bid, and the property was purchased at a low price and held in trust so Nelson wouldn't lose it. But the bureaucratic goal of creating fear of the tax man was more than accomplished in the media attention attracted by Nelson's celebrity.

The IRS uses fear and intimidation while talking about voluntary compliance.

What is voluntary about money forcibly extracted from The People at the point of a gun (imprisonment and confiscation) using as justification a law that is equivalent in length to fifty-five Bibles? Those who dissent against Government policy open themselves to audits and abuse of power. The laws are so muddled that they can be interpreted to mean almost anything, and the cost of trying to defend one's self, even against baseless claims, can lead to bankruptcy. With the courts predisposed to side with Government, most small taxpayers are bludgeoned into "voluntary compliance."

ROBIN HOOD AND THE TAX MAN

Myths and legends have been an integral part of society since long before the written word; in ancient times they were often passed on at gatherings and around campfires. Since their earliest origin, they have been used to create a historical background for society, to reflect moral standards, to create tradition among adults, and to pass cultural values on to future generations.

The means by which society passes on myths and legends has become richer and more diverse through time, and now all genres of writing and art are included. From the plays of the Ancient Greeks to today's cinema and whatever new innovations may arise in our future, myths and legends should continue to be passed on to posterity as a bridge to societies irreplaceable intellectual heritage. New myths and legends should be created to reflect changes in current societal values for changing those from our past debases our historical heritage. Unfortunately, propagandists see a ripe opportunity for using historical myths and legends to subtly attack those values which they perceive to be an impediment to molding society toward their political objectives.

Those promoting socialism have been particularly adept at

co-opting different "meanings" to their cause, realizing that if long-standing definitions can be changed, it becomes easier to promote their collectivist agenda, as the historical perspective of the original meaning is "replaced." We have previously noted word changes such as "Liberal Economics," "diversity," "tolerance," and "contribution." But the propagandistic attack has not been limited to words. It also extends to myths and legends. A typical example can be found in the co-opting of the legend of Robin Hood.

Any American child can tell you that Robin Hood "stole from the rich and gave to the poor." And for *stealing* he is touted as a hero? Because he was only taking from the rich, and giving what he stole to the poor, this somehow makes stealing an act of social justice? Is this a message we want to teach our children?

In point of fact, Robin Hood *was* a hero, but the issue was not a class struggle of rich versus poor. *The issue was taxation* that was keeping the poor in a condition of meager subsistence. The true story of Robin Hood highlighted Government oppression through taxation. What Robin Hood "stole" was excessive tax monies, confiscated from the poor and used to enrich and maintain Government officials. He returned the money to the powerless serfs from whom it had been forcibly taken in the first place. The Sheriff of Nottingham epitomized the high Government official being enriched by confiscation and exerting force to maintain the power of the ruling political elite.

To teach children that Robin Hood stole from the rich to give to the poor is a historical distortion that is used to promote socialist agendas, including the end justifying the means and of the illegitimacy of wealth. The Robin Hood myth has been co-opted to teach that it is moral to take from those who have more than you have. As previously discussed, "soak the rich" has long been the favored rhetoric of socialism and the political elite ruling class. Judging by how successfully the legend of Robin Hood has been debased is one more indicator of how far America has already travelled down the path toward socialism.

If The People are to live in a Free society that promotes the flourishing of all of humanity instead of only the elitist ruling class, excessive taxation must once again be viewed with the contempt it was given by our Forefathers. Severely limiting the politician's ability to tax must once again be restored to its true function as a limitation on the growth and power of Government.

CHAPTER 19

GUN CONTROL

MOST AMERICANS ARE AWARE THAT THE "right to keep and bear arms" is one of the basic Constitutional guarantees preserved in the Bill of Rights. This most basic of Freedoms, codified in the Second Amendment has been and will continue to be under constant assault from two distinct groups, who believe that all rights arise out of Government. The first group comprises those who wish to use Government to exert control over The People, including those who employ overt force, such as Marxists, tyrants, oligarchs, totalitarians and authoritarians, and those who generally favor economic pressure over confrontational force, including proponents of Keynesian socialism and social engineers. Freedom and Liberty are antithetical to these groups as they either advocate control for personal gain and/or power, or they promote the collectivist belief that The People are incapable of making sound decisions and must be carefully controlled in order to promote their concept of the greater good.

The second group includes those who believe in the benevolence of the State and that Government should and will protect them from the vagaries of the world. They also believe that disarming society makes them safer. A threat to Freedom arises when this second group extends their misconception that Government will protect *them* into the belief that Government is also going to protect *you and me*. The question of access to arms extends back into antiquity. Among the ancient Greeks, Plato believed that in order to secure control by his militaristic police state, The People should be disarmed. He taught that some citizens should be trained in the use of weapons, but that they should not be permitted to possess them. Instead, all weapons should be stored in State armories. Aristotle strongly disagreed with his teacher's theory. While conceding that possession of arms was one of the main determining factors of who would rule, Aristotle was opposed to State control of weapons. He believed in individual responsibility and taught that all citizens should earn their own living, participate in governance and bear arms, a view that followed directly from his strong belief that power should be reposed in The People. Aristotle wrote extensively, in numerous texts, on the importance of The People bearing arms, and he was keenly aware that this state of affairs conflicted with the ability of the rulers to exert their dominance, as reflected in his astute observation, "Both oligarch and tyrant mistrust the people, and therefore deprive them of arms.[55]

This maxim has persisted through the ages with all tyrannical and despotic Governments trying to disarm The People, either to preempt resistance to subjugation, or as a means of maintaining their dominance. Adolph Hitler noted, "The most foolish mistake we could possibly make would be to permit the conquered Eastern peoples to have arms. History teaches that all conquerors who have allowed their subject races to carry arms have prepared their own downfall by doing so.[56]

Of equal importance to an armed society being a deterrent to

---

55. Aristotle; Book 5, Chapter X
56. Adolph Hitler, April 11, 1942

subjugation is the individual's right to self-protection. Whenever The People are disarmed, they have no other choice than to look to Government to protect them. But of course, Government cannot offer a blanket security to The People because Government is almost never at the scene of a crime. Generally, only criminals and victims are at the crime scene.

Occasionally, crime is committed with bystanders present, but it is far more prevalent that criminals will attack their victims when they are alone and vulnerable. If law enforcement officers were present, it is irrational to believe that the criminal would be so stupid as to commit the crime. I am, of course, excluding those crimes where Government itself is the criminal.

Extending this common sense approach, we may note that if the victim is defenseless, the criminal armed, and the Government absent from the scene of the crime, then what is the almost certain outcome? The crime will be committed successfully. Government will arrive after the crime, scrape up the remains, and calm and reassure the victim's friends and survivors. In some cases, the criminal is even caught and punished at some later date, actions which have been shown to have very little deterrent effect on future crimes, and, of course, no mitigation effect whatsoever on the crime already perpetrated.

But if the potential victim, as well as the potential criminal, is armed, he or she is unlikely to be attacked in the first place because most violent criminals are cowards who will rarely attack someone unless they judge that they have considerable advantage. In those rare cases in which an armed individual is attacked, he or she, and any other potential victims nearby, have a far better chance of a favorable outcome by defending themselves than by waiting for Government to act. It is often a considerable period of time before Government even learns that a crime may have been committed. TV's depiction of squads of police cruisers arriving on the scene to catch the perpetrators in the act is nothing more than Hollywood myth. Ask a few officers how often in their careers they have confronted armed individuals during the act of committing a violent crime. When viewed from the perspective of the number of gun crimes being committed, it is an extremely rare occurrence. But *all victims* are confronted by armed perpetrators during the commission of their gun crimes. Fear of a victim potentially defending herself is far greater than any fear that the police will catch them in the act or even at some later date.

Thomas Jefferson is often incorrectly credited with a trenchant commentary on the consequences of preventing The People from enacting their own defense. It was actually written by the Italian philosopher Cesare Beccaria (1738–1794), but was quoted in Jefferson's commonplace book.[57] "Laws that forbid the carrying of arms…disarm only those who are neither inclined nor determined to commit crimes…Such laws make things worse for the assaulted and better for the assailants; they serve rather to encourage than to prevent homicides, for an unarmed man may be attacked with greater confidence than an armed man. It is a paradox that many who reject the use of force on a personal basis, and reject yours and my right to use force to protect ourselves, readily endorse the use of force by the State. They mistakenly do so in the belief that they are somehow maintaining order or are somehow making society safer. This exemplifies the idealistic belief in the way society should be, instead of the reality of the way society is, and totally disregards the rather clear verdict of recorded history.

Fear of legal repercussions, never particularly effective as deterrent to crime, seems to have an even more diminished effect in modern times. Today's prisons may be overcrowded, stuffed past capacity with the huge numbers of drug prohibition inmates, but they are also equipped with modern amenities such as television, air conditioning,

---

57. A sort of scrapbook kept by many educated people in early modern times.

and recreational facilities. The result is that many convicts live in conditions that may be cramped, but are nonetheless more comfortable and secure than their previous living quarters. In addition, many will get out early due to modern social tendencies, tight budgets, and overcrowding itself. More will be said about the problem of prison overcrowding in the next chapter on crime.

To the extent gun control restrictions are increased, honest and good people become less able to protect themselves, and they live in greater fear. As a given society is disarmed, criminals will gradually shed the instinct of fear. Knowing that houses are occupied by defenseless people who expect the State to protect them, potential criminals will surely be emboldened. But where homeowners are even potentially armed, the criminal runs the risk of getting shot. The same dynamic applies to other sorts of targets, for example a convenience store where the owner, clerk, or even a customer or two might be armed.

My mother was a crack shot and knew how to use most types of firearms. She could even shoot birds on the wing with a shotgun, a feat many seasoned hunters find difficult. After my father died, Mother was trying to decide if she could live alone for the first time in her life. Her choice was made more difficult because one of her good friends had been brutally tortured and murdered in the small Texas border town where my family lived. Ms. Russell, as she was known to all the area kids, myself included, was a large woman who had never married and lived alone after the death of her family. She was head librarian for the school district and had convinced my mother to give up teaching fifth grade late in her career to become an elementary school librarian.

They shared a love of reading and literature and were close friends. Then one day—it was before Dad died—Ms. Russell was found dead in her home, naked and tied to a chair. The details of her torture at the hands of some depraved inhuman psychopath, before she finally met death, are too gruesome for description. Mother accepted the death of her friend with great strength of character, but we all knew the brutality and torture weighed heavily on her, and we were thankful she had Dad to help her through. The killer was never found, and the crime remains unsolved to this day, all the resources of Government having again demonstrated their impotence. Even though she lived alone, Ms. Russell never owned a gun.

After Dad died, I asked Mother to come and stay with me, in another Texas city, but she wanted to live out the rest of her years near her friends. Sitting at the kitchen table, Mother told me how she was struggling with what she should do. She asked if I thought she should move into an apartment. I asked her if that was what she wanted to do, and without hesitation she told me she wanted to stay in our family home where she had over forty years of wonderful memories. But then she asked if I thought that was crazy because of what had happened to Ms. Russell. Genuinely concerned for herself, she also didn't want my brother and me to worry about her being there alone.

I told her she should live wherever she wanted, and pointed out that Ms. Russell did not have the ability to protect herself. With Mother following me, I took a shotgun from the gun closet, loaded it and stood it next to the head of her bed. I know it gave her comfort because she kept it there until her death from cancer years later, and it only saw the inside of the gun closet when small children were in the house.

Even in her seventies, Mother was most capable of defending herself as long as she was armed. This gave her comfort, and she was able to live alone without fear. She could protect herself because firearms equalize the vast differences between weak and strong, old and young, male and female. Indeed, guns are frequently described as "the great equalizer." If Government and the collectivists had been successful in disarming society through their incessant attacks on The People's right to possess the means of their own defense, what chance would Mother have had if attacked? Present crime statistics demonstrate the sobering reality that being attacked is a possibility of which we should all be aware. How could Mother have defended herself against an intruder or robber, or even the very same sadist who had tortured her friend? How much would her level of fear have increased, knowing that she had no means of defense? How much would her level of independence and confidence, and her pursuit of happiness in her old age have been decreased if out of fear she had regretfully decided to move? How much bolder would a criminal have been, knowing that she was aged, alone and defenseless?

Mother was not the type of person to protect only herself. Our neighbors, the widow next door and our Hispanic friends across the street, were also safer because she was armed. In a crisis, Mother would not have hesitated to grab a gun and help defend them. Even in her seventies, she was very capable and willing to do so. She would not have waited helplessly for Government to come after the fact and count the bodies and fill out the paperwork. Mother would have done her best to see that it was her friends who survived.

Some argue that by defending herself or our neighbors, Mother would be unjustifiably assuming the role of judge and jury, possibly even executioner, and that this is somehow unfair to her attackers. John Locke unequivocally agreed with Mother's right to defend herself, and addresses this argument in his Second Treatise on Government:

> ... the Law, which was made for my Preservation, where it cannot interpose to secure my Life from present force, which if lost, is capable of no reparation, permits me my own Defence, and the Right of War, a liberty to kill the aggressor, because the aggressor allows not time to appeal to our common Judge, nor the decision of the Law, for remedy in a Case, where the mischief may be irreparable.

What Locke is saying in West Texas lingo is that since the sheriff can't get there in time, and the harm to Mother may be irreparable, she has every right to defend herself and shoot their butts off, which includes killing them if she deems it necessary. Clearly The People's rights are being violated by the attackers, not the criminal's rights being violated by any act of self-defense.

It is a Natural Right of mankind to protect herself, her family, her home, and her property. Earlier, I stated that when I speak of "mankind," I do so in the traditional, bigender sense and with only the aim of brevity in mind. *All* rights of mankind include all human beings with the exception of some rights which communities see fit to deny children until they reach adulthood. I reiterate the point here because it is probably more important to afford women the means of their own protection for as we have previously noted, weapons make acts of defense much more equal with acts of aggression which tends to benefit the weak and elderly.

The right of self-protection is such a basic law of nature that few mammals in existence will not protect their young from acts of aggression by their own kind. And only the weakest and most timid of animals will not stand in their own defense. Certainly none of the higher mammals exhibit such timidity. Since self-defense is a Natural Right, it is immoral for Government to deprive The People of the means to defend themselves and their loved ones.

It is inevitable that technology will continue to progress. It is only reasonable that criminals and the Government will utilize the most advanced weapons available. If The People are relegated to using antiquated or outmoded weapons, it is tantamount to hampering the ability of self-defense. It is therefore a right of all mankind to avail themselves of even the most advanced weapons they determine are necessary for their own defense. Only weapons of mass destruction, which can indiscriminately kill vast numbers, such as nuclear or biological weapons, are not weapons of self-defense.

Defense is not an act of aggression; it is an act of protection. Even the noted pacifist Mohandas Gandhi recognized the importance of self-protection when he said, "Among the many misdeeds of British rule in India, history will look upon the Act depriving a whole nation of arms as the blackest."[58]

MYTH OF THE WILD WEST

We have previously noted that the story of Robin Hood has been perverted from its original intent as an allegory about oppressive taxation, and the myth of the Wild West is another example of how Government and the media try to cloud the reality of history, in this case to support their anti-gun agenda. It is doubtful that anyone who has debated the issue of reasserting the right of The People to carry guns for self-protection has not heard the argument that we cannot return to the Wild West. The term "Wild West" has come to mean Hollywood's version of that period in American history encompassing the latter half of the nineteenth century in the western United States. Shoot-outs in the street. "Bad guys" taking over towns and terrorizing the honest citizens.

Lawlessness. Indians portrayed as stupid or savage. Revolvers that shoot twenty times without the need to be reloaded. And often all twenty shots are fired at someone ten feet away, and every one misses its mark. Bar room brawls in which chairs are broken by smashing them into men's faces without knocking out any teeth, or breaking any bones. Men being thrown through glass windows without getting the slightest nick from all the broken glass.

Well folks, prepare yourselves for a shock. It never happened. It is all Hollywood myth. In all of what we now call the old West, there

---

58. Mohandas Gandhi, An Autobiography, pg 446

were fewer than fifty shoot-outs in the street. Dueling had long since gone out of style. In modern times, more than fifty people have been killed in New York or Los Angeles or Chicago in one weekend.

Portrayal of the Indians as savages might sell box office tickets or soothe the nation's conscience for a despicable genocide of many who were peaceful, nature- loving people, but it has no basis of historical fact. The bad guys never took over a single town. Most of the settlers and townsfolk of the day were tough, seasoned Civil War veterans, men not likely to allow a few punks to come in and take over their town. Almost all women of the day could shoot and were not shy about protecting their families. Neighbors supported neighbors, and common protection was universally practiced, especially by those living in remote areas. With The People armed, motivated and able to protect themselves, they did not live in fear. They did not depend on Government to protect them, and most of the Old West had very little crime.

While most western towns were peaceful, two exceptions may be noted: frontier mining camps and towns serving as trail drive terminuses. These raw frontier towns attracted very few women and supported a disproportionate number of saloons and gambling halls, which served the large and fluctuating population of adventure-seeking young men. There were a high number of fistfights, some knife fights and even some gunfights, amplified by alcohol and competition over the insufficient female population. However, these skirmishes were generally engaged in by willing participants, and were not a product of criminal activity. Overall, the days of the Old West, when The People almost universally carried arms, were relatively crime free compared to the rampant crime in the latter half of the twentieth century when significant numbers of The People have been disarmed.

What about present day armed societies? The People of Switzerland are armed. At age eighteen, all able bodied young men report for defensive military training. When they go home, they take their modern military weapons with them. Swiss national police statistics for the year 2006[59] record thirty-four killings or attempted killings involving firearms, along with sixty-nine cases involving bladed weapons and sixteen cases of unarmed assault. An additional eighty-nine cases of assault involving firearms resulted in bodily harm to the victim compared to 526 for bladed weapons.

Just as an armed and modern day Switzerland has exceedingly little crime, it was the same in the Old West. People did not depend on Government to protect them.

They protected themselves. The truth of the Wild West is that it was one of the most orderly and crime-free periods in American history.

PERSONAL CARRY LAWS

Do you think that the police want to be forced to leave their "off duty" guns at home? Many law officers carry personal weapons when off duty. In some locales it is even required. Do you think they would feel safer without them? Do you think that society is any more threatened because of these personal weapons they carry? Do you think society would have been more threatened by my mother carrying the means of her own defense? Is there any reasonable argument that a law depriving my mother of the means to defend herself would prevent criminals from obtaining weapons? Of course not. It is absurd. And yet we are bombarded by a media with a mission to achieve that end.

In the later part of the twentieth century, many states in the U.S. began to once again legalize the right of The People to carry arms. It had not gone unnoticed that states that already had such laws seemed to have lower crime rates than those that did not, a view publicized

---

59. *Polizeiliche Kriminalstatistik* der Schweiz (PKS)

and promoted by Second Amendment support groups such as the National Rifle Association.

Anti-gun activists tried their best to explain the statistics away, but their efforts were decimated by John Lott's and David Mustard's rigorous statistical study in connection with the University of Chicago Law School. They performed a nationwide comparison, on a county-by-county basis, of violent crime between 1977 and 1992 before and after implementation of concealed carry laws in the studied areas. Lott offered the following conclusion:

> Our most conservative estimates show that by adopting shall-issue laws, states reduced murders by 8.5%, rapes by 5%, aggravated assaults by 7% and robbery by 3%. If those states that did not permit concealed handguns in 1992 had permitted them back then, citizens might have been spared approximately 1,570 murders, 4,177 rapes, 60,000 aggravated assaults and 12,000 robberies. To put it even more simply criminals, we found, respond rationally to deterrence threats... While support for strict gun-control laws usually has been strongest in large cities, where crime rates are highest, that's precisely where right-to-carry laws have produced the largest drops in violent crimes.[60]

The study by Lott and Mustard is in complete agreement with observation that the U.S. cities today with the stricter gun laws have higher crime rates.

If some people wish to continue to rely on Government to protect them, we must all honor and defend their right to do so. However, to permit those same people *to force the rest of us* into relying on Government for our own protection is clearly an immoral act, for self-defense is a Natural Right of all mankind. Clearly, it is a right that we

---

60. "More Guns, Less Violent Crime", Professor John R. Lott, Jr., The Wall Street Journal, August 28, 1996, (The Rule of Law column).

must consistently defend, for those who believe all rights arise out of Government will perpetually be trying to deprive The People of their own means of protection.

A COLLECTIVE RIGHT?

The proponents of gun control have been undaunted by the success of local pro-gun legislation. The facts have not borne out their argument that The People would be safer if private gun ownership were further restricted or outlawed altogether. In the early years of the twenty-first century, they tried another tactic—an entirely new theory about the Second Amendment. Noting the language of the amendment, " A well-regulated Militia, being necessary to the security of a free State, the right of the people to keep and bear Arms, shall not be infringed" the anti-gun advocates developed the theory that the right to keep and bear arms really was a right of the Government itself—the right to have a "well-regulated militia." Under this remarkable invention, The People had no individual right to defend their homes and persons; the only justification for gun ownership was in case they were needed by the Government to form themselves into a militia. This view was put forward in the case *District of Columbia v. Heller,* and found wanting by the Supreme Court in 2008, the majority stating that "the Second Amendment protects a personal right to keep and bear arms for lawful purposes, most notably for self-defense within the home."

The Heller decision applied only to Federal gun control laws, so a second case, *McDonald v. Chicago*, was pushed through the courts to see if the justices would extend the concept to state and local laws, and on June 28, 2010, they did just that, with Justice Samuel Alito writing, "It is clear that the Framers ... counted the right to keep and bear arms among those fundamental rights necessary to our system of ordered liberty."

GUNS VS MISSILES?

Another popular argument for disarming The People is that the complexity of weaponry in modern warfare makes self-defense futile against the army of the State, so the rationale of The People being armed as a deterrent to State oppression or foreign invasion is moot. As noted previously, the more important element of the right to "keep and bear arms" is for self-protection, but even this futility argument is specious.

We need not spend considerable time debunking this argument as we have an excellent historical example. Afghanistan has never been successfully conquered. Not even the most technologically modern armies in the world (ancient or current) have been successful in conquering Afghanistan. Not even Alexander the Great was able to subjugate The People of Afghanistan. The Soviet army attempted to occupy Afghanistan in 1979 with over 100,000 soldiers engaged in active combat. After failing to subjugate the Afghan people, and with terrible losses in human life, military equipment, and Russian rubles, they officially ended their final withdrawal ten years later, on February 15, 1989. Within two years, the Soviet Union had ceased to exist, but Afghanistan was still unconquered.

In the power vacuum following the withdrawal of the Soviets, an organized fundamentalist religious group called the Taliban eventually emerged.

Reminiscent of rule in now failed communist countries they ruled through extreme violence and authoritarian control including oppression of women and elimination of all potential opposition. Often this included extermination or imprisonment of the educated and capable.

Just as the various communist countries failed, it would have only been a matter of time before the Taliban would have been displaced for the same economic reasons that permeate this book, though the time frame might have been longer and the suffering of The People greater because of the poverty-stricken, war-torn condition of Afghanistan.

Before the lengthy process of economic collapse and chaos could play itself out, the American army invaded on October 7, 2001, displacing the Taliban, in response to its harboring of the al Qaeda religious terrorists responsible for the attack on the U.S. of 9/11/2001. There is considerable difference between the war by the Soviet army and that of the U.S. in that the goals were opposite. The U.S. is not trying to conquer and occupy Afghanistan, but rather is supporting the new Afghan Government against a minority of religious zealots, while at the same time trying to weed out Al Qaeda.

However, it is instructive to note that not even the vaunted military of the United States, aided by NATO allies and regional powers such as Pakistan, have been able as of this writing to achieve the capitulation of a tiny, but very committed segment of the population … precisely because they have the availability of arms and are willing to die for their cause. The number of American dead in Afghanistan reached 1,000 on May 18, 2010, and the conflict has in no manner been decided. History will eventually record whether The People of Afghanistan are able to find a means to live in Freedom under a responsible domestic government, but the example of Afghanistan debunks the "armed-individuals-are-helpless-against-a-modern-army" myth, and is without ambiguity.

CONCLUSION

Self-defense is a natural right of all species. When The People are disarmed, they are forced into the intolerable position of helplessness against an aggressor and reliance upon the State for protection, which is then used as a justification for more authoritarian rule. Attempts at disarming society promote greater fear and more crime, not more security. Our right to keep and bear arms must be guarded very closely, for it is an anathema to those who believe in the authoritarian rule of the State. They fear it quite simply because it is one of the safeguards in our Constitution which has helped to keep us Free from those who would usurp our rights to their "benevolent" and all powerful State.

CHAPTER 20

CRIME AND PUNISHMENT

WHAT IS THE PROPER ROLE OF Government with regard to crime and punishment? The police power of the State is one of its most basic functions. The People rightly expect that their Government will keep the streets safe and apprehend and punish those who violate the rights of others. But of all the legitimate functions of Government, it is perhaps the most likely to be abused.

Moreover, just as it is fair to say that the State can never wipe out all criminal acts, and must be satisfied with keeping crime "under control," so it is also true that it is not possible to completely wipe out abuse of police power, and those who value Freedom will have to feel a sense of accomplishment if they can reduce it to a minimum.

We're a long way from that in the world today, and while it would be foolish to say that abuse of the police power in the United States is comparable to that in, say, North Korea, I believe it is nonetheless true that it is a greater problem here in our country than it is in many, if not most, of the nations of the First World.

As the dramatic revolutionary socialism of the early twentieth century gave way to a more insidious creeping socialism in the second half, countries incrementally gravitated toward ever more utilization of police power, disguised as benevolence, with more application of force and restrictions under the guise of "necessity" for protection against crime. Like frogs boiling in the pot of water, most Americans have never given a passing thought to the growing threat that is eroding our Liberty.

If we in the U.S. live in a truly free society, how can we have more people in prison than any country in the world, both in actual numbers and as a percentage of the population? At the end of 2008, America was incarcerating 2,424,279 convicts.[61] America imprisons substantially more of its citizens than communist China, which has a population more than four times as great. Additionally, we have even more people on probation from prison than we have behind bars. In the U.S. over five million of our citizens are either on probation (4,270,917) or parole (828,169). This represents an astounding one out of every 45 adults.[62] The only thing limiting Federal, state and local Governments from incarcerating even more of The People is space, in spite of the fact that construction of prisons has experienced one of the biggest growth spurts at any time in history, except possibly for the Nazi death camps and communist gulags.

Prisons have become crime factories fostering long periods of forced association among hardened felons and those who have committed lesser crimes (many of whom are incarcerated for the first time), where the seasoned criminals influence and instruct the newer convicts. The cost to society, both in actual dollars and in stigmatized lives, has been steadily increasing (limited only by bed space). If these facts cause you concern, I hope you will consider this chapter very carefully, and with an open mind. I believe they represent an

---

61. OLR Research Report, February 13,2008; 2008-R-0099

62. 1 Sabol, William J., PhD, West, Heather C., PhD, and Matthew Cooper, Bureau of Justice Statistics, Prisoners in 2008 (Washington, DC: US Department of Justice, December 2009), NCJ228417. p. 8

intolerable condition that is unacceptable for any free society, and an escalating threat to our Liberty.

If I were to tell you that we could eliminate a majority of all crime in a matter of months...

If I were to tell you that it is Government policy which is amplifying the problem of crime, which is then used as justification for an assault on Liberty...

If I were to tell you that this is history repeating itself through institution of the same failed social tinkering that has occurred (and failed) before in America...

If I were to offer reasonable proof of all of these assertions...

Are you willing to help end this madness? For that is exactly what I intend to show, asking only that the reader keep an open mind and consider the destructive reality of what is actually taking place, rather than merely accepting what the social engineers are telling you should be happening.

Perhaps the most fundamental problem is that our Government is treating something that should be an economic debate, while instead it is treated as moral imperative. In the process, it ignores the negative societal consequences that result when Government employs the economic act of "prohibition."

PROHIBITION

Today the word "prohibition" has become synonymous with the period that began in 1920 when the importation, manufacture, sale and transportation of intoxicating liquors were banned in America due to passage of the Eighteenth Amendment to the Constitution and ended in 1933 when it was repealed by the Twenty-first Amendment. Prohibition has ceased to be a generic term and has come to be referred to as a failed attempt to solve a perceived problem by the direct action of banning it by law. It was called the "Noble Experiment" because its principal advocates were not self-interested special interests, but rather moralists who were trying to make America a better place by ending the problem of drunkenness. Whether noble or not, the experiment failed because morality is not a matter that can be controlled by Government action.

So today, Prohibition means not only the excesses of the Roaring Twenties, with its speakeasies, organized crime, bootleggers, bathtub gin, and moonshine, but Prohibition stands as a prime example of the law of unintended consequences. By banning intoxicating beverages, Government unintentionally created a black market, which criminal elements rushed in to fill. They battled one another for market share, not with clever advertising, but rather with machine guns. They used the enormous profits they earned from their activities to buy off politicians, law enforcement officers and judges. To the extent that "untouchable" people were working to enforce the law and do battle with the organized criminals, their efforts were an abysmal failure.

Stripped of its cultural context, the word prohibition means simply the act of forbidding something by law. It is legitimate for Government to prohibit activities in which a person violates the natural rights of another. Using Locke's list of rights as an example, Government properly prohibits someone from taking a life (murder), liberty (kidnapping) or property (robbery, burglary, etc.). But when Government takes prohibition into the economic sphere, problems are created. By prohibiting an economic commodity though services such as prostitution, other services are also frequently prohibited. Government interferes with the right of people to own property or make individual choices (and to pursue happiness). So, instead of enforcing a right, Government becomes the violator of a right.

Intoxicating beverages are commodities. So are turnips, oranges, cotton and aluminum. So are other drugs, or products that contain drugs. A drug, or psychoactive substance, is a substance that crosses the blood-brain barrier, and therefore acts directly on the central nervous system, resulting in changes in perception, mood, consciousness, cognition, and behavior. The most utilized and abused drug in the world is caffeine, a natural insecticide found in certain plants including coffee, tea, and chocolate. Another heavily consumed drug is nicotine, a natural pesticide occurring in plants of the nightshade family such as tobacco. The drug in intoxicating beverages is the chemical ethanol (C2H5OH), a potable alcohol produced by the distillation or fermentation of vegetable products containing certain sugars or starches.

Caffeine, nicotine, and ethanol are drugs legally obtainable to adults in the United States. The commodities come "packaged" as: coffee, cigarettes, beer, etc., and are purchased over-the-counter although in the case of intoxicating beverages, and increasingly, tobacco products, sales are heavily regulated by the Federal, State, and even local Governments.

All of these drugs have both positive and negative effects on their users, although it has become clear in recent years that in the case of tobacco products, the negative effects vastly outweigh the positive. But positive or negative, all the drugs I have mentioned are legal for adults to purchase in the United States.

Other examples of drugs include marijuana, cocaine, and a host of commodities for which the sale or possession is prohibited by Federal law. But why are some drugs legal and others are not? It can hardly be maintained that the distinction is based on the harm to society that can be done by the "controlled substances," as illegal drugs are euphemistically known in legal circles. The presently illegal drug marijuana is relatively benign as compared to the legal drug alcohol, not to mention the legal drug nicotine, which in its tobacco packaging kills and maims, through diseases such as emphysema, significantly more humans than all other drugs combined.

Many supporters of drug prohibition see it as a moral act. These drugs are bad for people, they say, and therefore the Government is justified in prohibiting them. This is, of course, precisely the argument used to justify passage of the Eighteenth Amendment. The basic problem with that line of thinking is that it ignores the unintended consequences of prohibition. You simply cannot prohibit the workings of the laws of economics; yet today, we continue to imagine that by legally prohibiting the use of drugs such as marijuana we can in fact prevent their use, and we are reaping the unfortunate consequences of that policy in exactly the same way as occurred with respect to alcohol prohibition in the 1920s.

People who support this sort of Government intervention through force may not realize the evil that intervention inflicts on society. If it is a question of basic morality that they believe should be shared by all mankind, then they are willing to use the force of Government to impose their moral ideal upon those who do not share it. They see increased Government authoritarianism as a necessary tool to achieve a higher morality for mankind. This reflects an obvious belief in the use of Government as an activist solution to achieve greater good or to solve perceived social ills.

We are more and more coming to realize that most of the food we Americans consume in excessive quantities are bad for us. Our high calorie, high fat, high sodium, high cholesterol, high carbohydrate diet is literally killing us. Would that justify a Federal Food Police force, which would drive hamburger purveyors underground, and sentence people caught snarfing Oreos to thirty-day prison terms? Would it justify taking children away from parents under the guise of being abused because they are obese?

Or looked at it another way. What is the difference between prohibiting the consumption of a substance and *requiring* the consumption of a substance?

What if a majority of drug supporters were to achieve political dominance and decide that all people should take some variety of psychoactive drugs for the betterment of society? What if they passed laws *mandating* that all citizens be *required* to take certain drugs, and were willing to use the force of Government to impose their ideal? What if drugs were developed that made humans docile and obedient to authority, and the Government forced The People to take them? Would those who presently use the force of Government to enforce their moral imperative become willing or docile drug takers?

Or would they assert that they have a right to make their own decisions affecting their personal lives, and would they rebel? Aren't the more than thirty million Americans who freely admit to frequent illicit drug use, and who feel oppressed by current drug prohibition, rebelling now by disobeying the laws because they believe they have a right to make decisions on their own behalf?

This obviously becomes a clash of ideals. One side believes in moral justification or acting to better society, and the other believes just as fervently in individual Freedom and the right to choose what is best for them.

It does not matter whether the drug is alcohol, as in the 1920s, or marijuana of our generations. It does not even have to be a drug. It could be wheat or corn or peas or potatoes. All are economic commodities. As such, they are inescapably linked to the laws of supply and demand which constitute the basic laws of economics. Herein lies the answer to our dilemma of why the U.S. is imprisoning more of The People than any country in the world.

Commodity prohibition is not a moral act with only moral consequences; it is an economic act with devastating economic and societal consequences. If prohibition is used as a moral act in violation of the laws of economics, a set of forces is put into motion over which mankind has no control.

The most basic law of economics dictates that if we do not have enough of any commodity to meet the demand, the price of that commodity will increase. For example, if we have a severe freeze which damages a significant portion of this year's orange crop and we no longer have enough supply to meet the needs of all those who wish to purchase oranges or orange juice, there will be a sharp price increase.

Economic prohibition of oranges will produce an even greater price increase as supply is interdicted due to the increased risk of fines and imprisonment. The price of oranges will continue to rise until the increasing potential profit eventually entices someone to take the risk and begin smuggling or illegally growing oranges.

This brings into play the second most basic law of economics which dictates that when you do not have enough supply of a commodity to meet demand and the price begins to increase, it will continue to increase (making it more profitable), until more people are enticed to provide that commodity, and the price is brought back down by the effect of the increased supply. However, normal commodity "risk" usually involves such factors as how perishable the item, tenuous supply sources, problematic supply routes and all other factors that could increase the potential for loss. Risk is much more difficult to mitigate when supplying a commodity that is illegal, due to penalties and punishment, and there is heightened potential for total loss (rather than partial).

Prohibition establishes an artificially high price that will not abate significantly, even when there is sufficient supply, because of the increased risk due to illegality.

Government uses the increased crime its prohibition policies foster to grow in size, justifying an increase of law enforcement and prisons, and usurpation of the basic rights of individuals. Economic prohibition is one of Government's most successful tools for creating more Government and for increasing authoritarian dominance over

The People. This is easily observed in the consequences produced by America's ongoing "war on drugs."

We cannot defeat or ignore these laws of economics. They are at work whether we acknowledge them or not. Regardless of whether the commodity is oranges or marijuana, the resulting detrimental effects of prohibition are the same. Ignoring the basic laws of economics through enactment of commodity prohibition can have devastating consequences for society. Alcohol prohibition of the 1920s and 1930s is a graphic example.

At some point America will legalize drugs! No matter how strong your moral fiber, you cannot defeat the laws of economics. We will legalize drugs for the same reasons that alcohol was legalized with the repeal of the Volstead Act in 1933. The price we are each paying in dollars, in fostering crime and through a perpetual loss of our personal Freedom, will continue to mount until Americans are finally forced to admit that we cannot legislate morality. Unfortunately, the enormous amount of wealth we will have squandered on this reenactment of 1920s Prohibition can never be recovered, and rights that have been usurped by the State will be very difficult to recover.

For every 10,000 prohibition prisoners we put in jail, there will be 20,000 ready to take their place on the streets. More interdiction means less supply and higher prices, enticing more to risk whatever penalty we impose. High price induces the growth of gangs. Gang warfare over control of turf and distribution are a predictable consequence. The parallel between the growth and dominance of gangs in the 1920s and the growth of gangs today is a predictable outcome of prohibition.

Today, warfare among gangs in Mexico who are competing to supply America's drug needs has produced such a dangerous climate that travel advisories have been issued warning about the danger of crossing the border. And the huge illicit profits are used to corrupt the system, to buy off law enforcement and judges and to buy protection from corrupt Government officials. In the past four and one-half years, during a crackdown on the drug cartels in Mexico by President Felipe Calderon, in which even the army has failed to stop the traffickers, over 40,000 Mexican citizens have lost their lives in the resulting violence.

The segment of society using drugs becomes increasingly more estranged from Government as they are forced to become criminals in order to make choices they perceive to be a basic right. They also learn that to exercise what they perceive as a basic right to make choices of their own behalf, they must do so in the shadows.

Universally known names from alcohol prohibition of the 1920s were AL Capone, Joe Kennedy, and La Cosa Nostra. Today's parallel examples are Pablo Escobar, Manuel Noriega, and the Medellin Cocaine Cartel. The preeminence of all was brought about by the artificially high price of the different commodities, the drug alcohol in the 1920s and marijuana and cocaine today. There is no greater fuel for the growth of gangs and for increasing gang warfare than commodity prohibition. It is probable that even the term "organized crime" was first used to describe the activities of groups engaged in the illegal activities of making and distributing alcohol during Prohibition. Once created, that legacy of crime has extended to the present day. A graphic example of the effects of prohibition on crime is a comparison of the murder rate.

[The chart below illustrates the homicide rate in the United States from 1900 to 1998. It is important to note that each of the most violent episodes in this century coincide with the prohibition on alcohol and the escalation of the modern-day war on drugs. In 1933 the homicide rate peaked at 9.7 per 100,000 people, which was the year that alcohol prohibition was finally repealed. In 1980, the homicide rate peaked again at 10 per 100,000. *Source: US Census Data and FBI Uniform Crime Reports.*]

Murder in America
Homicides per 100,000 population
1900 - 1997 (FBI Uniform Crime Reports)

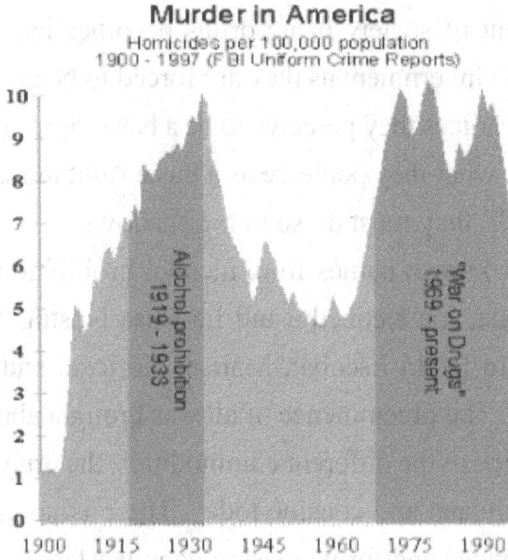

SOME FACTS ON CRIME

Though numbers supported by interest groups vary widely, it is almost universally agreed that a significant majority of all crime is drug related. Crime not only surrounds the activities of supplying the drugs but also includes the crimes committed by users in order to obtain drugs. With prohibition of drugs acting as a crime factory, there is an ever greater need for courts, which serve as clearing houses, and for prisons, which serve as warehousing facilities.

Our legal system is clogged past capacity, to the extent that few cases today even go to trial, which damages an important part of our Constitutional framework. Northwestern University School of Law professor Robert Burns sounds a clear alarm in his book *Death of the American Trial*. He shows that the number of Federal civil trials has declined 60 percent since the mid–1980s. In 2002, less than 2 percent of all cases ended in a trial—down from 12 percent in 1962 and 20 percent in the 1920s. *Less than 5 percent of criminal cases now go to trial*; most result in plea bargains. Even so, the system is so clogged that most trials are postponed from months to years. The court system would certainly collapse if it were to try an additional one-third of the cases (much less all 95 percent)! Also note the significant decrease in cases actually being tried between the early 1960s and mid–1980s, which coincides with the implementation of present day drug prohibition. Contrast today's system with Thomas Jefferson's belief in "trial by juries in all cases," which prevents excessive and unwarranted use of law.

The warehouse system is also clogged. Our prisons are full. Our local jails are full of convicted felons that our prisons cannot accept because they are so crammed past capacity. "At year end 2006, 23 States and the Federal system operated at more than 100 percent% of their highest capacity. Seventeen States operated at between 90% and 99% of their highest capacity. The Federal prison system was operating at 37% above its rated capacity at yearend 2006."[63] This has created a revolving door of early release.

State prisons are also jammed past capacity. In 2011 the Supreme Court even ruled that the State of California must reduce its prison population by more than 30,000 inmates due to pervasive overcrowding. And the State of California is unlikely to build more prisons because it is totally bankrupt although not technically bankrupt. Only the State of Illinois is more indebted.

The average time a person will now serve for the crime of homicide

---

63. Sabol, William J., PhD, Couture, Heather, and Harrison, Paige M., Bureau of Justice Statistics, Prisoners in 2006 (Washington, DC: US Department of Justice, December 2007), NCJ219416, pp. 5-6

is less than seven years. Seven years for murder? It is a fact. The jails are so clogged with prohibition prisoners that we have no place to keep violent and hardened criminals: the people who assault you, your spouse or your child. We have no choice but to put them back on the streets where many are repeat offenders. Isn't it reasonable that these facts are contributing to serious crime's *real* victims?

America now imprisons a greater percentage of its people than any country in the world! More than Russia. Even more than Communist China, which rules over one fourth of all The People on the face of the earth. And the numbers are rapidly growing. As ACLU researcher Elizabeth Alexander reports, "Between 1970 and 2005, the number of men, women, and children locked up in this country has grown by an historically unprecedented 700%. As a result, the United States locks up almost a quarter of the prisoners in the entire world. In fact, if all our prisoners were confined in one city, that city would be the fourth largest in the country."[64] The number of people imprisoned in America is unconscionable, but especially so in a country which claims to be the champion of Freedom and Liberty for the world!

What is Government's solution to the problems of crime? More! More jails. More prisons. More officers. More secret police. More so-phisticated equipment. More radar blimps. More electronics-equipped planes. More helicopters. More ships. More speedboats. More listen-ing devices. More phone taps. More searches. More seizures. More personnel to make it all function. In short, using more money to create more Government! This is (and has been), we are told, the solution. And guess who gets to pay for it all? But where are the benefits to The People? Prohibition of drugs benefits all those who derive wealth, power, privilege, and status from association with Government, but it defies the laws of economics and is amplifying crime, for which

---

64. Alexander, Elizabeth, "Michigan Breaks the Political Logjam: A New Model for Reducing Prison Populations," American Civil Liberties Union (November 2009), p. 3.

it claims to be the solution. Prohibition cannot work, so the question now becomes how much destruction to resources and lives, and how much increased crime will be tolerated before the tipping point is reached and Americans realize the war on drugs was lost before it was even begun.

DYNAMICS OF DISTRIBUTION

The of the biggest misconceptions regarding drugs is that they are spread by drug pushers. It is very unlikely that your child would buy drugs for the first time from a stranger. Danger to children from interacting with strangers is learned at an early age. However, if your child is approached by one of his peers, a friend whom he knows and for whom he has some trust, the outcome may be quite different. It is a natural biological trait for human beings to be curious. They want to explore. They want to try new things. This is a trait of almost all mammals. It is also characteristic that this trait is heightened in the young.

Drugs are rarely spread by drug pushers. Pushers function more as various size cogs in the supply chain. Drugs are *spread* by drug users. Why? Generally because of the price. If the price of drugs is too high for a user to support his desired use (or habit), the easiest method of affording drugs is to sell them on a small scale and use the profit to purchase drugs for their own use. Let's look at a very common example. A user purchases one ounce of low-quality marijuana for one hundred dollars. It is divided into four quarter-ounce bags and sold for forty dollars each. Three are sold, paying for the initial investment (plus a tidy profit), and the fourth is "free" for the user's personal consumption. Since this activity is illegal, who becomes the most promising target for sale? People the user knows and trusts and who they believe will not inform on them. His friends. Possibly your kids! In this manner, a huge percentage of users become salesmen for the system. They inadvertently promote usage, rarely, at least *at first,* for profit, but rather just to pay for their own use of drugs.

But then something else begins to happen. It is natural that those friends whom they have introduced to drugs will look to them for safe supply. As some of the newcomers are faced with the same high price dilemma (to support their growing desired use), they also begin to introduce drugs to their friends. Soon they are buying more and more. As in any commodity, bigger purchases mean a volume discount on price. Our original user now finds himself in the position of buying kilos (about 2.2 pounds), instead of ounces. Now, instead of supplying only his own drug needs, his drug purchases have evolved into a small business. Since marijuana is a weed and will grow anywhere, users may discover they can grow enough in their bedroom closet to net thousands of dollars, since high quality weed buds are literally worth ten times as much by weight as silver. Money may not grow on trees, but it is certainly attached to weeds. For more than a decade, marijuana has surpassed corn as the largest cash crop grown in America. What new vistas are in our original user's economic reach?

That new car? That new boat? Illegality also breeds secrecy. From earliest childhood we learn not to "tell on" our friends, and since everyone is interacting with people they know and trust, they feel safe. And they usually are! But now that they have become "dealers," they are a primary target of the legal system. Even though the percentage of those caught is very tiny, the actual number of individuals convicted is very high, and the destruction of their productivity is an additional cost that is seldom calculated by those who think in numbers of compliance.

ADDICTS AND PRICE

So far, we have only addressed the casual user. What about those addicted to hard drugs? What about the person who would steal or even kill you to support his habit? Once again, the answer is in the artificially inflated price. In order to understand the price dynamics of addiction, let's investigate an extreme example of a $500-per-day heroin addict. What exactly does that mean? It means that this poor soul has become addicted to the point that it will take $500 worth of drugs each day to completely satisfy his habitual needs. A lesser amount of heroin will help "keep the wolf away," but given the choice and money, he will "use" $500 worth of drugs. But a lesser amount becomes critical for him. True heroin addiction is far more of a struggle to avert feeling gut-wrenchingly sick than it is to feel good. We have all seen the television depiction of withdrawal. For most addicts, Hollywood's depiction is somewhat over-sensationalized. But for a few, the symptoms of withdrawal become so severe that the addict can no longer function without the minimum amount, with symptoms including insomnia, diarrhea, abdominal cramps, nausea, sweating, chills, runny eyes and nose, anxiety and irritability, and in very extreme cases hallucination.

Our addict is either in a state of feast or famine. In periods of feast, his drug needs are met, and he is of little danger to anyone. He lies around in the stupor of his drug-induced high and has his mental trip to who knows where (or cares for that matter). He feels good, and stealing from, or assaulting someone is the last thing on his mind.

In periods of famine, however, our user's entire focus shifts to obtaining drugs. More correctly, his focus is on obtaining enough money to buy the drugs he must have to satisfy his needs. He feels bad. As time passes the addict's sense of anxiety and panic grows because he knows from past experience that the symptoms of his withdrawal are going to increase and his condition will progressively deteriorate. In this state he becomes a danger to everyone with whom he comes in contact. His family is no more immune than yours. He usually begins with stealing from his own family, until he is cast out, at which time he often progresses to burglary. Each time he commits a crime to satisfy his need, it becomes easier. He is "rewarded" with need satisfaction? Haven't heard of this phrase? In time, many progress past burglary to assault, or even worse. Steal-reward. Assault-reward. Kill-reward.

No number of laws or jails can prevent this cycle in a free society. Do you want to give up *your* Freedom so society can attempt to prevent destructive behavior in this individual? Our addict does not care about your morality! His entire focus is on need and reward. However, there is a simple way to end his need to commit crime. To end the destruction he creates. To end the stealing. To end the assaults. To end the killing. Simply allow him to satisfy his basic need and let him wallow in Never Never Land.

For the addict, it is the high price that compels him to commit crimes. If our heroin addict went to the hospital and purchased the same amount of drugs which cost him $500 on the street, they would only cost him a couple of bucks. If drugs were legal he could *afford* them. The addict's focus is not on committing crimes; his focus is on preventing the onset of withdrawal. If he is able to satisfy that need, he ceases to be a danger. Our lives and those of our children are safer. Instead of society being harmed, the problem becomes focused on the addict who must live with the choices he is making. This is why, for example, caffeine addicts are safe people. They can afford their drug.

Some will point out that lowering the price of a commodity will normally result in more purchases. Heads up comparisons are difficult to find when the commodity is drugs, but comparisons we have do not necessarily support this conclusion. While hard drugs are illegal in Holland, the Dutch have had a tolerant policy toward marijuana for many years, and prices are modest as compared to America. One might predict low price would result in far greater usage. This is not the case. Statistics show Americans smoke twice as much marijuana as the Dutch on a per capita basis.

This may be because societal mores cannot as easily be brought to bear in America because of the secrecy surrounding marijuana usage. Possibly illegality skews recruitment of new addicts. Or possibly more of the young are tempted into trying it due to the allure of doing something they shouldn't be doing such as eating the "forbidden fruit."

One tenet of Freedom is that mankind has the right to make choices on his own behalf. If a man chooses self-destructive behavior, society has every right to reason with him and attempt to help him. Society does not have the right or the responsibility to use force to prevent men from making destructive choices that do not infringe on the rights of others. Equally important, Society has no obligation to take care of him for choosing to bring about his own destruction. That should be the role of charities, not of Government. Local charities are a better judge of those who are truly deserving of help than Government regulations, which always paint with too broad a brush.

BUREAUCRACY OF A SINGLE CRIME

Consider for a moment the number of bureaucrats who can become involved for a single crime. Number one is the operator/dispatcher who directs an officer to the crime scene.

Beyond that you may have an arresting officer, someone to transport the criminal, a booking officer, jailers for each of the various shifts, multiple support personnel to cook, clean, etc.; an investigating officer; a prosecuting attorney; a defense attorney also paid by the State if the defendant has no resources, as with most addicts; clerks who keep track of the paperwork; transportation officers to the courtroom;

a bailiff; court reporter; a judge; and the judge's support personnel.

If the person is convicted, you now have a continuation of all of the above personnel involved in the previous jailing and transportation phase until the convict can be transferred to the State or Federal facility. Then the entire chain of Government "employment" begins again. You have transportation officers of the "new" system both state or federal; indoctrination officers; clerks; support personnel; jailers, etc.—which are now associated with the prison system. Add it all up and it costs us about $40,000 per year to keep our criminal locked up after he is in the prison system—$40,000 *each*! And after the usual "early release," the "rehabilitated" prisoners are transferred into the parole system and we begin an entirely new bureaucratic drain on our resources.

The cheapest thing involved in the prison system is building them. The politicians will scream for more prisons and fight over the money to build them. This is a misdirection from the real cost. It is far more costly to operate prisons than to construct them, though both go to the bottom line of resources forever lost to society. As one typical example, a 2008 report of prisons in the State of Connecticut calculated that the average per inmate cost of incarceration in 2006 was $45,164 per year, with a low at the Willard/Cybulski Correctional institution of $29,493, and a high at the Northern Correctional Institution of $100,385.5 As expected, it costs even more for Federal Prisons, with America having the highest cost of any country in the world. It is also estimated that the cost has been and is currently growing faster than any other country in the world. Due to health costs alone (as the prison population ages), the costs are expected to increase more than 10 percent per year.

What is the accounting "bottom line"? We can send those we now incarcerate to damned fine colleges for less money than we can keep them in prison, and demographics of an aging population predict that costs are on the verge of skyrocketing. The path we are on is financially unsustainable in a free society and would be an intolerable burden to even the most totalitarian.

SAVE THE CHILDREN

One of the most effective propaganda tools of all time is to evoke the mantra of saving children. Because every parent fears their child's life might be lost to drugs, saving children is one of the most widely utilized themes for justifying drug prohibition and the attending government usurpation of civil liberties. It is probably the most singularly unifying reason among those who support drug prohibition. But there is one *major* problem regarding save-the-children-from-drugs argument. With the trillions of dollars spent on prohibition of a handful of drugs, with all of the broken families and stigmatized lives, with the horrendous economic cost and loss of productivity, with the growth of the police state mentality, with significant loss of civil liberties, and with prisons jammed so full, we have to contract with county jails to hold overflowing prison inmates, *it is easier for our children to buy marijuana or cocaine than it is for them to buy beer or alcohol.* If you do not believe the truth of this statement, don't trust the propaganda of Government statistics and percentages of compliance; simply ask the kids. Almost all of them either know where they can buy, or know whom to ask and find out where to buy drugs, while buying alcohol is far more problematic. *Prohibition fosters rather than decreases the availability of drugs for children.* There is a simple explanation. Businesses that sell alcohol to minors risk the loss of their licenses and livelihood. Drug deals are consummated in the shadow world of illegality where the price has become high enough that suppliers are willing to take the risk. And as we have seen by the dynamics of distribution, the kids start out buying from their peers who are selling drugs as a means of affording the high price. The observable fact that children have easier access to drugs because of drug prohibition is one of the most ironic and disturbing of all of the unintended consequences produced by those who think they can use Government as a solution for greater good. Dictated by the laws of economics, high price caused by prohibition is the problem, not the solution!

CHAPTER 21

SIEGE MENTALITY

THE VAST MAJORITY OF THOSE WHO enforce our laws are honorable citizens to whom society owes great gratitude. But as law enforcement becomes more centralized, it tends to develop a siege mentality, an us-versus-them attitude on the part of law enforcement personnel, which holds a dangerous hidden potential among a small percentage of the enforcers. This situation represents a threat to Freedom, which is amplified because the persons involved are the front line engaging in the daily application of force. We see this in the centralized police forces of every totalitarian state.

Abuse and corruption are handmaidens of power, and law enforcement is one form of the direct exercise of power. Petty corruption is endemic, but it can be held at tolerable levels through administrative procedures, an independent judiciary, and a free press, among other factors. The siege mentality problem, however, goes beyond mere petty corruption; it appears whenever police power ceases to be exclusively applied to dealing with individual crimes, and begins to be used to achieve political, social or ideological ends sought by those who control the police organization itself. In this process, the police force begins to resemble a military, rather than strictly a law enforcement organization, and we may hear it called not just the "police," but the "secret police." It is at this point that the siege mentality problem rears its ugly head.

Fortunately, society has a defense against this danger, and that is to maintain a decentralization of the powers of law enforcement, placing the greatest degree of primary authority so that it resides at the local level. Decentralized police powers will always be more conducive to the protection of Freedom with the single exception of those situations where the local population is itself extremely polarized, and one group has the power to intimidate another. Examples of this are the Tutsi-Hutu conflicts in Rwanda and Burundi; conflicts between the indigenous peoples and the introduced Russian population of the republics of the former Soviet Union; and of course, the American south during the Jim Crow era. Even in these cases, however, a form of centralization is the true root of the problem in that the police forces are controlled (centralized) by the dominant group at the expense of the oppressed group. Such situations may be described as *locally* centralized, in that they are not truly representative of the community as a whole.

To the extent that the function of law enforcement is centralized, the imposition of Government authoritarian rule is made easier. The enforcers have fewer feelings of allegiance to those they do not know. The People are less trustful of enforcers they have little control over and often oppose rules they have little direct hand in creating.

This is why an oppressive State will tend to prefer using outside forces to put down local disturbances instead of using local enforcers who might feel more kinship with The People.

In the Tiananmen Square Protests of 1989 in China, as communist regimes across the world were beginning to collapse, the leaders of the communist Peoples Republic of China faced an escalating dilemma as protests broke out in cities across the country. Most important were disturbances in the capital, Beijing, where local police were reluctant to use force against the unarmed protesters who had occupied Tiananmen Square. Elements of the twenty-seventh Army of the People's Liberation Army were rapidly moved across China from distant Hebei province, out of "necessity" to "maintain order" in Beijing. The twenty-seventh Army was commanded by Yang Jianhua, nephew of Yang Shangkun, then President of the PRC, an iconic figure in the communist leadership as he was one of the few remaining leaders who had personally participated in Mao Zedong's famous Long March of the 1940s. Having positioned loyal army units from outside Beijing, the Marxist strongman Deng Xiaoping (1904–1997), who was the effective ruler of China from 1978–1990, ordered the protest crushed, and with The People unarmed and reduced to throwing rocks and Molotov cocktails, totalitarian rule was brutally reestablished under the treads of tanks by Yang Jianhua's troops, who felt little kinship with The People of Beijing.

This outcome stands in stark contrast to the 1991 attempted coup in the Soviet Union, and those protesting for Freedom led by Boris Yeltsin (1931–2007). Many local troops stationed in Moscow were persuaded to defect and protect the Russian White House. Others defended the popular mass demonstrations or withdrew rather than engage the protestors.

In the modern makeup of political views and prejudices, it is generally true that people who think of themselves as liberals tend to glorify civilian bureaucrats, while distrusting military and police officers, those who call themselves conservatives, do just the opposite. In truth, all aspects of Government need to be viewed through a skeptical lens. Law enforcement is not immune to the increased corruption accompanying centralization of Government, and is an extension of the principle that the degree of corruption is commensurate to the degree of increased power, as stated in the well-known dictum of Lord Acton that, "Power tends to corrupt, and absolute power corrupts absolutely."

Moreover, the corruption of those Government workers who are armed, and thus able to administer deadly force, is more serious than the corruption of garden-variety bureaucrats; a siege mentality among armed enforcers can be especially frightening and destructive of Freedom.

Military sieges produce an uncompromising mentality for those wrapped up in the moment of conflict. One classic example, and the deadliest siege on record, is the Nazi siege of Leningrad (1941–1944), lasting 849 days with an estimated 4.5 million casualties.[65] But the polarization and determination caused by a siege mentality is not a modern phenomenon, and is evidenced by conflicts throughout history. The siege of Petersburg (1864–1865) in the American Civil War produced an estimated 70,000 causalities[66], and the siege of Jerusalem in the First Jewish-Roman War in AD 70 produced casualty estimates ranging from 60,000 to 1,100,000.[67] It is a trait of human beings that the us-against-them mentality can be so amplified that rather than capitulate, many will literally starve to death and others will engage in starving them. As the duration of a siege is extended, the two sides increasingly view each other in ways that are less human and more adversarial.

My point here is not to denigrate the fanaticism, or heroism, of the besieged or besiegers in a wartime situation. For the besieged, often, the willingness to endure suffering rather than surrender may have important strategic consequences. By tying up the German Army for more than two years, the Leningrad resistance very possibly saved

65.Glantz, David (2001), *The Siege of Leningrad 1941–44: 900 Days of Terror*, Zenith Press, Osceola, WI, ISBN 0-7603-0941-8. p. 220

66. a b Grant, p. 231 http://en.wikipedia.org/wiki/List_of_battles_by_casualties#Sieges_and_urban_combat

67. Josephus, *The Wars of the Jews* VI.9.3

Russia from Nazi conquest. The fanaticism of the besieged may also have a logical basis in that the fate of the captured was often worse than starvation, particularly in Medieval times when long, slow, torturous death was the potential fate of the conquered. Similarly, the besiegers often suffered equally or worse, but knew that discontinuing the siege could be disastrous for themselves and their country.

But what justification can there be for such extreme fanaticism in domestic situations, where there is no actual siege, but only the mentality? Any sense of heroism disappears, and all that remains is the fanaticism.

As authority is centralized away from local control, an increased siege mentality relationship develops between The People and the enforcers. Each side becomes increasingly more suspicious and fearful of the other, and the us-against-them attitude, the siege mentality, grows apace. Human beings have varying abilities to resist the negative consequences of this trend, but unfortunately, some men have specific personality traits that subconsciously make them respond by an intense bonding to their fellow enforcers which exacerbates the effect such that, under the right circumstances, there is no abuse of which they are not capable. They are convinced that their function is necessary, right and just. They only need the capable leader to involve themselves in the most heinous of atrocities, and the psychological dynamic of the conflict draws them to both sides, one as perceived victims (of persecuted causes) and the other as perceived preservers of order. When this tendency operates without the benefit of a local ethos to keep both sides in check, the conflict is often escalated, resulting in the imposition of draconian authority. Government often uses the conflicts created by centralization of power to justify the growth of more Government and to usurp rights of The People, based on an alleged imperative to preserve order.

On the other side of the line, the increasing siege mentality is at work as well. Frustrated by an inability to achieve political goals through legitimate means, some people inevitably become radicalized and begin to pursue their goals through violent tactics, of which the most notable is terrorism. Although it is by no means a new phenomenon, terrorism has become an accepted tool of many of the disaffected in modern times. From the Basques of Spain to the Tamils of Sri Lanka, ethnic and other groups have sought to solve their political problems, real or imagined, by seeking to sow fear among The People of the groups against whom they feel and perhaps are oppressed. One thing that is new is the scale of terrorist activity, particularly on the part of Islamic fundamentalists such as those who belong to al Qaeda and similar organizations. An in-depth analysis of the nature of the terrorist threat has been dealt with by many other commentators, good and bad, and is not relevant to this book.

However, it is clear that the terrorists of the al Qaeda type are a threat to The People of all nations, both directly and because the response of the threatened, exhibits many of the signs of siege mentality. Freedom is thus jeopardized by both those who, if they were victorious, would impose one of the most repressive regimes ever devised, and from those who, in determining policies to protect The People from such a fate, are potentially threats to Freedom themselves.

Whether activated by a fear of terrorism or some other cause, another threat to Freedom in a condition of siege mentality are those who subconsciously worship authority and who seek enforcement for the perceived status associated with it.

They believe in rigid authority to preserve order. This personality type is easily molded into blindly following and obeying the authority they so cherish. When ordered to violate your Liberty, they will not hesitate. They perceive themselves as the last heroic line of defense between lawlessness and order. The State becomes the focal point of their authority worship, and they derive perceived status and respect from their association with it. In turn, the State readily uses and promotes them as tools for the imposition of its authoritarian policies.

When led to extreme application of force, these types are easy to recognize. The Nazi SS and death camp personnel and the Soviet KGB stand out as twentieth century examples. But when the exercise of force is less blatant, they become like chameleons, integrated into the bureaucracy of the State. They are like smoldering coals waiting only for the right wind to unleash their power. When that power is unleashed, it will attempt to consume all Liberty standing before it, because Freedom is the antithesis of the authoritarian rule to which these men pay homage.

Since centralization of power dramatically increases the authority and perceived status the authority worshipers seek, it is one explanation of why enforcement activity becomes a focal point of their ambition. Society must be ever watchful, for centralization of power can unleash even inhuman abuse if circumstances are ripe and if the wrong leaders can falsely justify their abuse of The People. The latent authoritarianism of this type only awaits the proper circumstances and orders to make the transition to outright oppression, using the guise of "maintaining order." They are never "responsible"; they are only "obeying orders." They will never consider the moral implications of what they are doing because they fundamentally believe that the most moral of all activities is the preservation of order instead of the preservation of Freedom.

As I have said, but feel compelled to repeat, the vast majority of enforcement personnel are not corrupt or dangerous and do not blindly follow authority. Most are good, honorable, and honest people who provide a necessary, and often thankless service to society. They routinely put their own well-being at risk to protect The People. They present no danger to our Liberty, and many will work to help us restore it. They suffer as much from a siege mentality and polarization of society, caused by centralization of power and imposition of unjust laws, as you and I do. Their jobs are made less rewarding and more difficult by the increasing wedge of mistrust created as the power of law enforcement is more centralized.

There was a time in America when law enforcement was a neighborhood occupation. The policeman was a friend of those he protected. He was given respect, and he had respect for those under his protection. Children were taught to seek him out if lost, or in time of trouble. As we have centralized authority and disarmed The People, we have created more fear than respect. The neighborhoods have little say in who protects them. They have become suspicious of the police who can then expect little help from The People. Unjust laws produce disrespect for more just laws. This makes it easier for law-breakers to be accepted back into society instead of being shunned.

Furthermore, open disapproval and shunning by one's peers is a far greater deterrent to non-violent crime than incarceration or rehabilitation. Laws intended to legislate morality, creating crimes where there is no victim, will inevitably disaffect large segments of the population, leading to disrespect for the enforcers and for the law in general. Suspicion and mistrust between the enforcers and The People grows in proportion to centralization of power, imposition of authoritarian rule, and the sheer volume of laws.

It is also important to understand, as the worldwide economy totters ever closer to collapse, that the siege mentality from centralization of law enforcement may become pivotal during the chaos which would surely follow such an event. It used to be easy to imagine such an eventuality as so unlikely that it need not be factored into the equation of policymaking. Doomsday economic scenarios were thought to be little more than the imaginings of conspiracy theorists and crackpot economists. But it is impossible to maintain that view any more. As European nations and American states face literal bankruptcy as a result of their socialist policies, and riots demanding the continuation of untenable spending spread from place to place, it is clear that the struggle between preserving order and Freedom could easily be elevated into a struggle that will define whether our descendants will be Free, or slaves of the State. As worrisome as terrorism and the potential for overreaction to terrorism are, it may tragically turn out that the most serious cause of a destructive siege mentality is the bankruptcy of collectivist economics.

PART IV. REBUILDING AMERICAN FREEDOM

★ ★ ★

CHAPTER 22

A PROGRAM FOR FREEDOM

Up to this point we have discussed the nature of Freedom and its relationship to human achievement. We have traced the history of this relationship, and found that the degree of Freedom men and women have enjoyed has waxed and waned over time. We have seen how, in the past century, there has been an intellectual, political and from time-to-time military battle between the forces of Freedom and those who believe in centralized control of human decision-making—with themselves always as the controllers.

We have discussed a number of important challenges to Freedom which exist at this particular moment, in the early years of the second decade of the twenty-first century. I state the point as simply as I can. Freedom is declining in absolute terms, in this country and in many others throughout the world. We face a potentially catastrophic reduction in the extent to which The People are able to make decisions about their own lives. *What is to be done?* "[68] What corrective actions

---

68. Written in 1902, *What is To Be Done?* is Vladimir Lenin's most important book about tactics addressing three main issues, "the character and main content of our political agitation; our organizational tasks; and the plan for building, simultaneously and from various sides, a militant, all-Russia organization."

can we take to return America to the pathway of Freedom and the flourishing of humanity that it produces?

That is the purpose of this chapter. Some of the remedies I will propose are broad goals that can be realized through legislative action or through Amendments to our Constitution. Others are everyday actions that we can take such as helping to build consensus, or to holding our representatives accountable.

CONGRESS

Thomas Jefferson noted over 200 years ago that once a person is elected to public office, he can generally maintain the position for as long as he so desires. This tendency, which Jefferson so accurately observed, has been amplified today by campaign finance laws and favorable redistricting that make it almost impossible to challenge a sitting legislator. The reelection rate in Congress has long averaged over 96 percent, and most people remain in office for decades after being elected.

Jefferson's concern notwithstanding, the Founding Fathers were virtually unanimous in thinking of the U.S. House of Representatives as the Government body that above all others should be considered a short-term commitment of volunteer public service. They never intended Representatives to become professional politicians with what has effectively become lifetime tenure. Their concept was that a respected local citizen—farmer, lawyer, businessman, etc.—would agree to set aside his personal affairs for a few years and *serve* the community by representing them in the capital. The House was the "people's branch" of Government, and a bulwark against the possibility that an elitist ruling class would erode the rights and Freedoms that the Founders had so ardently strived to protect in the Constitution and Bill of Rights. They sought to make sure the American Congress would never become a privileged class as were the titled classes of the monarchies of Europe.

Today we can see clearly that their concerns were well-founded. Once elevated to a permanent position with a high expectation of reelection, our politicians no longer feel accountable to The People. They have indeed begun to act as a privileged class. They have exempted themselves from the laws they pass which govern The People. They have voted themselves extra compensation in the form of ever larger salaries, special health care benefits and luxurious pensions. And as their tenure extends itself, they justify even more abuse as tradition, building upon previous abuse by those who have come before them. The People's supposed representatives have indeed become professional politicians. As such they cannot be said to represent The People because there is a fundamental conflict of interest. A professional politician derives his or her compensation, power, privilege, status, and graft for the corruption from association with Government. Given natural human tendencies, many are seduced by power and are unlikely to support the basic ideal of preservation of the Rights of The People. To do so would be tantamount to reducing their own power and influence. With no intention of leaving office and returning to life among The People, and with their lifelong goal being to exercise the power they derive from Government, many have exhibited a tendency to vote themselves more power, rather than less.

Impose Term Limits on Senators and Members of Congress. The People must reassert their rights over Government as a prelude to meaningful change. Therefore we must amend the Constitution to limit the time any individual may hold office. This should not exceed a cumulative maximum of two terms. A member of the House of Representatives should serve no more than a total of four years, the Senate twelve years. This would reestablish our Forefathers concept that the House of Representatives should be more an act of voluntary service rather than tenure, complete with perks and privileges, in a professional body. As to the Senate, I will write more later in this chapter. For now, I will simply note that by serving for a potential twelve years, they will be able to ensure continuity.

Repeal the Seventeenth Amendment. Most of the key elements comprising the Federal Government of the United States are well known to the world. However, this author believes that a key element conceived by the Founders has been lost, and is rarely studied today. It provided a key element of restraint against the leviathan machine of Government.

The Constitution set up a complex set of checks and balances, including an executive branch, a bicameral legislative branch and a judicial branch, each with interlocking dependencies and different areas of authority. This was conceived as a way to prevent any element of Government from garnering too much power. What has been lost is that the *states* were also granted a seat at the shared Federal table of power. The states have lost their representation in the system of checks and balances so artfully crafted by the Constitution, and the result has been progressively harmful by empowering the growth of the Federal Government at the expense of the states. This situation is traceable to one particular action: the Seventeenth Amendment to the Constitution, adopted in 1913. The amendment changed the way Senators are elected with the unintended consequence of negating one of the key checks and balances conceived by the framers of the Constitution.

The Senate was designated in the Constitution as the representative body of the states, and its members were to be chosen *by the various state legislatures*. Our Forefathers intended that the House of Representatives be The People's voice, but they conceived the Senate as representing *each state's government*. They also believed Senators would have to face fewer distractions, and that they would be less vulnerable to the influence of large outside interests. At least selection by state legislatures provided a means to see that the Senate was more representative of statewide and regional interests than of large national and international financers and corporations.

It may seem counterintuitive that The People can be better served without direct election of Senators. However, the Founders were right in their design, and the harm done to Freedom by the Seventeenth Amendment is observably growing with time. The amount of money necessary to fund Senatorial campaigns has grown to the extent that Senators are more beholden to their fat cat contributors than to The People of their States. *Often, a Senator's largest contributors do not even reside within the States they represent.*

Thus the effect of the Seventeenth Amendment has been a significant *nationalization of Senate elections.* States' rights issues have been pushed to the rear as more emphasis is placed on national issues. Perhaps most destructive of all, states find themselves beset with expensive, unfunded mandates from the Federal Government. In addition, the Executive Branch is ceded more power by default when a complicit Senate does not stand up for states' rights. We find unelected bureaucracies in charge of various agencies and commissions wielding broad powers over the States; over and over these bureaucracies frustrate state governors and legislatures seeking to balance their budgets, to keep taxes down and to provide workable solutions to often unique problems that impact their state. The rightful power of the states is being usurped with each new mandate and each new decree. The latitude and scope of this shift of power is now increasing at a staggering pace, placing an ever greater financial burden on the states and simultaneously hampering productivity of their businesses and the Freedom of their People.

Direct election of Senators was a topic of great debate in the late 1800s. In fact, by the time the process for the Seventeenth Amendment began, many of the States had already instituted policies of statewide elections for their Senate representative rather than being chosen by their legislatures. The direct election proponents sought to place power in the hands of The People rather than the cloakrooms of the state legislature. Unfortunately, the Amendment had the unintended consequence of upsetting the careful balance of interests in the Federal Government, by removing a key check—the involvement of the states in national decision-making.

It is imperative that we restore the states' seat at the table of power by repealing the Seventeenth amendment, thereby putting selection of Senators back into the hands of state legislatures.

<u>End Special Treatment for Congress</u>. Congress should abide by all laws imposed on the American people and *should be banned from exempting themselves from any law*. The single exception should be unitary exemption from misdemeanor laws, which might prevent presence for voting, for example, by delaying a Congressman for a traffic violation while on his way to an important vote. Congress should be subject to all felony laws and penalties, including tax violations, bribery, collusion, conspiracy, etc. Congressional offices should also be required to abide by any regulation or restriction imposed on any other organization, including labor, safety, environmental, and civil rights laws. A major purpose of this requirement would be to reduce the likelihood that burdensome laws would be passed at all.

Congress should also be barred from voting itself pay raises, and its salary should be fixed. One means of achieving this would be to have congressional pay increase by the *lesser* of either the Consumer Price Index or two percent, and should be adjusted every two years in line with election of the House of Representatives. Members of Congress should collect pay only when in office and there should be no pension or lavish retirement accounts of any kind. All monies in the Congressional retirement fund should be immediately relocated to the Social Security fund, and Congress should participate in the same social programs as are available to The People.

Reform Congressional Rules. When the siren lust for power becomes especially great, Congress finds means to avoid the restrictions provided by its own rules. Probably the most blatant way this is accomplished is to temporarily suspend the rules. Once the rules have been suspended, The People are literally subject to whatever points of abuse and/or corruption the offending legislature decrees. Suspending the rules is only one of a myriad of corrupt procedural tricks and machinations used by Congress to circumvent its restrictions and to force its agenda on The People.

Let's consider a recent example of another type of subterfuge Congress employs. The lame duck Congress of 2010 was attempting to pass a so-called "food safety" bill granting new regulatory powers to the FDA and providing for thousands of new agents, much to the delight of large agribusiness and their lobbyists. Small family farmers and ranchers were fighting the proposal because they knew sooner or later they would find themselves unable to afford compliance with the onerous regulations and mountains of paperwork that inevitably grow from such laws. There was stiff and growing opposition, and with Congress' term of office rapidly drawing to a close, and with a pending massive shift in power to the incoming opposition, the Democrat House leadership used an egregious procedural trick to force their "food safety" legislation through without debate or vetting. Here's how it worked: In 2009, the Senate had amended the Military Construction and Veterans Affairs and Related Agencies Appropriations Act and sent it back to the House where is should have gone to a conference committee to address the differences between the versions passed by each chamber. The House had never acted on the bill and, with the year almost at an end, it might never have become law. But it proved to be a procedural vehicle to bypass rules and enact the food safety bill and a host of other legislation. While new bills must pass a committee vote, the defense bill had already passed through the committee process. On the floor, an amendment completely stripped the bill of its original contents; then another series of so-called amendments replaced the now-nonexistent content with a conglomeration of pending bills that the powers-that-be desperately wanted to enact before the deadline. Included was the food safety bill. The House leadership then circumvented returning to customary parliamentary review by creating a Special Rule (House Resolution 1755, which passed by only one vote) to bring up the bill immediately. To add insult to injury, the bill was renamed the "The Full-Year Continuing Appropriations Act, 2011."

The newly named House Resolution 3082 was then introduced in conjunction with the new Special Rule. It would be considered "in order," meaning it would not go through the committee process *and* all normal procedural measures would be circumvented. Reading of the bill was waived and no "points of order" were permitted. Debate was limited to final passage (no amendments permitted) and for only forty minutes. HR 3082 was introduced and passed by only six votes. The "Military Construction and Veterans Affairs and Related Agencies Appropriations Act" was transmogrified into the "Full-Year Continuing Appropriations Act, 2011" and *passed in less than two and one-half hours* from the time "Special Rule 1755" was installed. The bill with its significant expansion of power and reach of the FDA—not to mention empowering thousands of new Government agents—was never even read but was simply railroaded into law. This is an unconscionable abuse of power. Unfortunately, it is only one example of what has become an alarming trend of accepted operations in Congress.

Here are two practical changes that we can immediately make that would have prevented the political chicanery of our example. First, support, and demand that your Congressman support, a "Read the Bills Act" which would provide that all bills be published online at least seven days before any vote including procedural votes on them. Furthermore, every word of every bill must be read in its entirety out loud in each chamber before a vote may be taken. The only exception to the 7-day Rule would be a declaration of war.

The second thing we can do is to promote a "One Subject at a Time Act," which would require that each bill must deal with one subject and *only* one subject. Sometimes known as "riders," bills which cannot pass on their own merit are often attached to important or popular legislation which frequently involve last-minute budget appropriations. In some instances unpopular "riders" have also been attached in an attempt to kill legislation. The One Subject at a Time Act will prevent Congress from passing unpopular measures by attaching them to popular or urgent bills that have majority support. It will also prevent the creation of behemoth conglomerations of bills which become so large as to be beyond comprehension, such as the longest bill ever enacted by Congress, the 2010 "Affordable Health Care for America Act," popularly known as "Obamacare," that contains 314,900 words on some 2,700 pages. It is also important to note that both Democrats and Republicans have been equal opportunity offenders when it comes to producing behemoth bills. Of the ten longest bills, five were introduced by Democrats, and five by Republicans.

As a further restriction of the One Subject at a Time Act, the title of the bill must describe what the bill will actually do. This will prevent propagandistic titles such as the "Protect America Act" which give no indication of what the bill entails, and often has little to do with the bill's actual subject matter.

Another abuse by Congress has been development of the process of "earmarking" funds. Earmarks are mandates inserted into appropriations bills directing funds to specific projects, usually in the district of the Congressman initiating the earmark. The most serious criticisms of earmarks are lack of accountability, transparency and conflict of interest. Most, though not all, earmarks can legitimately be associated with what has come to be called "pork barrel" spending, "bringing home the bacon" to the Congressman's district or to favored special interests. The Constitution clearly gives Congress the power to direct appropriations, and doing so is often perfectly legitimate and desirable.

The abuse would be curtailed if all earmarks were vetted through the One Subject at a Time Act by considering each individual earmark as a unique subject, and therefore requiring a separate bill. As such, they would also be subject to the Read the Bills act providing Internet publication, additional transparency, and time for debate.

THE EXECUTIVE BRANCH

<u>End the Abuse of Executive Orders and Presidential Directives</u>. The ongoing struggle for power and dominance extends among all the competing interests in Government, and the constitutional concept of checks and balances is designed to maintain proportionality so that no particular branch garners powers not intended for it to wield. In the Executive branch, two of the most egregious violations of this principle are the abuse of "executive orders" and "presidential directives."

Executive Orders are formal instructions from the President to his staff and should be used for the purpose of carrying out the legislative will of the Congress. As a distinguishing element of Presidential power, even the term "executive order" was unknown before the early 1900s. President Franklin Roosevelt dramatically increased the power of the Presidency through use of this new tool. In 1942, during World War II, Roosevelt issued Executive Order 9066, allowing certain areas to be declared as military zones and paving the way for the internment of Japanese Americans. Today, this action is rightly regarded as one of the most egregious abrogations of civil rights in US history—American citizens herded into what may reasonably be called concentration camps for no other reason than their ethnic ancestry.

An earlier example of Rooseveltian executive overreach, perhaps even more devastating in the long run, was Executive Order 6102, which probably exacerbated the duration and severity of the Great Depression. During the Wilson administration of 1917, Congress had passed an act declaring emergency powers to deal with World War I. In 1933, fifteen years after the war had ended, Roosevelt convinced Congress to pass an amendment declaring the emergency *still existed*. He then used the powers he was thereby granted to confiscate all of the privately owned gold in the United States by executive order. Those who did not comply faced the following penalty:

Section 9: Whoever willfully violates any provision of this Executive Order or these regulations or of any rule, regulation or license issued there under may be fined not more than $10,000, or, if a natural person may be imprisoned for not more than ten years or both; and any officer, director, or agent of any corporation who knowingly participates in any such violation may be punished by a like fine, imprisonment, or both.

Few actions in the history of America have affected a more sweeping usurpation of power to Government. Keynesian inflation could not be used to tax The People so long as they put their assets into gold, so Roosevelt simply confiscated the gold at a fixed price and then dramatically increased the price of gold once the deed was done and the gold confiscated. Those among The People who had been prudent in their economic affairs were decimated by the unconscionable sweep of Roosevelt's pen.

There seemed to be no limit to this new Executive determination of power until the Supreme Court struck down Executive Order 10340 by President Harry Truman who tried to nationalize all of America's steel mills. But that example aside, restraint on the use of executive orders has been virtually nonexistent, encouraging succeeding Presidents to ever greater abuse. *Executive orders have even been used to declare war,* a power that is unambiguously reserved to Congress under Article 1, Section 8 of the U.S. Constitution. Although Congress has pushed back, the Executive Branch still does not practice restraint, and even the issue of war declaration through executive order remains largely unsettled.

One thing is certain: The power being wielded by the Executive Branch under the concept of executive orders was never intended by our Forefathers. The legal theory used to derive such fiat powers from the Constitution is questionable at best, but that does not seem to matter with a Supreme Court intent on aggressively arrogating power to the Federal Government.

Unfortunately, this abuse of power is continuing to grow and is untenable if we are to live with Freedom.

Another extension of the concept of executive orders is the use of presidential directives. These powers purportedly arise from agencies or departments that have been delegated power by Congress. While most of the directives thus far issued have been routine administrative announcements or arguably responsible national security directives, the practice is growing, the criteria used for justification is diminishing, and the potential for abuse is rife.

The People have no recourse other than to severely limit, restrict and define or eliminate the power of the Executive Branch in the issuing of executive orders and presidential directives.

Prevent Unelected Bureaucrats in Agencies and Commissions from Legislating. Much like a business, Government must organize itself around rules, practices, and hierarchies in order to function. Government executives and bureaucrats are often perceived as serving in a capacity similar to executives in the private sector. Their rules and practices are viewed as analogous to those which businesses must employ in order to function. But there exist vital and important differences. Government and businesses are so distinct in their functions, means, and objectives that comparisons are superficial at best.

Businesses appeal to desires and needs, and are constrained by the choices of individuals, who make their decisions known each time they purchase or reject products or services. Executives face perpetual evaluation through competition in the marketplace. The means and rules businesses employ in organization and function likewise face the restriction of successfully appealing to the purchasing needs and desires of The People. Inefficiency or disapproval by a significant number of their customers leads to failure or replacement in the business world. Government is different. Rather than engaging in appealing to its customers, that is, its constituents, Government exercises force, either using threat or a punishment, to achieve compliance with rules, regulations, and laws. Nowhere is this distinction more apparent than in the case of the dozens of more-or-less independent agencies and commissions Congress has created and scattered throughout the Executive Branch.

Agencies and commissions can and do become mini-tyrannies, and their Executives become mini-despots. They have little concern for the desires or needs of The People who are their supposed customers because their jobs are secure, and they face little accountability. Evaluation and advancement are more focused on growing their department in numbers of employees and/or size of budget than with approval or disapproval of The People. Because bureaucrats are unelected, they have no direct accountability to the voting public, and although they are theoretically accountable to Congress, their activities are rarely scrutinized. Once created, these agencies and commissions strive to grow in virtual perpetuity.

From where do these agencies and commissions derive their legitimacy? The People have lent Congress the power to construct our laws, but Congress is now delegating that power—the power to make rules and regulations that are in practice indistinguishable from laws—to unelected, unaccountable bureaucrats. And this legislative power ceded to the bureaucrats is only part of the problem.

Congress has also allowed them to serve the functions of judge, jury, and even enforcer of the rules they make, all of which are beyond their rightful duties which should include only investigation and prosecution. Congress has to delegate this authority because of the extraordinary expansion of Government. Given its penchant for highly intrusive Government, Congress would find it virtually impossible to pass all of the necessary legislation. With the Courts already crowded by the overuse of litigation, excessive criminal prosecution for victimless crimes and other reasons, it would also be unfeasible to place the additional burden of agency regulation on the Federal judiciary. Thus Congress has circumvented the judiciary and placed enormous power unintended by the Framers of the Constitution into the hands of its chosen bureaucrats.

Congress has now abdicated so much power to the regulatory agencies and commissions and spawns that these entities have become a direct threat to Liberty and Freedom. Their greatest abuse is the creation of law and public policy by fiat. These agencies simply declare and act as though they have regulatory power and authority; and they generally impose unreasonably onerous penalties to discourage anyone from challenging them. A typical and often used penalty extending far back into the twentieth century is "a fine of ten thousand dollars a day, per occurrence." This type of penalty is favored where normal interaction should produce multiple infractions.

To appreciate the power behind this type of penalty, consider a company that has hundreds (or thousands) of customers and is accused with being out of compliance for six months. *Every infraction* in that six-month period could produce an additional $10,000 fine for *each day* they are out of compliance. As a practical matter, the amount of the fine is arbitrarily applied because the potential maximum often approaches absurdity, but the threat of economic ruin is very real and has a chilling effect on dissent. Also, because violations are adjudicated in an "administrative court" of the agency itself, an accused violator will be facing both an "administrative judge" and lawyers, who are employed by the same agency that has issued the accusation. Is this supposed to be impartial justice? To be sure, if the defendant loses in the administrative court, he can often appeal to the real judicial system, but this places the additional burdens of time and drain on resources required by a secondary fight in the new arena. Another tactic is for the agency to use its power of injunction to shut down a business that protests while the matter is being adjudicated, which can take years in the courts. Even if their business is not shut down, facing millions of dollars in potential fines and years of costly legal battles against Government lawyers, most medium and small businesses are bludgeoned into "compliance." They simply cannot pay the legal fees or take the risk. The bureaucrats view the ruthless use of these tactics as a primary tool for establishing and asserting their authority as they protect their turf and extend the power of their agency.

The accumulation of power is generally attended by the growth of arrogance and hubris. The regulatory bodies created by Congress are now even beginning to challenge the body that ostensibly gave them legitimacy to begin with.

Regulatory agencies with the power to create law by fiat most certainly were never intended by the Framers of our Constitution. It circumvents the checks and balances intended by our Forefathers. Even a majority of Congress cannot easily change regulations created by these agencies if they are supported by an arrogant executive branch or even a determined political minority in the legislative branch.

Having failed to achieve much of his agenda in his first two years in office, and after his policies were strongly rebuked in the election of 2010, President Obama decided to achieve through executive orders and regulatory authority what he has been unable to achieve through legislation. He is not the first President to have done so, but the scope of his legislation by regulatory fiat goes far beyond that of any predecessor.

The Environmental Protection Agency (EPA) has been instructed by the White House to enact regulations to limit greenhouse gas emissions similar to those which failed to pass in Congress. The Executive Branch asserts these powers citing a 2007 Supreme Court ruling that allows the EPA to determine whether carbon dioxide is a hazard to human health. Do we really want a regulatory agency to have the power to circumvent or negate the rightful decision-making power of Congress? At the time of this writing, a bill is being circulated in Congress to strip the EPA of the authority to set greenhouse gas emission limits, but it will face many hurdles, not the least of which is the stated intent of President Obama to veto the bill.

In a second example of regulatory overreach, the Federal Communications Commission (FCC) has recently passed controversial new "net neutrality" regulations of the Internet. The issue is not the good or ill resulting from the regulations, but rather the precedent set by the FCC's new self-created powers to regulate the Internet, which has to date remained remarkably free of Government interference. Using a benign regulation to get a foot in the door is a tactic used by bureaucrats to gain legal precedent. Then, over time, the powers are expanded into more controversial areas, and made more onerous. Once the Government allows agencies to create regulations by fiat, it can be followed by the right to tax; bureaucrats worldwide are salivating over the prospect of taxing the Internet.

<u>Force Congress to address its rightful duties and stop passing its responsibility to unelected bureaucrats</u>. I urge you therefore to support and demand your Representative support the "Write the Laws Act:"

- Congress must write specific legislation with no details left to the bureaucrats.

- All allegations of wrong-doing must be tried in Judicial Branch courts, not by bureaucrats

- All punishments must be rendered by judges, not bureaucrats.

- Executive Branch agencies must be limited to investigation and prosecution.

- Citizens must be held blameless against any Government actions that violate these rules.

- Previous legislation granting legislative and judicial power to bureaucrats should be identified so it can be repealed.

<u>Give the President the Temporary Power of the Line-Item Veto</u>. Until the practice of bundling unrelated legislation by the Congress can be addressed by the One Subject at a Time Act, we should give the President the power of line-item veto. This will allow the President to strike down unrelated segments of laws without having to veto the entire piece of legislation. Used properly, it will provide a means of fighting pork barrel politics, and the practice of forcing unpopular legislation by attaching it to critical legislation. However, the Line-Item Veto should not be considered a substitute for the more important One Subject at a Time Act, and should only be considered a stop-gap measure pending enactment.

THE JUDICIAL BRANCH

The function of a Supreme Court in a Free society is to preserve the rights of The People by assuring that Government does not infringe upon or usurp individual rights or circumvent the restrictions placed on it by the Constitution and the Bill of Rights. It is not to rectify social injustice: That is the domain of elected representatives of The People, the Congress. Neither is the purpose of a Supreme Court to "legislate from the bench," for to do so is to ignore all the political and social input necessary in the legislative process. The proper function of the Supreme Court, and the Judicial Branch as a whole, must be viewed in the context of how its duties relate to the other branches of Government in the exercise of their rightful duties.

The true purpose of a Constitution in any Free society is to place severe limitations on Government. It is to prevent centralization of power and imposition of authoritarian rule. Most of all, it is to guarantee the rights of individual human beings against those who would transgress those rights, including a majority of their fellow citizens, and especially their own Government. All lawful decisions of any Supreme Court should reflect these principles with the realization that the greatest threat to Liberty is Government, which the Court's foremost purpose should be to restrain.

It is intolerable that our elitist, Ivy League educated Supreme Court Justices[69] often perceive themselves as agents of social change, and have shown an increased willingness to continue to usurp more and more of The Peoples' rights and transfer them to the Federal Government.

Here are some potential corrective measures to restore the balance of power now threatened by the Supreme Court:

<u>Allow Congress the Power of Withdrawal of Jurisdiction</u>. One means

---

69. Presently all nine Supreme Court justices attended Ivy League Colleges.

of correcting abuse of power by the Supreme Court is through appellate jurisdiction in the legislature and by selective withdrawal of jurisdiction by the legislature. To ensure that change will not be frivolous or easy to achieve, withdrawal of jurisdiction should require a super majority.

Narrow the definitions of the Commerce Clause, Necessary and Proper Clause, and General Welfare Clause of the Constitution. Such actions, probably through the Amendment process, would be designed to reflect the original intent of the Constitution and curtail the ongoing "interpretive expansion" of the powers by the Court. In the case of the Commerce Clause, this would return the meaning to the intent of expediting the movement of goods and services between the States. The Necessary and Proper Clause should be made clearly applicable to only the "foregoing powers," which are the specifically enumerated powers. A second option would be to eliminate this controversial clause altogether. Narrowing the definition of the General Welfare Clause would reflect Madison's original intent that it must be tied to one of the specifically enumerated powers, and that it was not to be construed as granting any power but instead to be regarded as a statement of purpose.

Change the Oath of Office of Supreme Court Justices. The new oath should include a specific pledge honoring Article 1, Section 8 of the Constitution (Enumerating Powers) and the Ninth and Tenth Amendments[70].

Consider Terms and Term Limits for Justices. Should Supreme Court Justices continue to promote the myth of the Constitution as a "living document" that only they can "interpret," and the above remedies

---

70. The 9th reads: "The enumeration in the Constitution, of certain rights, shall not be construed to deny or disparage others retained by the people." And the 10th reads "The powers not delegated to the United States by the Constitution, nor prohibited by it to the States, are reserved to the States respectively, or to the people."

cannot be instituted or fail to resolve the Supreme Court's usurpation of power, we should have a national debate, and either change how Supreme Court Justices are appointed or have a term limitation of one term limited to six years. It is this author's personal belief that this should be *only a last resort* after failing to achieve a return to true Constitutionalism by implementing the previously suggested remedies.

<u>Strengthen the Jury System</u>. Trial by jury is one of the oldest civil rights, dating back as far as the Magna Carta, in AD 1215. It is an important tool in our struggle to maintain or reassert Freedom without resorting to insurrection. It empowers a minority to defend itself from the majority who would disregard the rights of others. It empowers The People to defend themselves against a Government which has circumvented its Constitutional limitation or barriers. It is a means by which The People are protected from unjust laws. And yet recently, Government has succeeded in diminishing the power and importance of this foremost right.

One of the most important duties we have as citizens in a Free society is to participate as a juror at every possible opportunity and to understand the rights, duties, and responsibilities charged to us in our part of the process.

It has become common practice today that the true responsibility of jurors is kept hidden from The People. This is accomplished through common dogmas developed by attorneys and judges who are agents of the Government. In a typical case, only the jury is truly independent and representative of The People. A Government employee, the judge, interprets the law, decides which evidence can or cannot be admitted and instructs the jury on the parameters of his decision. Prior to the trial, there is a period of jury selection during which both sides are able to question the jurors in order to discover bias. This is appropriate. However, the questioning has come to include any philosophical disagreement the prospective juror may have in prosecuting the particular law at hand. And the system even goes so far as to require an oath by jurors that they will uphold the decisions of the court and the law as decreed and interpreted.

What about unjust laws? An individual who refuses to take the oath is excluded from the jury; thus only those who already agree that the law is just can serve!

All this maneuvering is specifically designed to confuse and manipulate jurors by withholding an understanding of the true power of their position so that they will not exercise the power to determine that the law is unjust with regard to the case in question and, therefore, that the defendant is not guilty.

Jurors do not have the right to strike down laws; their decisions do not set legal precedent since they are trying only the particular case at hand. But jurors do have the inherent right to judge the law as well as the facts in the case before them.

This right of *jury nullification*, as it is known, was common understanding in the early years of the Republic. It was enshrined in the Constitutions of several states, and remains explicit in some of them, including Maryland, Indiana, Georgia and Oregon, with regard to all criminal cases, and in many others for specific kinds of cases, especially libel. But even when these conditions hold, Courts routinely conspire to prevent jurors from understanding this right, and there is probably no courtroom in the country in which a defense lawyer would be permitted to argue that the jury should find his client not guilty because he was charged on the basis of an unjust law.[71]

What a far cry this is from the beginning of the practice of the rights of jurors in America. In 1735, a New York newspaper publisher named John Peter Zenger was put on trial for libeling the Royal

---

71. An attorney who tried to make the argument brilliantly portrayed by actor Paul Newman in the 1982 movie, "The Verdict," for example, would almost surely be gaveled down and severely reprimanded.

governor of the colony. Zenger had indeed printed many criticisms of the Governor in his paper, the *New York Weekly Journal*, but they were all true. That didn't matter, according to British libel law, so all the prosecution had to do was to prove Zenger had in fact printed the accusations. Zenger's attorney, Andrew Hamilton, admitted that he had done so, but went on to make a brilliant argument for liberty.

The case, he argued, was about liberty and political power :Power, Hamilton told the jury, may justly be compared to a great river. While kept within its due bounds it is both beautiful and useful. But when it overflows its banks, it is then too impetuous to be stemmed; it bears down all before it, and brings destruction and desolation wherever it comes. If, then, this is the nature of power, let us at least do our duty, and like wise men who value freedom use our utmost care to support liberty, the only bulwark against lawless power, which in all ages has sacrificed to its wild lust and boundless ambition the blood of the best men that ever lived....

The jurors agreed, and found Zenger not guilty. The case became a celebrated incident in the buildup to the American Revolution and was frequently cited by the Founders in the course of their deliberations on the Constitution. It is the very source of our notion of freedom of the press.

Jury nullification has been an exceptionally valuable tool in ridding the nation of bad laws. In the early 1800s, juries refused to convict several persons accused under the misguided Alien and Sedition Act. Later, northern juries set free many who were accused of harboring slaves in violation of the heinous Fugitive Slave Laws. During the Prohibition Era, the practice of jury nullification was an important expression of The People's resistance to the Twenty-first Amendment, and helped make its repeal in 1933 inevitable.

Opponents of jury nullification frequently point out that the practice can be used for unworthy causes as well, such as the unconscionable verdicts delivered in several cases by racist juries during the Jim Crow era. But it is interesting to note that whether used for good or ill, jury nullification can ultimately promote justice. The racist nullification verdicts incensed the nation, and helped end laws which mandated segregation and racial discrimination, just as the admirable nullification verdicts in the Fugitive Slave Law led to the end of other unjust laws. It seems clear that jury nullification is a powerful tool for justice, and that in the end it allows the will of The People to be expressed. Above all, it is a great bulwark against the power of Government, whenever that power, like a swollen river, becomes destructive and wreaks desolation upon Liberty.

We are beginning to see the fringes of a new nullification movement today in the areas of taxation and drug prohibition. As Government abuse increases, we can hope that more Americans will seek a remedy, once again discovering their true rights as jurors. This power can be brought to bear against those who believe in Government control of our lives through the use of law as an instrument of social change rather than as a means of preventing infringement of rights.

Jury nullification is also a limited form of protection against centralization of authority. If Congress has imposed unjust laws, it becomes incumbent upon each individual community to resist those laws, for the defendant has a right to be tried by the peers of his community, who through a vote of not guilty may reject the Congressional decree. The imposition of the law must be proportioned to the support of the community when exercising their rightful duty as jurors.

There is little greater threat to our Liberty than ignorance of our rights. Today, few areas require more illumination than the area of jury rights. The jury power held by The People when known and understood becomes a sturdy cornerstone in the continual struggle for Freedom.

We must support modifying the legal system to include an

explanation of jury nullification to all prospective jurors and the right should be taught in civics classes as a prerequisite to graduation from high school. This would include the duty to judge guilt or innocence as well as to judge the validity of the law.

ECONOMIC POLICY

<u>Pass a Balanced Budget Amendment</u>. It is the natural tendency of Government to spend beyond its means, so long as it is permitted to do so. We must pass a balanced budget amendment to the Constitution. *A Federal balanced budget amendment is one of the most crucial actions we can take toward restoring Freedom.* The amendment should restrict Federal spending to an amount not to exceed 15 percent of GDP (gross domestic product) with a provision allowing for a temporary breaking of this cap during times of Congressionally declared war against other nations and extreme naturally occurring events. Amending any of the provisions of the balanced budget amendment should require a supermajority.

Recognizing that as fluctuations might occur from time to time in the natural course of events, we should return to the original Constitutional intent of proportionally billing the States (based on House representation) whenever the budget is not balanced for a period of two years[72].

<u>Audit and Reform the Federal Reserve System</u>. According to its official mission statement, the duties of the Federal Reserve System are to conduct the nation's monetary policy; supervise and regulate banking institutions; maintain the stability of the financial system; and provide financial services to depository institutions, the U.S. Government, and foreign official institutions. Similar institutions exist in several other countries, and are referred to generically as Central Banks. The

---

72. See discussion below on repeal of the Sixteenth Amendment

Federal Reserve is one of the most powerful and secretive institutions in the world.

Central Banks began in Europe in the seventeenth century—the Bank of England, for example, was founded in 1694. The concept has been controversial throughout American history; Alexander Hamilton strongly supported the idea, and pushed through legislation to found the First Bank of the United States over the vigorous objections of Thomas Jefferson. Presidents Andrew Jackson and Abraham Lincoln were other nineteenth century opponents of a Central Bank for America, and their efforts, along with popular sentiment, prevented the establishment of a Central Bank following the demise of the Second Bank of the United States in 1836. Various attempts were made to re-establish a U.S. Central Bank, but were thwarted until 1913 when the Federal Reserve System, or the Fed, as it is commonly called, was established.

While the public largely acquiesced to the notion of a central bank in the decades following, intellectual opposition has grown, spurred by comprehensive theoretical grounding created by the exponents of the Austrian School of Economics, expounded by Ludwig von Mises and Friedrich Hayek.

Many people have come to believe that the practical effect and true mission of the Fed is to preserve the wealth and power of world-wide bankers, financiers, and money changers; to insure gradual and continuous inflation as a form of hidden taxation of The People; and to foster perpetual indebtedness to the secretive "owners" of the bank, presumably elitist global financiers. Cogent economic analysis has implicated actions of the Fed in causing both the Great Depression and the housing bubble leading to the current economic crisis of the twenty-first century. Creation of debt by the Federal Reserve since President Nixon took America off the gold standard in 1971 and is now approaching crisis levels and has *de facto* bankrupted the nation.

In the unfolding of the financial crisis since 2008, the Fed has created so much additional debt that paying it off will amount to nothing less than the impoverishment of future American generations, who will surely regard our generation with ignominy. The debt being created by the Fed is being used to bail out the largest banks and financial institutions from losses incurred by risky and unsound business practices. It is not a small coincidence that virtually all of the senior officials comprising the Fed hail from the very banking interests receiving the greatest bailouts.

While opinions may differ on "behind the scenes" motives of the decision-makers at the Federal Reserve, several facts stand out. Policies of the Fed determine the value of our money, the interest rates we must pay in order to borrow, and the ultimate health of the economy. Secrecy promotes some degree of corruption, self-dealing and abuse in *every* endeavor of Government. It is time that we tear back the veil of secrecy. The way to start is by an open and complete audit of the Federal Reserve and by legislating transparency going forward. If the Fed cannot operate openly and transparently, without succumbing to partisan political influence, then it should not exist. Freedom becomes an illusion if the Federal Reserve is allowed to create unconscionable debt and then mortgage America's future to elite global financiers and foreign Governments.

Break up "Too Big to Fail" Financial Institutions. Financial institutions that are "too big to fail," meaning so large that their failure would result in irreparable harm to our banking and financial systems, are too big for the well-being of any nation. The answer is not to reward the incompetent and profligate by rescuing them with taxes and penalties imposed on The People.

In 1994, Congress removed restrictions on interstate banking and branching by the Riegle-Neal Interstate Banking and Branching Efficiency Act (IBBEA). This effectively eliminated all barriers to interstate banking on the State level. Prior to IBBEA, it was illegal for banks to accept deposits from customers outside of their home states. Since IBBEA, growth of enormous banks, along with corresponding insurance interests has dramatically accelerated. After Government creation of these behemoth banking institutions, they were declared "too big to fail," and the politicians bailed them out after the financial crisis of 2008, putting the taxpayers on the hook for the failure of big banks induced by risky behavior in pursuit of profits. To make matters worse, the Government actually consolidated some of the more seriously failing institutions. In other words, they made failing banks that were already too big even bigger just as Japan did after its market collapse. The taxpayers were put on the hook to guarantee solvency for failing banks.

We must once again raise barriers that prevent interstate banking and branching. Furthermore, we must prevent circumvention of these restrictions by "holding companies" or any other mechanism that will thwart the intent of preventing interstate banking. The biggest criticism of this action will be the difficulty of small banks being able to service the needs of the largest customers. This can be accomplished by allowing the creation of Bank Cooperatives on a regional basis that can "share" a single loan above a certain amount. This will restore the impetus of financial banking decisions being made at the local level by those most familiar with the needs of the community, and will energize jobs by better serving small local businesses instead of draining local resources to support loans to big customers by big banks.

End Bailouts and Takeovers of Business by Government. In addition to bailing out "too big to fail" banks and financial institutions, recent Government actions have also bailed out AIG, the largest insurance conglomerate in America, failing big businesses such as General Motors and Chrysler and the bankrupt mortgage behemoths Fannie Mae and Freddie Mac, which continue to issue unsound loans and pay multi-million dollar bonuses to their executives. Furthermore, policies at the FED are creating an economic climate of transferring vast sums of money from The People to the banking industry, supposedly to restore solvency. The results are unprecedented debt and unemployment not seen since the Great Depression. These rates are much higher than the manipulated statistics being reported; in addition, food and commodity prices are rising worldwide and there is little prospect for improvement in any reasonable timeframe.

Government intervention into the marketplace beyond maintaining a level playing field destroys jobs, reduces productivity and stifles economic well-being. Just as preventing the natural cycles of fires in our forests destroys their well-being and precipitates eventual conflagration, interfering in the cycles of economics that restore economic health are ultimately destructive. To force the American taxpayer to pay for the risky behavior and unsound business practices of the elitist financiers is counterproductive and unsustainable. Many argue this may be the greatest "looting" in history.

Those in Congress who supported the bailouts and takeovers in 2009 were seriously punished in the elections of 2010 when dozens of them lost their seats, and a new spirit of reducing spending and Government interference in business permeated the House of Representatives in particular. It is imperative that this movement continue in 2012 so that the Senate and Executive Branch can be impacted not only by example, but also by putting people in office who will be committed to never again undertake such reckless actions. In regard to the automobile and insurance takeovers, the Government should immediately divest itself of all ownership and control of those companies. Fannie Mae and Freddie Mac should be eliminated entirely, and a procedure put in place that will ensure the mortgages they hold will become subject to private sector control. Never again should tax dollars be used to prop up failing institutions. If bailouts continue, overreach and corruption will grow with time, and the bankers will come to count on the bailouts as they know they will face no consequences for their reckless behavior.

Restore Sound Money. It is imperative that America return to a sound monetary system. Consider this chart showing the explosion of debt since Nixon ended the gold standard.

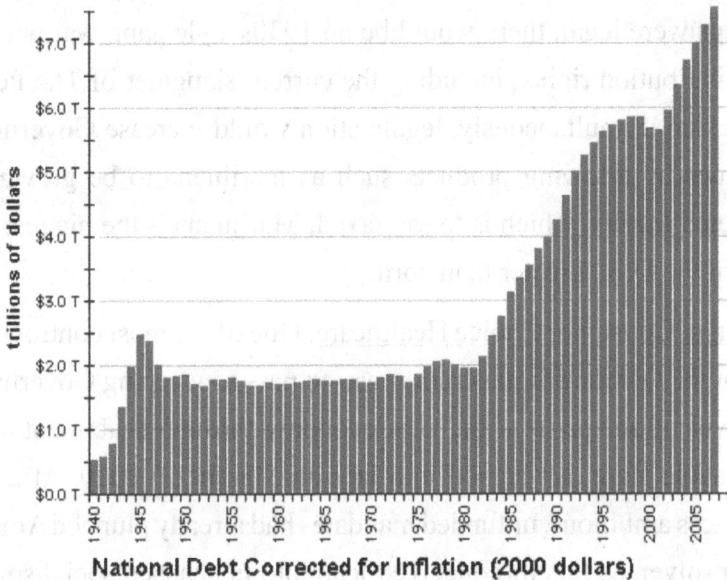

National Debt Corrected for Inflation (2000 dollars)

Source: U.S. National Debt Clock
http://www.brillig.com/debt_clock/

Voters should support and urge their representatives in Congress to pass the existing Free Competition in Currency Act (HR 1098) which will repeal the legal tender law now giving the Federal Reserve a monopoly over the money supply. Also, parts of the laws which give the U.S. Government a monopoly over the creation of coins should be repealed. The power of the states to coin money is strongly implied in the Constitution where it says the states can only coin money in gold and silver, and federal and state taxes including capital gains taxes on precious metal coins and bullion should be prohibited. This will reduce inflation and the severity and length of recessions.

End Drug Prohibition. The prohibition of recreational drugs, especially marijuana, is indefensible in terms of basic Freedom, but it is included here as an economic issue because of the enormous consequences for the economy. Ending the so-called "war on drugs" would benefit the economy by dramatically reducing Government expenditures in the arenas of law enforcement and the prison system. If drugs were legal, there would be no 1930s style gang warfare over turf distribution rights, including the current slaughter of The People of Mexico. Simultaneously, legalization would increase Government revenues by allowing products such as marijuana to be grown and marketed legally, which is to say taxed. Marijuana is the biggest cash crop in the U.S., greater than corn.

Return to Consumer Choice Healthcare. One of the most controversial acts of the Obama administration was to pass a sweeping Government takeover of one sixth of the U.S. economy through enactment of the Affordable Care Act signed into law on March 23, 2010. At a time when less ambitious, unfunded mandates had already plunged America into insolvency, this ill-conceived leap into unabashed socialism was a recipe for economic disaster.

Furthermore, the act is an unprecedented expansion of the powers of an unelected administrative bureaucracy by requiring the Secretary of Health and Human Services to issue almost 2,000 separate decrees. This centralization of power to a single unelected bureaucrat is more than just imprudent; it is a direct threat to Freedom and economic prosperity.

The manner in which the law is constructed is so blatantly uncon-stitutional that it should be declared as such by a unanimous vote of the Supreme Court.

However, the court has become so politicized as to be unreliable in preserving our rights and Freedom, and the majority position of the court can literally change with the failure of a geriatric heartbeat. The People must act to ensure we preserve our Freedom.

While some portions of the bill may be laudable, the overall consequences of the Affordable Care Act are destructive to innovation, job creation, and small businesses.

Support repeal of the Affordable Care Act. Make your opinion known to your legislators and hold them accountable. Support defunding of the act until a legislative majority can be achieved in Congress that will repeal this legislation.

TAXATION

Revenue from taxation is the lifeblood of big Government and socialism. It is a tool of oppression whereby supporters can be favored and advanced, and detractors can be punished and thwarted. Taxation is also a regulator of economic activity as businesses move responsively from areas of high taxation to areas with more moderate taxation, transporting jobs and prosperity with them. Excessive taxation can also produce "confiscatory stagnation" and become destructive to jobs, economic activity and prosperity.

Reform and Simplify the Tax Code. In the United States, the tax law has become so voluminous and distorted that it has ceased to function with clear and concise meaning, and has instead become a document of pure "interpretation." This is a clear pathway to abuse of The People as the interpretation is determined by bureaucracy and enforced through intimidation and punishment. The growth of unrestrained Government, fueled by excessive taxation and/or creation of debt has been the major factor in the destruction of almost every great State in history.

We must consistently vote to limit taxation and hold accountable the politicians who refuse to do so. Reform in America must be inclusive because most Government revenue is raised from unseen taxes, such as excise and sales taxes on things like gasoline and telephone usage, rather than the income tax.

Taxes should be uniformly applied, simply understood and without exceptions and loopholes. Furthermore, a supermajority vote in Congress should be required to raise taxes.

Repeal the Sixteenth Amendment to the Constitution. The sixteenth amendment allows the Government to institute an income tax without apportioning it equally among the states, as originally required by the Constitution. Income tax makes up only about one-third of taxes collected by the Federal Government now. Repealing the Sixteenth Amendment would force a more fair and equitable form of taxation such as transaction taxes. Repeal would end the debacle that has become the Internal Revenue Service with its voluminous tax code filled with loopholes. Repeal would also reinstitute another of the checks and balances that has been lost; Constitutionally, when the Federal Government produces a deficit against the taxes it collects, the States would be respectively billed their proportionate share, calculated by the number of Representatives.

Imagine for a moment the reaction of the State Governors and legislators if they were to receive a bill for their proportional share of the Federal debt! And if State legislators still chose their representative in the Senate,[73] imagine how vested they would be in insuring that there was no profligate spending at the Federal level for which they could be billed!

LAW

Law in twenty-first century America has now become more a tool of the socialist "Nanny State" than a means of protecting The People

---

73. By repeal of the Seventeenth Amendment (see earlier discussion).

against the infringement of their individual rights. The sheer volume of laws has become a direct threat to Freedom and Liberty. Fostered and created by a disproportionate representation of lawyers as legislators, every new law promoting social modification rather than preventing infringement of rights adds to the wealth and power of the legal profession and increases the size and growth of Government.

Make Laws That People Can Understand. Many laws and regulations are written in a format of "legalese" that even trained professionals have difficulty deciphering. Unintelligible laws and regulations are a means of monopolizing law as a profession and thereby eliminating the common man's ability to participate.

Laws should be written clearly and concisely without the obfuscation of legalese and should be interpreted in the spirit of what they say rather than the formalism of wording. Laws should also address only one topic at a time. We have already discussed some measures in this direction, including the "One Subject at a Time Act" and the "Read the Bills Act." In addition, we should end laws against victimless crime, including those addressing possession and use of drugs and other laws which penalize lifestyles which, although they may be unpopular, are both consensual among those participating and do not violate the rights of others.

End Asset Forfeiture. Asset forfeiture is seizing of the property of a person charged with a crime. It may make sense at first glance to demand that criminals forfeit the proceeds of their crimes, but the opportunity for abuse is so clear that it has become a moral hazard, particularly because in most cases the value of the seizures accrues to the police agency making the arrest. This distorts the responsibility of the police in several ways. They may choose to make arrests based on known available assets, rather than known illegal activity. They may time arrests with questions regarding the type of asset to be forfeited as motive. For example, arresting a drug dealer before the sale means police seize only the drugs which they cannot legally auction off. But by waiting until after the sale, they can seize the cash. Another abuse is to use the threat of forfeiture to force compliance with arbitrary bureaucratic regulations.

End the practice of law as a monopoly. This should include measures fighting barriers (such as legalese and requiring professional credentials) to the rightful self-practice of law.

Restrict Eminent Domain. The usurpation of private property for the presumed economic good of the collective is a travesty. Taking property from individuals and giving it to big business for the tax dollars a business project will bring to the community is an abuse of Government power and a flagrant violation of the natural right to property ownership.

MISCELLANEOUS

A) Voting—We must maintain procedures making voting an act of public responsibility and resist measures that make voting easily manipulated and unsecure. We should be suspicious of proposals for "online" voting as they are insecure and could be manipulated by outside interests. Votes could be purchased for little more than an addict's fix, or a pint of wine, and be rendered in the back alley over the purchasing offender's computer. At all polling places, we must demand that all voting machines produce a verifiable hard copy that will be used in recounting votes. Voting machine manufacturers try to create a myth of security so they can sell their products. In truth, electronic records can be accessed and changed. Hard copy backup largely averts that possibility.

B) Education—Fewer than half of the public schools in the United

States now teach civics, which is the study of rights and duties of citizenship. In other words, it is the study of Government with emphasis on the role of citizens—as opposed to external factors—in the operation and oversight of Government. The teaching of Civics should be a requirement for graduation in every State, and the curriculum should encompass study of the Constitution and Bill of Rights, as well as the civic responsibility and the duty of serving on juries.

C) As a means of fostering much needed reform in our education system, we should end the practice of granting teacher and professor tenure based on length of service, which often promotes incompetence and/or dereliction of duty.

D) Initiative and Referendum—The rights of The People are strengthened when they include binding Initiative and Referendum on statutes and constitutional amendments. Some states allow this; others do not, but should. In all cases, however, a two-third majority should be required for approval to insure that changes are not easily enacted.

E) Economic Islands of Prosperity—The U.S. should negotiate 200-year leases on properties strategically positioned around the world in emerging national markets to serve as Free Trade Zones, similar to the Hong Kong agreement that once existed between Great Britain and China.

CIVIL DISOBEDIENCE AND THE COURT OF LAST RESORT

When all other remedies have failed, The People have both the right and the responsibility to rebel.

───── CHAPTER 23 ─────

THE FREEDOM MANIFESTO

A Message of Hope And a Call To Action

THE MESSAGE OF THIS BOOK IS not one of despair and resignation. *It is a wake-up call to action.* The World is awakening to the reality that our current trajectory will inevitably lead to economic and social catastrophe. There is no denying that the mountain of debt we have created has led us to the precipice of ruin. There is no remedy that will be without sacrifice, but this is not the first, nor will it be the last challenge for those who love Freedom and Liberty.

The trust passed on to Americans by all who have fought for Freedom before us is an obligation we dare not neglect. Our struggle is between Government rule by an elitist few, and The People's right to rule themselves; between authoritarian rule and rule through choice and tolerance; between power monopolized by the privileged few and opportunity for all; between stores whose shelves are barren through chronic shortages with most goods available only to the favored of the State; and stores overflowing in bounty available even to the common man; between hiding one's thoughts in fear and speaking one's thoughts freely; between imposition of ideals through force and fear and promoting ideals through reason and persuasion.

Our Forefathers showed us that Freedom drives the economic tide that lifts all boats and induces the flourishing of humanity in all fields of endeavor. It is up to us to reinstitute the principles of Freedom which favorably changed the history of the world.

The message of Freedom is universal and does not apply only to Americans. All Freedom loving men and women should join in this debate, for the concepts found within the founding documents of the American Revolution are not limited by geographic boundary, population density, or any perceived complexity of the era in which they may be applied. They follow universal principles of nature and provide a roadmap for the flourishing of humanity.

THE OPPOSITION MESSAGES

The opposition messages of the twenty-first century are derived from the collectivist "isms" of the past century and a half. Foremost are Marxism and Keynesianism which promote socialism in different ways. Marxism promotes class warfare and the use of force. Keynesianism promotes subversion of economics through Government intervention and control. Both are destructive to Freedom and the well-being of humanity.

COUNTERING THE OPPOSITION

Revolutionary movements to effect change require simple, concise and condensed themes to spread their messages among The People. Rallying cries in America have been used since the earliest protests that later became the American Revolution. Now iconic cries such as, "No taxation without representation!" and "Remember Pearl Harbor" have become a part of heritage, but we must not forget that they also served a crucial purpose in their time.

Here are three succinct central messages that can help move toward the restoration of Freedom and Liberty in America, and which can also help perpetuate Freedom in the future of all humanity:

1. **Children have a right to be born free of debt.**
2. **Tolerance is the price we have to pay for Freedom.**
3. **Freedom is the driving force of human achievement.**

DEFINING THE STRUGGLE

The struggle is eternal. The forces of collectivism and Statism battle the forces of individualism and Freedom. Do all rights rise out of Government, which controls and micro-manages our lives? Or do all rights rise out of The People, whereby we only lend certain powers to Government and retain the widest latitude to make choices in our own behalf? Quite literally, who is sovereign over our lives and our bodies, Government or each individual? Do we want to live in fear of our Government as it rules through force, fear and intimidation, or do we want to be proud of our Government as it preserves our individual Freedom, promoting dialogue and reason? Do we want to consume our resources building prisons to hold one-fourth of all those incarcerated on the face of the earth, or do we want to use those same resources to build schools and restore America's place as a leader in education and innovation?

Do we follow Machiavelli, Marx, Lenin and Keynes with their historical legacy of misery, poverty and oppression? Or do we follow Locke, Jefferson, Madison and Adam Smith with their historical legacy of prosperity, abundance and Freedom?

Here is possibly a more poignant question of how we will shape our children's future: Can we refuse the Government slop that is currently leading us into subjugation?

THE FATHER OF ECONOMIC SOCIALISM

Early in his career, John Maynard Keynes struggled to explain inflation and held a much different viewpoint than the legacy he was to pass on later in life. In *Economic Consequences of the Peace* (1919), commenting on economic stagnation after the war, Keynes wrote these remarkably accurate observations:

> "Lenin is said to have declared that the best way to destroy the Capitalist System was to debauch the currency. By a continuing process of inflation, governments can confiscate, secretly and unobserved, an important part of the wealth of their citizens. By this method they not only confiscate, but they confiscate arbitrarily; and, while the process impoverishes many, it actually enriches some."

Keynes then goes on to observe that Government blames "profiteers" which he equates to capitalists and entrepreneurs for the inflation it was creating. He then shows that contrary to Government propaganda, "the profiteers are a consequence of and not a cause of rising prices." Keynes believed that if Governments continued this demonizing and creating hatred of the class of entrepreneurs, it could tear at the fabric of the social and economic order of the nineteenth century. "Lenin was certainly right" Keynes wrote; "There is no subtler, no surer means of overturning the existing basis of society than to debauch the currency. The process engages all of the hidden forces of economic law on the side of destruction, and does so in a manner which not one man in a million is able to diagnose."

Keynes later success was built on the opposite justification of Government intervention and control of economics, in the belief that the market could be manipulated in a manner to eliminate, or at least abate its normal cycles. By proposing massive Government spending in economic downturns, as a means of stimulating moribund economic activity, he also gave justification for massive expansion of Government. These ideas were promoted worldwide by many of the ruling elite who derived wealth, power, privilege and status from association with Government, and Keynes thinking grew in prominence.

Whether or not Keynes moved to accommodate the promoters of his success either consciously or sub-consciously, he continued to move in the direction of Government control of economics, abandoning much of his earlier thinking that conflicted with his increasing socialist underpinning. One key area was his unresolved earlier-described ideas on inflation. In *How To Pay For the War* (1940), Keynes showed that he had completely abandoned his earlier concerns about "debauching the currency," and indicated how to incorporate inflation into his theories though he died before setting them out in finer detail. Followers no longer need be concerned that Keynes thinking only applied to recessions, and his legacy has been propelled forward into the modern day. The minions of Keynes's economic socialism have now led us to the precipice of worldwide economic disaster. Those leaders blinded by the rhetoric of class warfare, those worried about preserving their premiere spot at the slop trough, and those desperate to preserve their office and power easily find a way to rationalize their actions in the writings of Keynes. Unfortunately, history has shown us time and again that socialism ends in utter chaos. The pathway America is on is totally unsustainable.

Consuming the seed corn of our children's future is no longer enough to support the gluttony of elitist politicians. They now eat up the seed corn of untold future generations. We must band together and "vote the bums out." This is not a task that we can accomplish alone. We must put aside some of our social differences when engaging in the political arena, and vote for those who will direct their efforts to smaller Government, returning to constitutionalism, paying off the debt and having a balanced budget henceforth. Those we elect must respect the rights of States as a better arena to address social issues. We must find our way back toward tolerance lest we be divided and misdirected from the greater issues. *But most of all we must unite.*

THE FATHER OF COMMUNISM, FORCED COLLECTIVISM, AND CLASS WARFARE

Karl Marx believed that the motivating force of history is class struggle marked by the exploitation of one class by another. The forced collectivist thinking of Marx was to spawn numerous "class struggles" across the globe in the twentieth century, which arguably caused more misery, death and destruction than can be laid at the doorstep of any other human being in history. The chaos of socialism caused the misery and death of hundreds of millions. The oppression is continuing to this day under both geriatric holdovers from the last century, as well as a new class of aspiring despots who point as justification to the ideas of Karl Marx.

But what did Marx teach that could so inspire men like Lenin, Stalin, Mao, Castro and Pol Pot? What is so appealing to people today? You may be surprised.

All of the remaining quotes in this chapter are from Marx's *Communist Manifesto*.

Marx wanted to *abolish individuality, Freedom, and independence.*

"And the abolition of this state of things is called by the bourgeois, abolition of individuality and freedom! And rightly so. The abolition of bourgeois individuality, bourgeois independence, and bourgeois freedom is undoubtedly aimed at.

By freedom is meant, under the present bourgeois conditions of production, free trade, free selling and buying."

Marx wanted to *abolish private property.* "In this sense, the theory of the Communists may be summed up in the single sentence: Abolition of private property."

Marx wanted to *abolish the family.* "Abolition of the family! Even the most radical flare up at this infamous proposal of the Communists."

Marx wanted to *indoctrinate children.* "But you say, we destroy the most hallowed of relations, when we replace home education by social."

Marx wanted to *abolish culture.* "That culture, the loss of which he laments, is, for the enormous majority, a mere training to act as a machine."

Marx wanted to *abolish countries and nationality.* "The Communists are further reproached with desiring to abolish countries and nationality."

Marx wanted to *abolish Freedom, Justice, religion, and even all morality.* "There are, besides, eternal truths, such as Freedom, Justice, etc., that are common to all states of society. But communism abolishes eternal truths, it abolishes all religion, and all morality, instead of constituting them on a new basis; it therefore acts in contradiction to all past historical experience."

Marx also put forth a plan for achieving his collectivist utopia, highlighted by his following list. It is poignant to note the number of milestones that have already been achieved, as well as the current struggle in society to adopt many of the rest:

1. Abolition of property in land and application of all rents of land to public purposes.

2. A heavy progressive or graduated income tax.

3. Abolition of all rights of inheritance.

4. Confiscation of the property of all emigrants and rebels.

5. Centralization of credit in the banks of the state, by means of a national bank with state capital and an exclusive monopoly.

6. Centralization of the means of communication and transport in the hands of the state.

7. Extension of factories and instruments of production owned by the state; the bringing into cultivation of waste lands, and the improvement of the soil generally in accordance with a common plan.

8. Equal obligation of all to work. Establishment of industrial armies, especially for agriculture.

9. Combination of agriculture with manufacturing industries; gradual abolition of all the distinction between town and country by a more equable distribution of the populace over the country.

10. Free education for all children in public schools. Abolition of children's factory labor in its present form. Combination of education with industrial production, etc. [I.e. indoctrination of children in Government – Author]

It is instructive to look back at the prescriptions of Karl Marx because we know how his utopia turned out in the countries which adopted his teachings in the twentieth century. Marxian socialism has been a dismal failure always ending in complete chaos. And yet, the empowerment of Government stimulates some to revive it from its ashes of destruction to subjugate new victims.

The great British statesman Winston Churchill illuminated the essence of socialism; "Socialism is a philosophy of failure, the creed of ignorance, and the gospel of envy, its inherent virtue is the equal sharing of misery."

In America we have not fully embraced socialism. Instead we have created a system dominated by Government that has been gradually tilting the economic balance from The People to the elite few. We still have the illusion of property ownership, but with the nationalization of the mortgage lending institutions, Fanny Mae and Freddy Mac, the Government now owns the mortgages on a majority of homes in America. Businesses still operate with a profit motive, but the intrusive and regulated society in which we live is no longer capitalist. As we have abandoned the principles that made America great and moved toward big Government, we have increased the disparity between rich and poor, begun the destruction of our middle class, and have created a debt that will impoverish future generations. We cannot continue down this path. We must change the trajectory of decline and despair. We must act together to restore the true tenants of Freedom. *We must unite.*

CALL TO ACTION

Marx ended his *Communist Manifesto* with what became an iconic challenge and call to action for his followers:

> The Communists disdain to conceal their views and aims. They openly declare that their ends can be attained only by the forcible overthrow of all existing social conditions. Let the ruling classes tremble at a Communistic revolution. The proletarians have nothing to lose but their chains. They have a world to win. **WORKING MEN OF ALL COUNTRIES, UNITE!**

Marx's words have reached out for over a century to those who would use class warfare to their own ends. It is time for the world to come together and assign Karl Marx's failed philosophy to the ash heap of history. A rational comparative observation of our past shows us the pathway that leads to happiness and abundance. *Freedom drives human achievement.*

Just as Marx called his followers to come together, those who love Freedom must now come together to set the world back on a sustainable path to the flourishing of humanity. *We must answer the challenge.*

The People disdain all proponents of class warfare. They openly resolve to resist enslavement by those who use force to usurp Liberty. Let a revolution in the marketplace of ideas combat those who would deny Freedom. The People have everything to lose without involvement. Nothing less than Freedom for humanity is at stake. Producers of the world, and **ALL WHO CHERISH FREEDOM, UNITE!**

www.ingramcontent.com/pod-product-compliance
Lightning Source LLC
Chambersburg PA
CBHW010240290326
41930CB00046B/3403

* 9 7 8 1 9 5 9 6 7 7 5 5 0 *